Antje Schirm

Credit Risk Securitisation

GABLER EDITION WISSENSCHAFT

Antje Schirm

Credit Risk Securitisation

A valuation study

With a foreword by Prof. Dr. Dr. h.c. Wolfgang Bühler

Deutscher Universitäts-Verlag

Bibliografische Information Der Deutschen Bibliothek
Die Deutsche Bibliothek verzeichnet diese Publikation in der Deutschen Nationalbibliografie; detaillierte bibliografische Daten sind im Internet über <http://dnb.ddb.de> abrufbar.

Dissertation Universität Mannheim, 2004

1. Auflage November 2004

Lektorat: Brigitte Siegel / Sabine Schöller

Der Deutsche Universitäts-Verlag ist ein Unternehmen von Springer Science+Business Media.
www.duv.de

Umschlaggestaltung: Regine Zimmer, Dipl.-Designerin, Frankfurt/Main

Gedruckt auf säurefreiem und chlorfrei gebleichtem Papier

ISBN-13:978-3-8244-8242-9 e-ISBN-13:978-3-322-81875-1
DOI: 10.1007/978-3-322-81875-1

Foreword

Credit risk has become the central focus of risk management in the last decade for a number of reasons. First, for a typical continental bank, credit risk is still the predominant risk category. Second, the new Basel Capital Accord of June 2004 allows for more advanced methods to assess the risk related with a bank's credit portfolio. Third, the markets to reallocate credit risk between agents experience the highest growth rate of all derivative markets. Fourth, from a theoretical and an empirical point of view, the modelling and valuation of credit risk is a more demanding problem than the analysis of market risk. Especially, the appropriate modelling of correlation effects, e.g. the correlation between defaults of different creditors or between default probabilities and recovery rates, is still not satisfactory resolved.

Collateralised Debt Obligations (CDOs) represent important derivatives to synthesise and reallocate the risk of banks' credit portfolios. These instruments are of specific interest as they, first, call for a determination of the whole loss distribution of a credit portfolio and not only for a few moments. Second and even more interesting, this loss distribution is carved into senior, mezzanine and junior tranches according to the needs and risk attitudes of the bank and the market.

Antje Schirm's dissertation represents the first academic study that thoroughly analyses the theoretical and empirical aspects of CDO valuation. The author makes three major contributions to the literature. First, she models carefully the general cash-flow structure for synthetic transactions. These transactions are typical for European securitisation techniques as compared to the predominant true-sale structures in the US. Second, she estimates a five-factor model to characterise the instantaneous spread of bonds in a Duffie/Singleton framework. These factors are related to the default-free term-structure of interest rates, a common risk factor and three rating related factors. Each factor is modelled as a Cox/Ingersoll/Ross process. Compared with a Gaussian framework, these processes pose a notable challenge to estimation, which is carried out by Kalman filtering. Third, she empirically analyses four European Collateralised Bond Obligation structures issued in 2001.

Antje Schirm's dissertation gives many important insights into the issues related with the valuation of CDOs using bond market data. Some of the most noteworthy findings are:

- The expected loss rate correlations under the physical and the risk neutral measure differ considerably.
- The choice of specific features of credit enhancement may have a big impact on the values of the individual tranches.
- The theoretical mezzanine premia are much larger than the observed ones. This difference boils down to a synthetisation premium of about 1% of the transaction nominal which is partly absorbed by transaction costs.

I strongly recommend this dissertation to anybody involved in the structuring and valuation of Collateralised Debt Obligations.

Prof. Dr. Dr. h.c. Wolfgang Bühler

Preface

This thesis is a result of my study period at the Center for Doctoral Studies in Economics and Management (CDSEM) and of my work with the Finance Group at the University of Mannheim.

First of all, I am greatly indebted to my supervisor, Wolfgang Bühler. His valuable suggestions and advice have helped me to raise relevant research questions, laying the foundation for the main contributions of this study to the credit risk pricing literature. His countless comments have allowed me to structure my results such that the key insights are easily accessible. Special thanks go to Enno Mammen for co-refereeing my thesis.

Research support from the German Research Foundation (DGF) made this work possible. I have benefited from the inspiring research environment at the CDSEM, a place where finance is integrated with theoretical and applied economics and where ambitious research is strongly encouraged. Many ideas in this work rely on fruitful discussions at seminars and conferences. I am very thankful to my committed colleagues of the Finance Group, namely Jens Daum, Christoph Engel, Christoph Heumann, Olaf Korn, Christian Koziol Jens Müller-Merbach, Peter Sauerbier, and Tim Thabe, not only for their patience and for their comments, but also for the encouragement they have provided. Many thanks go to Susan Atkinson for careful language advice.

Part of this work would not have been possible without an insider's view on securitisation. I am thankful to members of DZ Bank, Deutsche Bank, and HSBC, who gave me a patient introduction into the techniques of securitisation and have equipped me with transaction-related information, which is rarely available outside the financial sector.

All generations of my family deserve especially sincere thanks. My parents' love and encouragement, but also their enormous effort to support my projects wherever possible exceed all expectations. Finally, I would like to thank my fiancé Stefan for his endless love and support. I admire his courage.

Antje Schirm

Contents

List of Tables

List of Figures

List of Abbreviations

ABS	Asset-backed securities
APT	Arbitrage-pricing theory
AR	auto-regressive
approx.	approximately
assoc.	association
BCBS	Basel Committee on Banking Supervision
bps	basispoints
CBO	Collateralised bond obligation
CDF	Cumulated distribution function
CDO	Collateralised debt obligation
CDS	Credit default swap
CIR	Cox, Ingersoll and Ross (1985)
CLN	Credit-linked note
CLO	Collateralised loan obligation
CMO	Collateralised mortgage obligation
CSO	Collateralised structured obligation
c.p.	ceteris paribus
EMM	Equivalent martingale measure
EMU	European Monetary Union

EUR	Euro
IRB	Internal ratings-based
ISDA	International Swaps and Derivatives Association
i.i.d.	identically independently distributed
KF	Kalman filter
KfW	Kreditanstalt für Wiederaufbau
LGD	Loss given default
MAD	Mean absolute deviation
MBO	Mortgage-backed obligation
ML	Maximum likelihood
MYE	Median yield error
OC	Overcollateralisation
OECD	Organisation for Economic Co-operation and Development
OTC	Over-the-counter
OLS	Ordinary least-squares
PDE	Partial differential equation
PV	Present value
p.a.	per annum
QML	Quasi maximum likelihood
qu.	Quantile
RFV	Recovery of face value
RMSE	Root mean squared error
RMV	Recovery of market value
SDE	Stochastic differential equation
SME	Small and medium enterprise
SPV	Special purpose vehicle

Std dev.	Standard deviation
TS	Term structure
UK	United Kingdom
US	United States

List of Symbols

$\hat{}$	Characterisation of estimates
*	Superscript for parameter sets and random variables under the physical measure
$^-$	Superscript for pre-default market values
$\#(t^{pay}, risk = ...)$	Number of surviving reference claims in t^{pay} of a certain risk level
$\#D$	Poisson random variable
$\#mez$	Number of mezzanine tranches of a capital structure
$\mathbf{1}$	Indicator variable
$A_k(\tau, \phi_k)$	Function of maturity and parameter set determining zero bond yield component in CIR model
$\mathbf{A}_r(\phi_r)$	Vector of $A_k(\tau, \phi_k)$ determining riskless term structure
$\mathbf{A}_s(\phi_s)$	Vector of $A_k(\tau, \phi_k)$ determining three spread term structures
$B_k(\tau, \phi_k)$	Function of maturity and parameter set determining zero bond yield component in CIR model
$\mathbf{B}_r(\phi_r)$	Vector of $B_k(\tau, \phi_k)$ determining riskless term structure
$\mathbf{B}_s(\phi_s)$	Matrix of $B_k(\tau, \phi_k)$ determining three spread term structures
$C(t, \tau)$	Affine function of common credit factor
$CDF[\cdot]$	Cumulated distribution function of a portfolio or tranche loss variable
$CDS_{tr}(t)$	Value of a tranche credit default swap in time t

$CF_{tr}(t^{pay})$	Coupon- or premium cash-flow of a securitisation tranche in time t^{pay}
$CF_i(\tau)$	Coupon or principal cash-flow of a bond of issuer i in time τ
$Class\,(t,\tau)$	Affine function of class-specific credit factor
$D_{(\cdot)}(t,\tau)$	Any zero bond price/discount factor in time t with maturity τ
$D_{class}(t,\tau)$	Defaultable zero bond price/discount factor of a class
$D_{corp}(t,\tau)$	Defaultable zero bond price/discount factor of a corporate borrower
$D_r(t,\tau)$	Riskless zero bond price/discount factor
$\mathcal{D}$	Zero bond yield expectation due to diffusion stochastic
$E_{corp}[1]$	Standard exponential variable
$\mathbb{E}_t$	Expectation taken in time t under the risk-neutral measure
$H_{corp}(t)$	Compensator of bond/reference asset, with *corp* evaluating to *class*
$\overline{K}_{tr}$	Upper threshold of a tranche loss range
$\underline{K}_{tr}$	Lower threshold of a tranche loss range
LGD	Loss given default as a fraction of the pre-default market value
$M(t)$	Time-t-value of a riskless money-market account
$\mathbf{M}$	Covariance of measurement noise in KF-recursion with partitions $\mathbf{M}_r$ and $\mathbf{M}_s$ and diagonal elements $m_r(\tau)$, $m_{class}(\tau)$
$N_{corp}(t)$	Value of Poisson process in time t
$OC_{tr}(t)$	Overcollateralisation ratio of a tranche in time t
$PV(\cdot)$	Present value, usually of a loss variable or cash-flow stream
P_i	Principal exposure to an individual reference borrower
$P_{pool}(t)$	Current principal value of a reference portfolio
$P_{tr}(t)$	Current tranche principal
$\Pr_{\{\Upsilon_{corp}>T\}}(t)$	Survival probability in t until T

$RC_{orig}(0)$	Time-zero value of the originator's residual claim in a securitisation transaction
$R_{class}(t, \tau)$	Defaultable spot rate of a class
$R_{corp}(t, \tau)$	Defaultable spot rate of a corporate borrower
$R_r(t, \tau)$	Riskless spot rate
$\mathbf{R}_r(t, \phi_r)$	Riskless term structure in time t represented by five yields
$\mathbf{R}_r(t)^{pred}$	Prediction of riskless term structure in KF-recursion
$SA(t)$	Time-t-value of a spread account held by the SPV
$S_{class}(t, \tau)$	Spot spread of a class
$S_{corp}(t, \tau)$	Spot spread of a corporate borrower
$StdDev_{orig}$	Standard deviation of the value of the originator's consolidated stake in a transaction
$\mathbf{S}(t, \phi_r)$	Three spread term structures in time t represented by five spot spreads of every class
$\mathbf{S}(t)^{pred}$	Prediction of three spread term structures in KF-recursion
$\mathcal{S}_{pool}(t)$	Weighted average spread income generated by the reference pool in a period
$\mathcal{S}_{tr}(t)$	Weighted average spread payable to tranches in a period
$\mathcal{S}_{tr\,by\,SPV}(t)$	Weighted average spread of tranches issued via SPV
T	Maturity date
$\mathbf{T}(\phi^*)$	Transition matrix of state vector in KF-recursion with partitions $\mathbf{T}(\phi^*)_r$, $\mathbf{T}(\phi^*)_s$
$U[0,1]$	Standard uniform variable
$V_{class}(t, \tau)$	Coupon bond price of a class
$V_{corp}(t, \tau)$	Coupon bond price of a corporate debtor
$V_i(t, class, \tau)$	Coupon bond price observation in the market for a given class and payment dates τ
$\mathbf{V}_r(t)$	Prediction error variance of riskless term structure in KF-recursion

$\mathbf{V}_s(t)$	Prediction error variance of three spot spread term structures in KF-recursion
$W_k(t)$	Standardised Wiener process
$XS(t^{pay})$	Excess spread amount generated by reference portfolio at a payment date
$XS_{orig}(t)$	Excess spread amount at a payment date accruing to the originator from the reference portfolio
$XS_{SPV}(t^{pay})$	Excess spread amount at a payment date accruing to the SPV under a tranched-basket swap

$a_k(\tau, \phi_k)$	Function of maturity and parameter set determining zero bond price component in CIR model
$b_k(\tau, \phi_k)$	Function of maturity and parameter set determining zero bond price component in CIR model
c	Subscript for common factor
c_k	Function determining the transition density of factor k
$class$	Subscript for class-specific factors
$class = (risk, sec)$	Class assignment of a reference asset
$class = r, risk$	Indication of riskless and corporate term structures
$class = u, v$	Two distinct classes of reference assets
$corp$	Subscript for corporate bonds
d	Realisation of $\#D$
df	Degrees of freedom
dt	An instant
$f_k(t)$	Factors
$f_r(t)$	Riskless short rate
$f_r(t^{pay} - \Delta t^{pay})$	Variable riskless rate, payable for period length Δt^{pay}
$f_r^{pred}(t)$	Prediction of short rate in KF-recursion

$f_r^{update}(t)$	Update of short rate in KF-recursion
$\mathbf{f}(t)$	State vector with partitions $f_r(t)$ and $\mathbf{f}_s(t)$
$\mathbf{f}_s^{pred}(t)$	Prediction of spread factors in KF-recursion
$\mathbf{f}_s^{update}(t)$	Update of spread factors in KF-recursion
$h_{corp}(t)$	Default intensity of bond/reference asset, with *corp* evaluating to *class*
$\overline{h}_{corp}(t)$	Mean-loss rate of bond/reference asset, with *corp* evaluating to *class*
$i = 1, ..., I(t^{pay})$	A surviving reference asset in period t^{pay}
i	Subscript for individual observations
ii	Subscript for diagonal elements
jun	Junior tranche in a capital structure
$k = r, c, class$	Subscript for factors
$loss(t)$	Portfolio loss in period t
$m_{class}(\tau)$	Vectors with $class = 1, 2, 3$ collecting the main diagonal of $\mathbf{M}_s$
$m_r(\tau)$	Main diagonal of $\mathbf{M}_r$
med	A coupon-paying bond exhibiting maturity and coupon rate equal to the medians of the sample observations
mez	Mezzanine tranche or total mezzanine range in a capital structure
$mez1$	Superior mezzanine
$mez2$	Subordinate mezzanine
$p_r^{pred}(t)$	Prediction variance of short rate in KF-recursion
$p_r^{update}(t)$	Update variance of short rate in KF-recursion
$\mathbf{p}_s^{pred}(t)$	Prediction variance of spread factors in KF-recursion
$\mathbf{p}_s^{update}(t)$	Update variance of spread factors in KF-recursion
q_k	Function determining the transition density of factor k

r	Subscript for riskless bonds and rates
$r_{corp}(t)$	Defaultable short rate
$risk = 1, 2, 3$	Risk-level partition identified with the agency ratings Aa/Aa, A, Baa
s	Integration variable
$s = \Delta t^{pay}, ..., t^{pay}$	Period prior to payment date
$savings$	Savings on protection costs to the issuer due to loss allocation in arrears
$s_{corp}(t)$	Corporate short spread, with *corp* evaluating to *class*
sen	Senior tranche in a capital structure
s_{SPV}	Nominal basket premium rate payable to SPV
$s_\imath$	Par spread of an individual reference borrower
s_{tr}	CDO tranche premium
$sub = 1, ..., tr - 1$	Tranches subordinate to *tr*
t	Period
$t^{pay} = \Delta t^{pay}, ..., T$	Payment date in a securitisation structure
$tr = 1, .., \#tr$	Tranches in a capital structure
u_k	Function of maturity and parameter set determining zero bond price component in CIR model
$\mathbf{v}_r(t)$	Prediction error of riskless term structure in KF-recursion
$\mathbf{v}_s(t)$	Prediction error of three spot spread term structures in KF-recursion
ytm_{class}	Yield to maturity of a class
Δ	Discrete change
Δt^{pay}	Payment interval, coupon period
Λ_k	Market price of factor risk

$\Sigma(\phi^*)$	Transition variance of state vector in KF-recursion with partitions $\Sigma(\phi^*)_r, \Sigma(\phi^*)_s$
Υ_{corp}	Default event time as first-arrival time of a Poisson process
$\beta_{class}(t)$	Parameter vector of Nelson/Siegel term structure equations with entries $\beta^0_{class}(t), \beta^1_{class}(t), \beta^2_{class}(t), \beta^3_{class}(t)$
$\gamma_1, \gamma_2, \gamma_3, \gamma_4$	Functions determining the closed-form solution of a zero bond price in the CIR model
$\varepsilon_i(t, class, \tau)$	Regression residual of individual coupon bond price observation
$\varepsilon_r(t)'$	Measurement noise of riskless rates
$\varepsilon_s(t)'$	Measurement noise of spot spreads
$\eta(\cdot)$	White noise with given time-varying variance
θ_k	Unconditional factor mean
κ_k	Reversion rate
λ_k	Parameter determining a market price of factor risk
$\mu(f_k(t))$	Drift of a generalised Wiener process
$\sigma^2(f_k(t))$	Variance of a generalised Wiener process
σ_k	Factor volatility parameter
τ	Time to maturity
$\underline{\tau} = (\tau_1, ..., \tau_N)$	Vector collecting payment dates of a coupon bond
ϕ_k	Entry of ϕ relating to factor k
ϕ	Full parameter vector
ϕ_r	Parameter vector of riskless rate model
ϕ_s	Parameter vector of spread model

Chapter 1

Introduction

1.1 Securitisation: traded portfolio credit risk

Credit risk modelling has gained increasing attention since the late 1990s as a consequence of two developments. The reorganisation of the Basel Capital Accord ('Basel II'), under way since the publication of the First Consultative Paper (BCBS (1999)) aims at establishing capital requirements applicable to a bank's credit positions that capture the positions' risk contribution to the bank portfolio adequately. Not only the authorities are concerned with the quantification of the risk contribution of positions in a credit portfolio. Banks are incited to make use of their expertise regarding the credit risk inherent in individual exposures acquired through their screening and monitoring effort. Therefore, for both sides, the need for adequate credit risk measurement and forecasting arises, both requiring appropriate modelling techniques. Modelling requirements concern the assessment of the individual default riskiness, as conveyed by the exposure size, the probability of default, and the loss given default, or recovery rate, respectively. Moreover, the need for risk assessment extends to the quantification of a single position's contribution to the entire bank portfolio risk. The regulatory environment thus lays the foundations for the extensive development and assessment of credit portfolio risk models, both on a regulatory level and on the level of individual financial institutions.

Increasing risk awareness, amplified by the institutional and regulatory environment, has been parallelled by the development and current consolidation of markets for credit derivatives. These instruments permit the transfer of selected risk components of assets subject to credit risk. Whereas single-name instruments, namely credit default swaps (CDSs), spread options or total return swaps, refer to the pure default loss risk or spread change risk of individual reference assets, multi-name products permit a credit portfolio risk transfer between market participants. Regarding the underlying asset properties, multi-name derivatives take either the form of basket swaps or portfolio derivatives, both types differing with regard to the number of reference assets whose credit performance determines the contingent payoff specification. Basket derivatives normally refer to a small number of assets, such that the single-debtor default risk has notable impact on the derivative value. Portfolio derivatives, by contrast, refer to a defaultable debt pool in which the single-exposure risk contribution is small. According to the properties of the transferred risk profile, the payoff rules of basket swaps mostly refer to a given number of default events, such that protection against losses incurred by the nth default event is obtained under typical basket swaps. Portfolio derivative payments, by contrast, are explicitly linked to evaluated losses incurred as a consequence of asset default, such that senior/subordinated structures are established. The need for valuation of multi-name derivatives requires an adequate modelling approach to the underlying risk profile. The information requirements of the capital allocation purposes translate to the derivative pricing problem: Fair premia payable in exchange for single-name default risk exposure convey the market participants' view of the risk factors, i.e. default probabilities and loss severity. An appropriate solution to a multi-name product pricing problem has to consider the portfolio characteristics of the underlying, thus establishing the need for a credit risk portfolio model.

Whilst credit risk securitisation makes use of portfolio derivatives, securities available to investors may also be considered as portfolio derivatives themselves. With the issuance of notes whose contractual claims are backed by the uncertain bundled cash-flows generated by the defaultable debt portfolio, credit portfolio risk transfer can be achieved under a small number of contracts, by comparison to alternative means for risk transfer, such as individual loan sales or the acquisition of protection under single-name contracts.

Securities issued from those transactions are referred to as collateralised debt obligations (CDOs). Due to the entitlement of CDO investors to cash-flows generated by a specified pool of assets, they are categorised under the asset class of asset-backed securities (ABSs), generally subsuming note issuance programmes characterised by asset pooling and cash-flow bundling. Figure 1.1 depicts securitisation activity in Europe. Primary market volume is expressed in the cumulated portfolio nominal of those transactions that have been placed in the Euromarket or in the European domestic markets, transferring the risk of European debtors.[1] Note that a notable proportion of CDOs are privately-placed, thus not showing up in the figures. The disaggregation of total securitisation has been available since the third quarter of 2001.

In addition to ABSs, mortgage-backed securities make up for the remaining fraction of the total securitisation volume, using the same risk transfer techniques as ABSs, but being

[1] See The Bond Market Association (2003) (data reports) and Rajendra (2004) (Deutsche Bank).

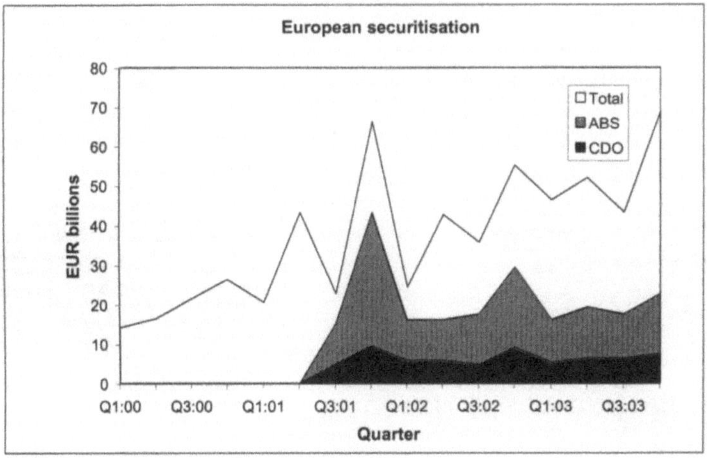

Figure 1.1: **European securitisation issuance.**
Primary market volume is expressed in cumulated portfolio nominals as reported by The Bond Market Association and, subsidiarily and consistently, Deutsche Bank. Figures include transactions placed in the Euromarket or in the European domestic markets referring to European debtors. Disaggregated data for ABSs and CDOs has been available since Q3:01.

exposed to extra risk factors other than counterparty credit risk.

Yearly securitisation volume has experienced steady growth, the issuance shortfall in the summer months is consistently compensated by increasing activity towards the end of the year. This discrepancy was largest in 2001 when a number of deals were postponed as a consequence of the uncertain credit market environment in autumn.

The correspondence between portfolio derivatives and CDOs suggests that credit risk transfer is not necessarily linked to the establishment of a full-blown ABS-structure. Alternatively, the heart of a CDO transaction, i. e. credit risk transfer, can be replicated under appropriately structured derivative contracts. In the European market, so-called synthetic CDOs account for the majority of transactions: Yoshizawa (2003) (Moody's) reports that 85% of those transactions obtaining a Moody's rating in 2002 actually made use of synthetic risk transfer.[2] The figures depicted in the graph above in principle include synthetic CDOs, however, only to the extent that securities have been placed publicly.

With respect to portfolio risk modelling, CDOs as derivatives on underlying credit risk fac-

---

[2] The figure relates to transaction numbers. As debt portfolios whose risk is being transferred synthetically tend to be of a large volume, the proportion of synthetic CDOs expressed in pool nominal is expected to be even higher.

tors constitute an appealing means for analysis. The quantification of credit risk variables and their interrelation in a portfolio context from historical default data is hampered by the fact that credit defaults are rare events. Extensive time series and cross-sectional coverage would be required for risk quantification, which is currently unavailable outside the financial sector. CDOs, by contrast, are market-priced securities. At least one piece of information on the pricing of credit portfolio risk is available: The premia that security investors claim for compensation for their stake in credit portfolio risk is a function of portfolio losses transferred under the senior/subordinated structures. Structures may however deviate from the basic portfolio derivative scheme due to the presence of additional protective features, maintaining the derivative relationship to underlying credit risk factors.

1.2 Contributions of the study

The work at hand relates multi-name derivative pricing information to a credit portfolio model that conforms with single-borrower market data. The present study constitutes the first academic and thoroughly documented approach to CDO valuation, addressing the two major issues on the research agenda from a strongly empirical perspective: payout or cash-flow modelling and stochastic underlying portfolio loss characterisation.

Firstly, CDO payout modelling relies on transactions actually observed in the marketplace for which issuance pricing information is publicly available. Hence, not only a modelling context for various payout structures is developed, but also a detailed comparison with observed issuance conditions is drawn up. Whereas the payout model attempts to maintain a maximum degree of generality and treats specific structural elements as deviations from the general case, the empirical pricing comparison takes the form of a 'clinical study': The general model is evaluated precisely for the contract structures of four synthetic transactions that accommodate the general payout rules. Payout analysis complements prior research on CDO pricing as follows: A detailed cash-flow model has been established by Duffie and Gârleanu (2001), accommodating the predominant form of credit risk securitisation in the US that perform full asset transfer mostly under ABS-like structures.[3] The present contribution, by contrast, shall relate to the European securitisation technique and thus departs directly from the representation of CDOs as portfolio derivatives, extending the basic senior/subordinated structure to more involved cash-flow allocation schemes observed in the marketplace. With regard to the existing literature, my point of view is shared by Boscher and Ward (2002), performing a comparative-static valuation

[3] Yoshizawa (2003) reports the proportion of synthetic US-CDOs rated by Moody's to amount to 30% in 2002 and 15% in 2001 only.

study under the portfolio derivative premise established above.

Secondly, the formulation of an underlying credit model puts estimation issues into focus: A stochastic default time/default loss mechanism is generated by a reduced-form model, kept tractable enough to be estimated from market spreads. Not only market-implied single-name loss expectations shall be captured, but also the effects of systematic, i.e. non-diversified, risk factors affecting CDO tranche valuation shall be measured on the basis of market data.

Loss modelling extends the reduced-form framework of Lando (1998) and Duffie and Singleton (1999a) by the inclusion of a factor structure. A dependence structure interlinking multiple asset default, both in the reference market and in the asset pool, is generated by a number of systematic factors that affect all or a subset of claims simultaneously. Hence, a central contribution of my work relates to defaultable term structure model estimation: Riskless term structure modelling techniques are extended to the multi-factor problem, where the observed comovement in credit spreads is exploited for systematic factor estimation. With regard to inference, insight is gained on estimation methodology, which makes use of Kalman-filter based maximum likelihood estimation of simultaneous pricing equation systems. With regard to economic implications, insight is gained on modelling the stochastic behaviour of a broad sample of European corporate bond prices and implied risk premia.

Whereas the stochastic characterisation of bond price behaviour is of high relevance with regard to model validation, the model application to the CDO pricing problem permits a comparison of CDO model premia with their counterparts observed in the market, hence providing insight on price discovery in a relatively young and highly sophisticated market segment.

1.3 Outline of the study

Besides giving a characterisation of CDOs in their institutional and regulatory environment together with a classification of forms encountered in the market, Chapter 2 is largely devoted to the identification of risk factors affecting CDO pricing and performance. The shift of the view from cash-flow allocation to loss transfer, as outlined previously, is considered in great detail, as it provides the basis for subsequent formal analysis. A brief literature review lays the foundations for the modelling approach. Model development and estimation using a panel of prices of defaultable bonds issued by European corporates, are presented in Chapters 3 and 4, respectively. The outline, estimation, and validation of the underlying credit model precede the CDO pricing application, as both the methods applied and the data used possess a high degree of relevance in their own right. The basic valuation model under the senior/subordinated premise is explored in great detail in Chapter 5 and evaluated for a large variety of tranche dimensions. I include a comparative-static model analysis by expanding the estimated model to scenarios differing with regard to the underlying factor structure, the overall portfolio quality, the impact of systematic factors, and the relevance of factor risk pricing to the valuation task. Structural elements providing protection to investors of synthetic CDOs, a specific class of so-called 'credit enhancements' cause the payout function to deviate from the basic scheme, thus meriting formal investigation that will be undertaken in Chapter 6. The CDO model serves as the basis for an empirical pricing comparison, performed in Chapter 7: For a class of CDO transactions that closely accommodate the modelling approach, referred to as 'synthetic CBOs' the model is implemented, taking the specific contract details into account. The model-implied CDO premia are compared to observed issuance premia of CDOs, such that deviations of CDO markets participants' risk perceptions from the estimated factor model are identified. Chapter 8 consolidates the results and concludes.

Chapter 2

Credit Risk Securitisation: Structures and Risk Factors

2.1 From cash-flow allocation to default loss transfer

2.1.1 CDOs within the asset securitisation context

Traditionally, credit risk securitisations have been set up in the institutional framework of asset-backed securities (ABSs).[1] The term ABS-transaction or -structure generally refers to a note issuance programme, where the interest and principal payments are effectuated from the cash-flows generated by a specified portfolio of assets. ABSs are normally classified according to the type of collateral assets, determining the characteristics of the future income stream to be made available to noteholders. ABSs are characterised by two features: firstly, the pooling of cash-flows from financial claims and secondly, the issuance of notes that transfer the respective cash-flows to capital market investors. The issued notes may vary with respect to their priority on generated cash-flows, an element known as subordination or tranching.

Almost all types of pooled collateral assets have defaultable debt character, i.e. a future payment obligation of a debtor of fixed magnitude, which is subject to the risk of payment shortfalls.[2] A short account of the most relevant ABS types is given, firstly, in order to identify the elements characterising credit risk securitisations within their institutio-

---

1 See Herrmann and Tierney (1999), p. 5 for CDOs within the context of ABSs.

2 ABSs securitising cash-flows other than debt play a marginal role and shall not be considered further. Examples are whole-business-ABSs (securitisation of all cash-flows generated by a firm), future-flow-ABSs (securitisations of claims whose contracts have not been written at the ABS origination time) and securitisations of special risks, such as catastrophe or weather bonds.

nal context and secondly, to highlight the peculiarities and specific forms of credit risk securitisations.

Pooling of a large number of assets has its origin in the securitisation of mortgage loans under the guise of mortgage-backed securities, or mortgage-backed obligations (MBOs).[3] As the collateral mortgage loans are themselves backed by real-estate property, default risk in case of cash-flow shortfalls of collateral mortgage loans is of minor relevance.[4] Instead, the unscheduled early redemption decision of mortgage debtors, referred to as 'prepayment risk', is considered as the main risk factor for MBOs. As early redemption of mortgage loans is favourable in the case of a falling interest rate environment, the prepayment option has essentially the character of an interest rate derivative, adversely affecting the valuation of issued notes. Whereas mortgage loan securitisation constitutes an established refinancing vehicle in the US, the German mortgage sector primarily uses an alternative traditional refinancing means: the 'Pfandbrief'. As opposed to MBOs, Pfandbriefe are direct liabilities of the originating mortgage bank towards investors, such that the property pool is subsidiarily liable only in case of the originator's bankruptcy.[5] The maturity of the Pfandbrief sector, which recently began to provide tailor-made structured solutions, clearly explains why the MBO market in Germany is comparatively undeveloped.

Not only pooling of collateral assets has its origin in the MBO-market, but also the structural feature of tranching, which had its first appearance under the form of collateralised mortgage obligations (CMOs).[6] In order to create securities that are exempt from the undesirable prepayment risk – essentially a costly short option to a tranche investor – at least two classes of securities are issued, the subordinate class being affected by unscheduled payments from the mortgage pool first. The adverse effect of interest-rate-induced prepayment risk is therefore shifted from senior to subordinate MBO-investors.

ABSs which securitise the cash-flows from defaultable claims towards households or small

---

3 The US agencies, being the most relevant MBO-issuers in the US since the 1970s, Government National Mortgage Assoc. ('Ginnie Mae'), Federal Home Loan Mortgage Corporation ('Freddie Mac') and Federal National Mortgage Assoc. ('Fannie Mae'), find a rough correspondence in the German Kreditanstalt für Wiederaufbau (KfW), securitising German mortgage loans under the 'Provide'-programme since 2000. See Sullivan, Collins, and Smilow (1987), pp. 383-389 for agency MBOs. See http://www.kfw.de for the complete issuance information of the Provide transactions.

4 See Fabozzi (2000), pp. 226-232 for the risk factors of mortgage loans translating to MBOs and pp. 240-251 on prepayment assumptions applicable for US-MBOs.

5 See Mortgage Bank Act (2002), § 6 for the liability structure of the Pfandbrief.

6 Whereas the US agencies issue both pass-through-structures and tranched CMOs (See Fabozzi (2000), p. 236 and p. 283), all KfW's Provide-transactions are actually issued as CMOs. Furthermore, the KfW throughout uses the synthetic securitisation technique for risk transfer, see section 2.2.1.3. See Childs, Ott, and Riddiough (1996) with regard to a formal valuation study of CMO tranches as derivatives on the underlying risk factors.

businesses of a homogeneous contract type, by contrast, are affected by the risk of the payment shortfalls of private borrowers.[7] Mainly used as a means for corporate refinancing, one or, within the structure of multi-originator programmes, several creditors aim to create liquidity by the transfer of receivables from their private or corporate customers, such as receivables from credit cards, leasing contracts, trade credits, or, in the US, student loans. These respective collateral pools are characterised by a large number of claims, yielding a high degree of granularity.[8] The identity and the credit-worthiness of the single entities are not disclosed to the ABS investors, the composition of a the collateral pool may vary during the tenor of the structure due to renewal of matured collateral assets.

Whereas the above-mentioned ABS-types are largely initialised for the purpose of liquidity creation, collateralised debt obligations (CDOs) are used by banks primarily as a means for an explicit transfer of credit risk to market investors, with the exploitation of favourable refinancing depending on the availability of funding from the transaction. The following elements are common to both synthetic and true-sale CDOs, collectively distinguishing CDOs from other ABSs, to which only some of the mentioned elements apply:

Corporate or sovereign debt. The collateral claims are obligations of either corporate or sovereign debtors whose credit-worthiness is often verifiable on an individual basis. In comparison to ABSs set up mainly for refinancing purposes, the collateral pool may contain a considerably smaller number of particular entities.

Credit risk transfer. Reference claims normally have standard defaultable debt character. The main risk factor determining the cash-flows available for interest and principal payments to issued notes is the default risk of the collateral assets, which is economically transferred from the originator to capital market investors. Section 2.2.1 shows that credit risk transfer is not necessarily linked to the construction of an entire ABS-structure, but may alternatively be achieved by suitable credit derivative contracts.

Bank origination. CDOs are originated by banks. Section 2.2.2 outlines the motivations for CDO-issuance as a part of the investment or commercial banking businesses.

Investor-driven tranching. Banks make use of their expertise as financial intermediaries during note issuance. From a financial engineering perspective, tranching is

---

7 See Fabozzi (2000) pp. 319-328 for the risk factors of the mentioned ABS-types.

8 Granularity shall be used to characterise a portfolio in which individual partitions are of negligible size when related to the entire portfolio value.

performed in order to create structured securities that meet investors' preferences with regard to the desired exposure level to the securitised credit risk.

The credit risk of collateral debt is the main risk factor affecting the wealth of CDO tranche investors. It is therefore straightforward to classify CDOs as credit derivatives whose value is determined by the default risk of a large number of entities, i.e. as multi-name products, as has been suggested in the introduction. Payments from CDOs are therefore claims that are contingent on the performance of the specified collateral pool, the later being determined by the occurrence of bankruptcy events during the tenor of the structure.

Pooling and tranching have the following implications with respect to the contingent claims valuation problem to be considered.

Pooling, i.e. the selection of a large number of assets providing the bundled cash-flow amounts from which contingent claims are to be served, means that a potentially large number of random variables affect actual cash-flow generation.[9] Therefore, barring the degenerate case that the cash-flows of several claims are perfectly correlated, the number of random variables determining cash-flow availability is at least equal to the number of claims in the pool, assuming the simplest form of default characterisation by a randomly-drawn default time. A richer model structure, capturing the evolvement of cash-flows and credit-worthiness over time extends default-related random variables to the time series dimension. Furthermore, not only the individual debtors' credit-worthiness determines default losses that are transferred to tranche investors. As CDO tranches differ with regard to seniority on random cash-flows, the entire range of possible cash-flow realisations is of relevance to the payoff of several tranche investors. Cash-flow variation is driven by portfolio diversification. An increase in pool diversification is achieved by increasing the number of financial claims, hence increasing granularity such that portfolio cash-flow variation is reduced. Dependencies between the default riskiness[10] of several claims, however, reduce the benefit from diversification, where, regardless of a possible model specification, stronger dependence among cash-flows generated by the collateral claims entails higher probabilities for events characterised by joint cash-flow shortfalls, thus increasing cash-flow variation.

Tranching creates a subordination scheme, also figuratively referred to as a cash-flow waterfall. Translated into a corporate finance perspective, tranching mimics a capital

---

[9] Riddiough (1997) identifies a security backed by bundled asset pool cash-flows to dominate a corresponding security backed by an individual asset in the presence of unverifiable liquidation motives.

[10] A conceptual definition is in order: The term 'riskiness' consistently refers to the expected value of losses for a defaultable claim, as conveyed by a default probability and LGD, whereas 'risk' may refer both to default loss risk and deviations of random variables from their expected values.

structure, where capital stakes are subject to a standard bankruptcy sequence, characterised by ascending priority of equity, mezzanine, and debt investors on the underlying asset value. However, unlike for the firm capital structure analogue, loss allocation does not yield a termination of contracts, as will be shown in detail. Essentially, claims from tranches are issued under the form of debt contracts, i.e. a specified principal is provided, on which scheduled interest coupons are paid. Under the debt construction, the sum of all tranche principals at note issuance may not exceed the aggregate principal amount in the asset pool. In case of cash-flow shortfalls in the pool, the tranches assume a defaultable debt character: The subordination scheme determines a mechanism for the loss allocation to tranche investors, the subordinate tranches being affected first.[11] In general, the tranche payoffs are not mutually independent: In addition to the relative tranche sizes, the funds available for the serving of subordinate tranches are clearly affected by the claims of more senior tranches. This assertion may also hold in the opposite direction: Funds distributed beforehand to serve interest claims of subordinate tranches in earlier periods are not available for senior claimants, as would be the case for cash-flows deposited in a riskless account. The coupon size of subordinate tranches may thus affect later payoffs to a more senior tranche.

Putting both sides of a CDO transaction together, the resulting structure may be regarded as a synthetic bank, regardless of its institutional implementation.[12] The asset side is composed by the claims on cash-flows generated by the collateral pool during the tenor. The synthetic bank is refinanced by the issued notes, composing the liability side of the structure, entailing future payment obligations. Alternatively, the structure may be constructed in a manner so that only losses as differences between contractual and actual payments of the asset pool are transferred to the capital market investors, hence creating the asset-backed risk profile synthetically. In this case, all payment obligations, both on the asset and the liability side change in sign, with the risk structure of the issued CDOs being unaffected. This construction is subsequently explained in detail, because it provides the basis for the formal analysis of CDO tranche risk.

The formal analysis is characterised by the modelling of a large number of cash-flows, or losses, respectively, on the asset side. On the liability side, the payoffs of several derivatives are determined by the asset pool performance, the payoffs and therefore, values of the derivatives possibly being mutually dependent. The formulation of a model for cash-flows or, taking the credit derivatives perspective, losses from defaults, in the asset pool is

---

11 The alternative case of actual cash-flows generated by the asset pool exceeding the scheduled cash-flows, for instance in case of early redemption of callable pool assets, is not precluded per se. As the principal amount is still available for tranche redemption, this entails reinvestment risk only.

12 See Hatstadt (2001).

deferred to Chapter 3. The construction of a capital structure conforming to the cash-flows generated by defaultable debt is explained subsequently.

2.1.2 Tranched default loss transfer

Cash-flows from a debt portfolio normally occur at regular coupon periods and under the form of a final redemption payment at maturity. The view of default risk transfer shifts the focus from transfer rules applying to (positive) cash-flows generated by the asset pool to allocation rules that refer explicitly to losses as (negative) deviations from contractual payment obligations in the asset pool. The loss definition must encompass both a defaulted principal amount and a possible non-payment of interest coupons, to be discussed in detail at a later stage.

By tranching, losses in specific ranges that occur in the asset portfolio are transferred to several investors. Figuratively speaking, the cash-flow waterfall translates into a 'loss cascade'. The tranche specification determines the range of loss amounts in the asset pool which is transferred to the investor. The lower and upper bounds of the loss range of cumulated portfolio losses are denoted by $\underline{K}_{tr}$ and $\overline{K}_{tr}$, subsequently referred to as 'tranche thresholds'. These determine the order of loss allocation, where $\overline{K}_{tr-1} = \underline{K}_{tr}$ the decrement denoting the directly subordinate tranche. The maximum loss amount that can be allocated to an investor of a given tranche is limited to the tranche size $P_{tr}(0) = \overline{K}_{tr} - \underline{K}_{tr}$, however, principal losses are accompanied by the loss of the coupon applicable to the defaulted principal amount. Besides providing a cap on loss allocation, the currently outstanding principal amount $P_{tr}(t)$ constitutes the basis for interest accrual.

As for all tranched ABS structures, tranches $tr = 1, ..., \#tr$ are generally subsumed under the classification senior, mezzanine, and junior, 1 indexing the most subordinated piece. Subordinate tranches shield senior tranches from default loss allocation, expressed as the degree of 'overcollateralisation'. The overcollateralisation ratio of a specific tranche is expressed as

$$OC_{tr}(t) = \frac{\sum_{sub=1}^{tr-1} P_{sub}(t)}{P_{pool}(t)}. \tag{2.1}$$

The index $sub = 1, ..., tr - 1$ denotes all tranches subordinate to the tranche under consideration, starting from the junior tranche. Note that the overcollateralisation level is time-dependent: whereas initially, the identity

$$\underline{K}_{tr} = \sum_{sub=1}^{tr-1} P_{sub}(0) \tag{2.2}$$

holds, a reduction of the outstanding pool principal $P_{pool}(t)$ due to losses in earlier periods yields a reduction of $OC_{tr}(t)$, thus c.p. increasing the probability of the tranche considered to be impaired by defaults in the asset pool.

In the simplest case, which will be examined in detail during the course of the study, tranche thresholds are precisely identified with loss ranges in the underlying debt portfolio such that a tranche investor is impaired by aggregate losses that occur during the tenor of the structure exceeding $\underline{K}_{tr}$.

The unique identification of portfolio loss ranges with tranche principals is lost in the case of the installation of additional protective features, generally referred to as 'credit enhancements'. These elements are introduced in order to alter the level of riskiness of particular tranches or the entire capital structure. The prominent forms of credit enhancements are presented in Chapter 6 together with an assessment of their impact on tranche valuation.

A senior tranche is issued at almost zero risk premium above a riskless interest rate. Regardless of the actual implementation of risk transfer, a structurer generally attempts to maximise $P_{sen}(0)$ such that the tranche is still considered as virtually riskless by market participants and attracts cheap funding or credit protection. The actual default risk transfer takes place in the mezzanine loss range $\underline{K}_{mez}, \overline{K}_{mez}$. Structured according to the investors' preferences, and generally subdivided into several layers, the mezzanine loss piece may already be affected by losses of a size around the expected values of losses in the asset pool. Mezzanine tranches create a leveraged position in portfolio credit risk, a security type that is difficult to purchase under forms other than securitisation.

A key difference between CDOs and single-name positions of equivalent credit quality is the difference in the loss realisation upon a default event: Whereas single-name debt suffers a sudden loss in market value upon default event notice due to forgone future cash-flows, loss allocation to CDO tranches is of continuous nature and occurs gradually. Despite a possibly identical expected value of losses from a single-name claim and a CDO tranche, the distributional properties of losses incurred by both positions may be quite different.

Whereas senior and mezzanine tranches usually obtain an agency rating when issued as bonds, the lowest loss range, the first-loss piece or junior tranche, is in most cases retained by the originator. Contractual provisos effectuating first-loss retention achieve a mitigation of the pool's quality uncertainty arising from the informational advantage of the CDO issuing party, causing an adverse selection problem prior to origination and a moral hazard problem with respect to the monitoring of securitised claims.[13]

In addition to its contract-theoretic optimality, first-loss retention is implemented due to prevailing cash-flow constraints: The junior claim effectively amounts to a spot position in the defaultable asset pool that is protected against losses exceeding a cap $\overline{K}_{jun}$. Value additivity among all stakes in the transaction becomes evident in the fair valuation of the originator's positions: With regard to protection cost, value additivity requires the expected value of junior risk compensation to be equal to the difference of aggregate risk premia obtained by the collateral assets and the protection cost paid to more senior tranche investors.[14] However, the volatile nature of the residual claim precludes the payment of a regular coupon from the residual cash-flow stream, further lowering the marketability of first-loss pieces.[15] Compared with the unsecuritised credit exposure, with a theoretically worst outcome amounting to a total portfolio loss including coupon claims, the maximum loss in the order of the junior principal is acceptable for a bank as a risk-taker – all the more so, as the junior claimant is compensated for first-loss risk retention by the residual cash-flow stream.

2.2 Classification of structures

2.2.1 Contractual form of risk transfer

2.2.1.1 Outline

The contractual form of risk transfer determines cash-flows that are relevant to valuation, encompassing both contractual payments incurred by the default loss transfer mechanism and residual risks to which investors may be exposed. The outline of the two securitisation alternatives, traditional true-sales and synthetic structures, therefore departs from the ins-

---

[13] With respect to moral hazard mitigation by first-loss retention, see Gorton and Pennacchi (1995). The volume in a single-name loan sale and the screening and monitoring effort are determined simultaneously as a function of first-loss retention. First-loss retention is modelled as a guarantee of a fraction $\gamma \in [0, 1]$ of the sold loan piece. With reference to the lemons problem, see Riddiough (1997). In the presence of unverifiable liquidation motives of pooled assets, tranching together with junior retention is shown to mitigate adverse selection risk at origination. Monitoring of repayment is optimally performed by the junior stakeholder to prevent moral hazard.

[14] For a simple senior/subordinated structure, value additivity translates exactly to the time-zero values of tranche losses. However, if enhancement is provided by a spread account, value additivity must take losses absorbed by the account's balance into account, see Chapter 6 for the specific positions.

[15] Clearly, a first-loss piece can be issued as an equity-like claim, paying the residual claim as a dividend. An appropriate synthetic transfer may be performed under a total return swap, see Tavakoli (2001), p. 248. However, as high-probability, low-damage risks, first-losses are rarely transferable under insurance contracts, notwithstanding the risks resulting from asymmetric information.

titutional implementation. For both alternatives, the structural conditions on contractual cash-flows precluding or minimising risks unrelated to default losses are explored in great detail. Residual risks, i.e. unscheduled payment shortfalls and non-default-related market risks may be considered a major concern to counterparties. It is subsequently shown that synthetic securitisation aims at eliminating risk factors caused by variables other than reference asset default in a cost-efficient manner.

2.2.1.2 True-sale transactions

2.2.1.2.1 Institutional implementation The traditional way to transfer credit portfolio risk is characterised by the sale of the defaultable debt in the institutional context of an ABS-structure, implemented as depicted in figure 2.1.[16]

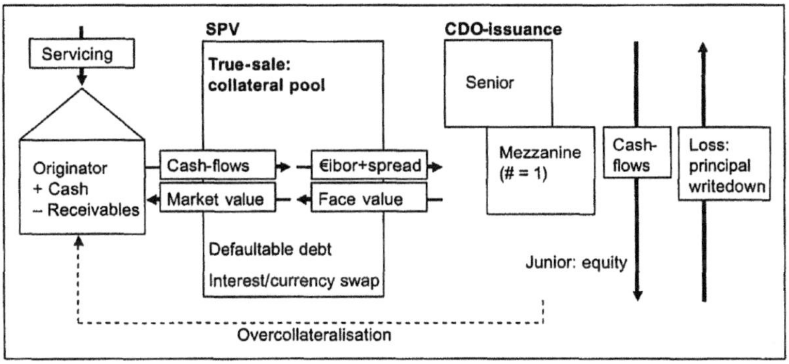

Figure 2.1: **Institutional implementation and cash-flows of a true-sale securitisation structure.**

CDOs are classified according to the marketability of underlying debt contracts, which take either the form of marketable securities, i.e. bonds, or non-traded bank loans. CDOs issued from true-sales are therefore subdivided into collateralised bond obligations (CBOs) and collateralised loan obligations (CLOs).

For true-sale structures, an initial cash inflow for pool acquisition is required. The contingent claims bearing tranched default risk are thus issued as funded notes at face value, the issuance proceeds then being available for claim acquisition. A true-sale structure is

[16] See for example Schorin and Weinreich (1998), pp. 1-3 and Standard & Poor's (1999), pp. 3-6 for funded securitisation structures. In addition to these general summaries, cash-flow diagrams of CDO structures are often given in the transactions' sales and rating information. Parties that are irrelevant to the valuation problem, such as external trustees or servicers have been omitted.

therefore characterised by the legal transfer of assets, either from the originator's balance sheet or acquired in the market, in any case entailing the payment of a principal value.

The transfer of the defaultable claims is achieved by the formation of a special purpose vehicle (SPV), a corporate entity whose purpose is the acquisition of collateral assets, refinanced by the proceeds of note issuance. Legally, this is achieved by selling contracts such that the SPV acquires the right both on future interest payments from the borrowers, which carry premia for individual default risk compensation, and on the principal redemption payment at maturity. Claim servicing is mostly performed by the originator under the existing lending relationship, who passes cash-flows to the SPV. Note that the SPV does not enter further transactions during the life of the structure, and in particular, that it is excluded from raising additional funds in order to fulfill payment obligations towards the CDO tranche investors.

Analogously to illiquid loan securitisation, the origination of true-sale CBOs seems attractive mainly for positions in bonds that cannot be sold directly due to low marketability. Hence, the initialisation of a true-sale funded by note issuance proceeds is not only a means for credit risk transfer, but also serves to free up funds that are then available for new business.

Furthermore, the opportunity of arbitrage gains by the repackaging process is mentioned in the practitioners' literature.[17] As opposed to the US, the availability of collateral assets is limited for Europe, where CBOs represent only a small fraction of traditional securitisations.[18] However, it will be shown below that CBOs are of interest in the context of synthetic structures transferring the credit risk of publicly-rated entities. CLOs play a prominent role in a bank-dominated system such as in Germany, where a large volume of bank loans to small and medium enterprises (SMEs) are available for securitisation.[19]

2.2.1.2.2 Cash-flow characteristics Given the SPV credit constraint, the funds available for distribution among CDO-investors are entirely determined by the coupon and principal cash inflows from the collateral claims to the SPV. Therefore, cash-flow availability has to be taken into account, both when setting up a true-sale CDO and when analysing and monitoring an existing structure.

---

[17] See Herrmann and Tierney (1999), p. 4 and for the discussion of arbitrage CDOs section 2.2.2.1.

[18] See Bakalar, Herrmann, Tierney, and Folkerts-Landau (2000), pp. 2-3 and Schorin and Weinreich (1998) p. 3 for US high yield bond securitisation and Herrmann and Tierney (1999) for the case for Germany.

[19] See Herrmann and Tierney (1999) pp. 19-34 for the analysis of the German corporate debt market under the aspect of loan securitisation. Henke, Burghof, and Rudolph (1998) pp. 11-24 discuss the requirements for credit risk transfer with a bank-dominated financial system in view.

Cash-inflows to the SPV are adversely affected by obligor bankruptcy risk. The cash-flow-related consequences of a default event of coupon-paying debt typically imply[20]

- the nonpayment of the face value at the contractual maturity of the defaulted claim
- the nonpayment of coupon claims upon default occurrence
- the inflow of a partial recovery payment. The recovery rate, expressed as the recovered amount in relation to the face value of the defaulted asset, is determined during the workout procedure. The actual amount is a random variable, with expectation increasing with the seniority of the defaulted claim according to the bankruptcy sequence. Furthermore, the time of receipt of the payment is a random variable itself, determined by the duration of the workout process.

There may be two reasons for non-payments to tranche investors, one due to scheduled loss allocation that is expected under the subordination scheme, the other due to unforeseen SPV insolvency. The risk of scheduled loss allocation is deliberately borne by CDO tranche investors, whereas counterparty risk towards a credit-constrained SPV, falling short of promised payments, should be precluded by the structure.

Defaults in the collateral pool cause the tranches not to be redeemable at initial face value due to the unavailability of defaulted principal payments in the collateral pool at maturity. The same holds true for the defaulted coupons of the asset pool. The mechanism of tranched loss transfer prevents a predictable shortage of funds. Default risk transfer is effectuated under a scheme comparable to sinking fund debt, however, with the relevant difference being that face value reductions are not linked to redemption payments.[21] The basic loss allocation scheme is characterised by dynamic principal write-downs of outstanding tranches, the most subordinate tranche being affected first.

With respect to cash-flow timing, payments to investors are due mostly on a quarterly basis because of the need of timely loss determination. Denoting the length of the coupon and loss determination period by Δt^{pay}, generally amounting to three months, the evolution of the face values of the respective tranches currently outstanding is dynamically determined as

---

[20] The institutional consequences of credit events are reflected in the defaultable debt valuation literature: The valuation of defaultable coupon-paying bonds in the reduced-form framework making use of the cash-flow decomposition is performed by Lando (1998), pp.102-106. The cash-flow sequence capturing coupon-paying debt default is referred to as the 'recovery of face value' (RFV) assumption in the valuation literature. See Duffie and Singleton (1999a), pp. 701 for the terminology. Duffie and Gârleanu (2001) adopt the decomposition in order to respect the cash-flow characteristics relevant for true-sale structures.

[21] See Duffie and Gârleanu (2001) p. 48 for the characterisation of traditional CDOs as sinking fund bonds.

$$\begin{aligned} P_{tr}(t^{pay}) &= \max\Bigg[P_{tr}(t^{pay}-\Delta t^{pay}) \\ &\quad - \max\left[\left(loss(t^{pay}) - \sum_{sub=1}^{tr-1} P_{sub}(t^{pay}-\Delta t^{pay})\right), 0\right], 0\Bigg] \end{aligned} \tag{2.3}$$

evaluated for all tranches $tr = 1, ..., \#tr$ in ascending order of seniority. $loss(t^{pay})$ denotes the aggregate loss in the asset portfolio occurred during the coupon period ending in t^{pay}. The rule determining reference losses $loss(t^{pay})$ is in principle a free contract parameter. However, the subsequent discussion of residual risks shows that the minimisation of SPV insolvency probability is closely related to conservative loss calculation.

The current principal evaluates to $P_{tr}(0)$ as long as cumulated losses do not exceed the tranche threshold $\underline{K}_{tr}$

$$\sum_{s} loss(s) < \underline{K}_{tr},\ s = \Delta t^{pay}, ..., t^{pay}. \tag{2.4}$$

The formulation takes into account that a tranche threshold is determined by the initial principals of all subordinate tranches, which are reduced by losses that have occurred during earlier periods, dynamically lowering the current overcollateralisation ratio of the tranche under consideration.

If two (or more) tranches are affected in period t^{pay}, losses are also allocated in ascending order of seniority, such that subordinated tranche principals are reduced to zero before more senior tranches are impaired.

A final principal redemption payment is made to the tranche investors of $P_{tr}(T)$, which amounts to the original tranche principal reduced by aggregate losses allocated to the respective tranche

$$P_{tr}(T) = P_{tr}(0) - \sum_{t^{pay}} \max\left[\left(loss(t^{pay}) - \sum_{sub=1}^{tr-1} P_{sub}(t^{pay}-\Delta t^{pay})\right), 0\right]. \tag{2.5}$$

The loss amount allocated to a tranche during the tenor of the structure is completely characterised by (2.5). However, issuance in the form of coupon-paying debt has to take the entire sinking-fund construction into account, dynamically described by (2.3). Most commonly, tranches are issued as par floaters, whose contractual coupons are determined by a riskless floating rate plus a constant spread s_{tr}.[22] Whereas the straightforward choice for the variable riskless coupon component is a three-month market rate, fixed at the beginning of the coupon period, the nominal premium for portfolio default risk compensation is determined such that the tranche under consideration is issued at par.

Conforming to standard coupon-paying debt, the coupon payment is determined in arrears, which does not only apply to calculation of the three-month floating rate $f_r(t^{pay} - \Delta t^{pay})$, but also to the weakly decreasing principal basis $P_{tr}(t^{pay} - \Delta t^{pay})$ on which current coupon payments are due. Tranche investors obtain a quarterly contractual payment of

$$CF_{tr}(t^{pay}) = (f_r(t^{pay} - \Delta t^{pay}) + s_{tr})\Delta t^{pay} P_{tr}(t^{pay} - \Delta t^{pay}). \qquad (2.6)$$

Note that portfolio losses to be allocated to tranche investors $loss(t^{pay})$ may be mitigated by recovery payments, causing loss amounts to fall below the full principal exposure. For true-sales, recovery cash-flows physically accrue to the SPV and are available for tranche redemption at maturity. Furthermore, an appropriate reinvestment policy must be specified, such that future income generated by reinvested recoveries meets the liabilities towards the trancheholders.

A retained junior claim, in the standard case not eligible to a regular coupon, assumes losses according to (2.3) only, where overcollateralisation $\sum_{sub=1}^{tr-1} P_{sub}(t^{pay} - \Delta t^{pay})$ evaluates to zero. The value-additivity-argument motivated for the junior claimant above, however, requires the originator to be appropriately compensated for first-loss retention: The residual claim on all portfolio cash-flows must be valued equal to losses borne by the originator. This requirement is fulfilled through a mechanism that is referred to as excess spread generation. Due to its relevance to the questions of structuring formally addressed within the valuation study, the mechanism shall be considered in more detail:

Excess spread generation only relies on (i) the self-financing property of the structure, and (ii) on contractual coupons that decrease with tranche seniority. Whereas the first requirement should be fulfilled due to the SPV credit constraint, the second is achieved through the ranking of nominal risk premia as an increasing function of a tranche's expected value of losses.

The following considerations presume that the riskless interest component of the collateral pool assets is swapped into the floating rate that compensates the CDO tranche investor for the provision of funding, as indicated in figure 2.1. A measure frequently used in order to quantify the relationship between cash-inflows from the collateral pool and payment obligations towards trancheholders is the weighted average coupon rate. Alternatively, by

22 See Bielecki and Rutkowski (2002), pp. 9-10 for the specification of single-name defaultable par floaters.

deducting the riskless interest component, a weighted average spread rate at origination is obtained, the measure to be used in this study. Consider the asset side of the transaction first: Every non-defaulted collateral asset, indexed by i, with principal exposure P_i generates an annualised spread income for single-name default risk compensation of s_i, applicable to the principal exposure. The number of surviving pool assets at any coupon payment date shall be denoted as $I(t^{pay})$ such that the dependence of asset pool spread income on the default history is accommodated. Expressed in relation to the outstanding pool principal, the weighted average spread generated by the asset side is defined as

$$\mathcal{S}_{pool}(t^{pay}) = \frac{\sum_{i=1}^{I(t^{pay})} s_i P_i}{P_{pool}(t^{pay})} \tag{2.7}$$

where $P_{pool}(t^{pay}) = \sum_{i=1}^{I(t^{pay})} P_i$.

Analogously, the weighted average spread on the liability side is defined as

$$\mathcal{S}_{tr}(t^{pay}) = \frac{\sum_{tr=1}^{\#tr} s_{tr} P_{tr}(t^{pay})}{\sum_{tr=1}^{\#tr} P_{tr}(t^{pay})}, \tag{2.8}$$

relating the premium liabilities towards tranche investors to the principal currently outstanding.

Leaving temporal mismatches regarding coupon payment dates aside, at initialisation

$$\mathcal{S}_{pool}(0) \geq \mathcal{S}_{tr}(0) \tag{2.9}$$

must hold to ensure payment of tranche coupons at every point in time. Equality characterises the limiting case, where all coupon proceeds received by the pool are allocated to tranche investors, for instance in the context of an interest-bearing junior tranche. Yet in the limiting case, the spread differential within the structure $\mathcal{S}_{pool}(t^{pay}) - \mathcal{S}_{tr}(t^{pay})$ is firstly, increasing in time, if the relation (2.9) holds with inequality, and secondly, increasing in portfolio loss severity. Upon loss occurrence in the collateral pool, principal reductions apply both to the asset and to the liability side. On the liability side, however, the accrual basis for the most subordinate tranche is reduced, bearing a higher spread than the defaulted claim in the collateral pool.[23] This mechanism causes the SPV to gain a periodical net cash inflow, referred to as excess spread. For the formal analysis, excess spread $XS(t^{pay})$ shall be defined on an absolute basis.

---

[23] Note that this argument extends to the inequality case: If junior risk is retained at zero premium, (2.9) causes the SPV to hold a positive cash balance from the first coupon date, hence providing additional protection against SPV insolvency.

The standard structure collects the excess spread on an account, whose final value accrues to the originator upon the consolidation of the SPV. The residual claim on excess spread compensates the originator for loss allocation to the junior tranche, taking the form of a lower or zero redemption payment at maturity. Value additivity requires both positions to be valued identically.[24]

The exposition of the cash-flows associated with funded structures shows that scheduled loss allocation aligns the cash-flows payable to tranche investors with the cash-flows obtained from the collateral pool. A remaining positive probability of SPV insolvency, however is inherent in traditional default risk transfer, which is due to deviations of actual cash-inflows from the typical defaultable debt scheme outlined above, violating the exact cash-flow matching conditions. In principle, only noncallable coupon-paying debt valued at par at origination with maturity equal to the tenor of the structure guarantees absence of insolvency risk, together with conservative loss allocation in the presence of uncertain recoveries. Those requirements are clearly unlikely to be fulfilled by the collateral available.

The inclusion of bonds trading at a discount due to prior quality deterioration, for example, is cheap for the SPV. However, when considering future cash-flows, a discount bond does not generate spread income applicable to its current credit quality, which would be required to meet premium claims on the liability side, the latter being calculated on a non-discounted principal basis. In face of recovery uncertainty, liquidity shortages may occur due to late or inadequate tranche principal write-downs. Furthermore, the convention of interest accrual on the basis of start-of period tranche principals $P_{tr}(t^{pay} - \Delta t^{pay}) \geq P_{tr}(t^{pay})$ tends to create coupon claims of trancheholders exceeding the coupon inflow from collateral surviving up to period t^{pay}. The risk of interest cash-flow insufficiency is largely mitigated by the non-eligibility of a retained junior tranche to interest payments, creating excess spread to a large extent, but a residual risk may remain.

Finally, the need to sell or replenish claims in case of maturity mismatches exposes even a cash-flow based structure with a static portfolio to market risk.

The risk of liquidity shortages does not comply with an intended absence of risk for senior tranches. Causing nominal premium shortfalls, it is still considered as undesirable by investors in rated mezzanine tranches. Accordingly, rating agencies are not only concerned with default loss risk borne by tranche investors, but also with structural integrity such that the SPV can meet its contractual obligations towards all investors of rated tranches.

---

[24] Schmidt and Ward (2002) discuss the analogous observation for a costless replication of a n−claims-portfolio via a portfolio of first to nth−basket CDS.

Some structural features mitigate remaining SPV insolvency risk.[25] A liquidity facility provided by the originator guarantees the payment of contractual cash-flows to rated tranches in case of SPV insolvency.[26] Furthermore, structures with little overcollateralisation through a non-interest bearing junior loss piece may incorporate priority rules on the basis of interest coverage tests.[27] The breach of a specified interest coverage requirement contractually triggers the redirection of interest payments to senior claimants, whose scheduled claims are fulfilled at the expense of the more subordinate claimholders, who either forego their scheduled coupons or suffer a deferral of payments until interest coverage is restored.

Market risk due to maturity mismatches is largely circumvented by the creation of tranches with different maturities. However, the uncertainty about the loss partition among maturity classes creates new SPV shortfall or market risks.

In addition to the credit risk-related issues, a proper credit risk securitisation requires the elimination of interest rate and possibly currency risk. Income from the asset side, generated on a fixed-coupon basis, is used to serve tranches normally issued as par floaters, hence requiring the credit-constrained SPV to attempt a perfect hedge. In traditional securitisations, however, hedges are difficult to implement using market-traded fixed-for-floating swaps because of the uncertain exposure size at future points in time.[28] Instead, hedging is generally assured through agreements with the originator of the structure, who assumes the risk of interest or exchange rate uncertainty. A risk transfer to an external counterparty providing the adequate interest or possibly currency swap must take the uncertain future principal basis into account. Whereas the assumption of pure market risk does not create problems to a financial institution, the uncertain exposure size effectively is a residual default-related risk factor still affecting the originator after the completed asset transfer.[29]

The requirement of cash-flow harmonisation, concerning the determination of suitable

---

[25] These are not to be confused with credit enhancements discussed below, as the underlying loss allocation mechanism is not affected.

[26] As further discussed in 2.2.2.2, this element affects the regulatory recognition of risk transfer adversely, see BCBS (2003), no. 504.

[27] See Schorin and Weinreich (1998) p. 10. Interest coverage tests basically correspond to a dynamic monitoring of the excess spread mechanism.

[28] Note the analogy to the credit default swap replication by an asset swap package for single-name risk transfer, see Duffie (1999), pp. 83-85. Whereas only one random default time enters the valuation of a single-name CDS, the random default times of a large number of borrowers determine the currently outstanding pool and tranche principals.

[29] The possibility of remaining market- or liquidity risks is recognised by the German supervision, see BaFin (1997), § 1, however, it is treated in a pure market risk context.

tranche principal reductions that accommodate losses from defaults in the collateral pool and the allocation of interest income of the pool to contractual tranche coupons, is judged as a major inconvenience to true-sale securitisations.[30] The necessity of extensive contractual documentation specifying allocation rules conditional on a large number of possible states together with dynamic monitoring of the structure causes non-negligible obstacles to the initialisation of true-sale CDOs. Furthermore, the risk of non-fulfillment of scheduled payments to mezzanine and junior tranches due to SPV insolvency reduces the marketability of those already highly-leveraged notes further, entailing higher risk premia.

In addition to those cash-flow related hindrances, the transfer of non-marketable loans towards borrowers of multiple jurisdictions to the SPV imposes legal constraints to the true-sale procedure.[31] Furthermore, the argument of a possible degradation of lending relationships due to the disclosure of the accomplished risk transfer is put forward as an obstacle to true-sale securitisations in a bank-dominated financial system.[32]

2.2.1.3 Synthetic securitisation

2.2.1.3.1 Institutional implementation Synthetic securitisation transactions are characterised by the acquisition of default protection on the capital market, whereas defaultable positions remain on the originator's balance sheet. Through the appropriate use of credit derivative contracts, a legal transfer of receivables is not required in order to achieve the transfer of portfolio credit risk. With respect to the creation of a synthetic bank, the asset side, generating future coupon and principal payments, is entirely held by the originator. A mere default risk transfer is not contingent on the provision of funding by investors, such that only the capital structure is transferred to market participants, protecting the asset side against losses from defaults.[33] Liquidity creation, a main motivation for issuing true-sale CDOs, is generally not intended. The fact that in Europe as opposed to the US, synthetic securitisation dominates true-sale volumes by far suggests that originating parties pursue rather different objectives with asset securitisation.

Synthetic CDOs can be classified as either synthetic CLOs or CBOs, depending on the

---

[30] See for instance Böhringer, Lotz, Solbach, and Wentzler (2001) pp. 10-11 for the disadvantages of true-sale securitisation. Those aspects relate to the incentives for synthetic securitisation, recognised by BCBS (2001a), pp. 15-16.

[31] See Böhringer, Lotz, Solbach, and Wentzler (2001), p. 10 for the institutional obstacles to loan sales.

[32] See Henke, Burghof, and Rudolph (1998), pp. 12-14.

[33] The relevance of this transaction type has recently been recognised by the rating agencies: Standard & Poor's (2003) and Yoshizawa (2003) (Moody's) extend their rating approaches to synthetic CDOs.

marketability of the underlying claims, analogously to true-sale structures.[34] The distinction according to marketability applies to the reference assets that underlie the credit derivative contracts among the parties involved. In the German market, synthetic loan securitisation plays a major role due to the predominance of bank loan financing of SMEs.[35]

Synthetic CBOs, however, largely differ from traditional CBOs with respect to the bond borrowers' credit-worthiness. Whereas repackaging of speculative-grade illiquid bonds represents the main objective for true-sale structures, pursuing the arbitrage motive to be discussed in section 2.2.2, underlying bonds of synthetic securitisations are liquid securities, often issued by investment grade debtors. Furthermore, the relevant issuers' default risk is often traded under single-name CDSs, such that a replication of claims issued from synthetic CBOs is in principle not precluded by collateral claim illiquidity.[36] Note that cross-default in case of asset mismatch even permits to protect an illiquid on-balance sheet exposure towards the reference entity of the derivative transaction. The basis risk that is incurred by a possible mismatch between the on-balance-sheet loss and the settlement payment under the swap is retained by the issuer.

From an institutional viewpoint, derivative credit risk transfer can be achieved through several contractual constructions.

The basic synthetic structure effectively boils down to a senior/subordinated portfolio derivative structure, whose implementation and cash-flow characteristics are illustrated in figure 2.2.

The issuance of senior/subordinate tranches does not require the inclusion of an SPV. The creation of a 'collateral pool' via an asset sale is replaced by the specification of the 'reference portfolio' whose default risk is to be transferred. Contingent claims of synthetic transactions bear losses in specified ranges of the reference portfolio. Loss ranges are set such that a standard subordination scheme is established, where the market investors provide credit protection under senior/subordinated derivative positions. Credit derivatives between the originator seeking credit protection and the counterparty can be set up in the form of portfolio default swaps, where losses falling in the specified range are exchanged for a regular premium. The use of portfolio default swaps is clearly limited to synthetic transactions, as a principal exchange does not take place and funding for reference

[34] See Jobst (2002a), p. 10 for this distinction.

[35] The 'Promise'-transactions, structured and issued by the KfW, present a prominent example of synthetic German bank loan securitisation, see http:// www.kfw.de for extensive documentation.

[36] Aside from on an own market review in 2001, where synthetic investment grade CBOs had their first appearance (see Chapter 7), some recent practitioners' literature is dedicated to this type of securitisation, see Hatstadt (2001), Humphries (2002) and Lehman Brothers (2003), pp. 12-14 for this relatively new securitisation type. It is also referred to as collateralised structured obligation (CSO).

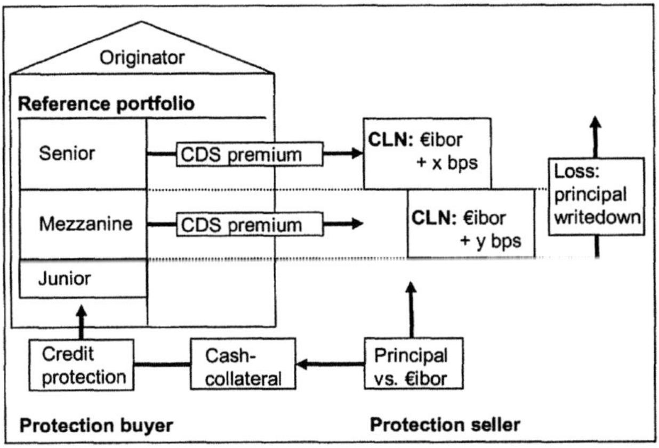

Figure 2.2: **Synthetic securitisation I: senior/subordinated portfolio CLNs.** Issued notes or portfolio default swaps (not depicted) represent direct obligations of the originator.

collateral acquisition is not required. However, as the CDS-transaction is vulnerable to counterparty default risk itself, it may not necessarily represent the optimal contract for risk transfer. Counterparty risk is ruled out by tranche issuance under the form of credit-linked notes (CLNs), as depicted in figure 2.2. The face value $P_{tr}(0)$ is provided by the protection seller at the origination date and invested in riskless securities. The deposited face value serves as cash collateral, which is available for the settlement payments to the originator to cover losses from reference portfolio defaults. The interest income on the cash collateral is accrued by the protection seller, who receives a premium as a spread on the outstanding exposure for default risk compensation. In case of reference portfolio default losses, funds are available with certainty to effectuate settlement payments to the originator, to be outlined in detail below.

The bankruptcy-remoteness of the cash-collateral, however, is installed by an agreement that exempts the riskless notes from the originator's bankruptcy mass, for instance through the transfer to a trustee holding the collateral on behalf of the originator.[37]

Alternatively, a structure may be set up including an SPV. Its function, however, differs from its counterpart's in true-sale structures. As opposed to true-sales, a principal exchange between the originator and the SPV does not take place. Instead, pure default risk of the reference portfolio is transferred to the SPV that provides credit protection for the originator in exchange for regular premium payments under credit derivative contracts.

[37] See Böhringer, Lotz, Solbach, and Wentzler (2001) p. 43 for examples.

The loss range transferred to the SPV may range from the transfer of the entire portfolio risk to the transfer of the loss range of a single tranche.[38]

A first example of the use of an SPV is given in figure 2.3, depicting a transaction where the full-portfolio default risk is transferred to the SPV.

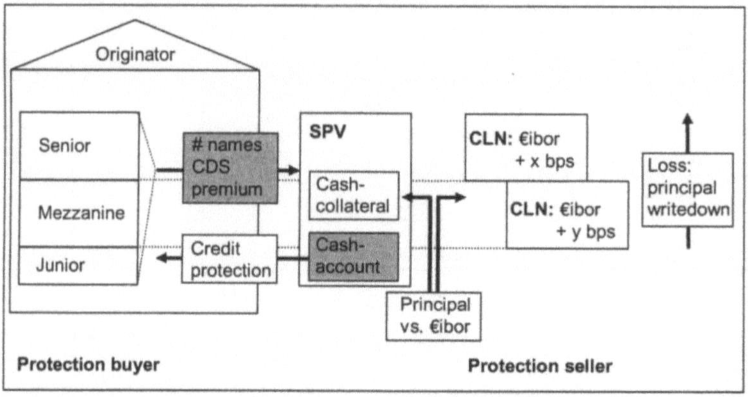

Figure 2.3: **Synthetic securitisation II: full-portfolio risk transfer via SPV.** Note or portfolio default swap (not depicted) issuance is performed by the SPV. Risk transfer from the originator to the SPV is effectuated under a number of single-name CDSs on underlying reference names. The cash-account held by the SPV may either accrue to the originator at final maturity or may provide additional protection to issued tranches.

As indicated in figure 2.3, a full-portfolio transfer can be straightforwardly implemented through plain-vanilla single-name CDSs on the particular reference names, such that the originator buys protection for each name from the SPV. The SPV in turn, holds a portfolio of protection-selling positions, to be refinanced and perfectly hedged through a waterfall capital structure of CLNs or CDSs.

An alternative structure, only transferring selected loss ranges under an appropriate portfolio ('basket') swap related to one or several tranches of the structure is shown in figure 2.4.

As opposed to the full-portfolio transfer structure, the premium applying to the entire range transferred from the originator to the SPV, is not separately identified from the single-name premia. A valuation of the relevant default risk is therefore required prior to

38 Besides covering the structures identified within an own market review, the following description relates to Standard & Poor's (2003), pp. 5, who highlight the differences between structures transferring full and partial credit portfolio risk via an SPV through appropriate derivatives. Hatstadt (2001), p. 4 performs his analysis on a the basis of a portfolio replicated through single-name CDSs.

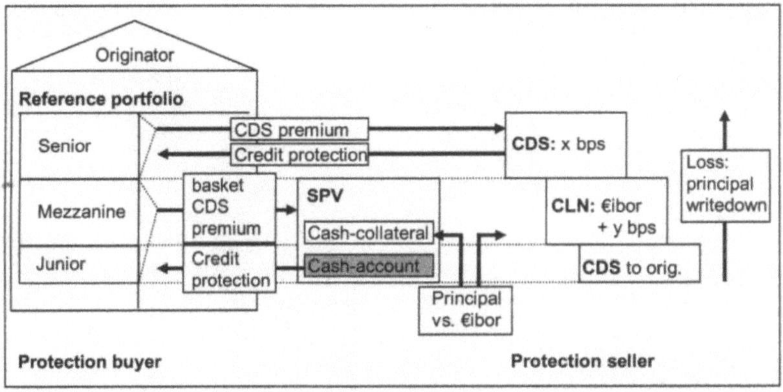

Figure 2.4: **Synthetic securitisation III: partial portfolio risk transfer via SPV.** Contracts with protection-selling investors are written both by the originator and by the SPV. Whereas the senior tranche is directly protected under a senior swap, subordinated tranches are issued by the SPV. The risk transfer from the originator to the SPV is effectuated under portfolio derivatives referring to the relevant loss ranges. Junior risk may be repurchased under a CDS, as illustrated in the figure or alternatively left unprotected, analogously to figure 2.2. Note or portfolio default swap (not depicted) issuance is performed by the SPV. Risk transfer from the originator to the SPV is effectuated under a number of single-name CDSs on underlying reference names. The cash-account held by the SPV may either accrue to the originator at final maturity as a residual claim or may provide additional protection to issued tranches.

the issuance of synthetic CDOs. Most commonly, the mezzanine loss range is transferred via one SPV, then issuing several tranches. Mezzanine tranche issuance is typically performed under CLNs that are automatically bankruptcy-remote with reference to the originator. Issued notes represent claims against the SPV only, which pays interest to noteholders out of the cash collateral and the portfolio default swap premium received from the originator.

For both structures that make use of an SPV, a junior tranche can either be simply left unprotected, or, if previously transferred to the SPV, be repurchased, as illustrated in figure 2.4. As a result of the whole transaction, the originator achieves a cap on losses at the mezzanine tranche threshold $\underline{K}_{mez}$, without being required to perform the true-sale procedure.

As depicted in figure 2.4, senior risk transfer is normally achieved under a direct portfolio default swap, requiring no collateral deposit. Due to the overcollateralisation provided by the subordinate tranches, it is referred to as 'super-senior', the term senior then applying to the highest funded CLN-tranche, which is either issued directly by the originator or via the inclusion of an SPV. As counterparty payment obligations under the super-senior CDS are considered as very unlikely to occur, the acquisition of a large volume of principal collateral seems inadequate for the desired exposure reduction, all the more so as collateral is generally not available to the originator's business.

Figures 2.3 and 2.4 include an additional position, a cash-account held by the SPV, that has not been discussed so far. It is added to the figures in view of the cash-flow analysis to be performed over the course of the formal study. The analysis carried out in Chapter 6 shall refer back to the illustrations when required.

An additional intermediary (not depicted in the figures) is often included between the originator and the SPV, providing protection on the entire reference portfolio under single-name CDS contracts in the same manner as described for the SPV above.[39] The respective construction is motivated by regulatory purposes discussed below and possibly by the structuring expertise provided by the institution. For the valuation exercise to be performed, the inclusion of the additional institution is in principle irrelevant, as the single-name CDS premia are already determined through the prices and terms of the reference claims.

2.2.1.3.2 Cash-flow characteristics From a financial engineering perspective, synthetic transactions are structured such that scheduled payments of true-sales are closely imitated. As opposed to the true-sale alternative, synthetic securitisation has an attractive feature in that the risk of payment shortfalls due to cash-flow insufficiency and limited liability of the SPV can be entirely precluded. It will be pointed out that this argument does not rely on the presence or absence of an SPV.

An exact replication of the sinking-fund bonds, backed by a funded collateral pool, but effectuating payments to all tranches with certainty, can be achieved by the issuance of CLNs. Premium payments to the note investors are determined according to (2.6). The riskless part of the coupon claim is generated by the interest income earned on the cash collateral, whereas the spread payment is either effectuated directly by the originator or served through the originator's premium payment to the SPV, respectively. The redemption of the cash collateral reduced by default losses borne by the respective tranche is determined according to (2.5).

The alternative CDS-issuance is accomplished analogously to single-name CDS terms. A regular premium is paid to the counterparty in exchange for credit protection in the specified reference portfolio. However, the contract is not terminated upon loss occurrence and the termination payment, as in standard single-name swaps.[40] Instead, the contract

---

[39] See BCBS (2001a), p. 28. This represents the basic structure for the KfW Promise loan securitisations, see Krämer-Eis, Schneider, and Tiskens (2001), p. 29.

[40] See Duffie (1999), pp. 73-74 for the pricing-relevant cash-flows of single-name CDSs.

remains active: Upon loss occurrence in the reference portfolio, the loss amount is paid by the protection seller. The principal as accrual basis for future premium claims is then reduced by the incurred loss amount applicable to the respective tranche, according to (2.3).

Assuming again that CDS premia s_{tr} are payable quarterly in arrears,[41] net periodic cash-flows to the protection seller resulting from the tranched CDS take the form

$$\begin{aligned} CF_{tr}(t^{pay}) &= s_{tr}\Delta t^{pay} P_{tr}(t^{pay} - \Delta t^{pay}) + P_{tr}(t^{pay}) - P_{tr}(t^{pay} - \Delta t^{pay}) \qquad (2.10) \\ &= (s_{tr}\Delta t^{pay} - 1)\, P_{tr}(t^{pay} - \Delta t^{pay}) + P_{tr}(t^{pay}). \end{aligned}$$

The representation encompasses the reduction of the principal exposure by the quarterly loss amount allocated to the tranche considered, described by (2.3). Instead of a reduction of his claim on final principal redemption, the protection seller incurs an immediate loss, payable to the protection buying counterparty.

Aside from the avoidance of the costly true-sale procedure, the substitution of cash-flow transfer of true-sales by synthetic loss allocation is attractive because of the exclusion of almost all risk factors other than pure portfolio default risk in the issued tranches.

One central advantage of synthetic risk transfer is the standardisation of loss determination, mitigating recovery uncertainty, which is seen as follows: Credit events that apply to the transaction considered can to a certain degree be specified according to the ISDA credit derivatives definitions, such that settlement payments may be detached from the random future cash-flow realisation.[42] Loss determination constitutes the relevant difference between synthetic CLOs and CBOs. The settlement procedure and credit event definition is flexible for synthetic CLOs, depending on the intended level of credit protection demanded by the originator. As for the funded alternatives, however, loss calculation still

---

41 This assumption does not comply with CDS terms, where premia are due upfront. It is made for convenience such that CDSs may be treated analogously to CLNs. It is however harmless, as CDS-issuance is mainly observed for super-senior tranches, whose principal exposure remains mostly constant.

42 See International Swaps and Derivatives Association (2003), art. IV for credit event definitions. The events related to reference obligor illiquidity generally trigger loss allocation earlier than the events related to bankruptcy, but imply minor losses. Credit event definitions adopted in the confirmation thus affect the probability of loss allocation, the expected recovery, the degree of protection provided to the originator and consequently, the premia of the issued tranches. A short discussion of the suitability of the credit event definitions for synthetic CDOs is given by Tavakoli (2001), p. 258.

relates to the cash-flows of non-traded defaulted assets.[43] Synthetic CBOs, by contrast, are characterised by cash settlement according to the ISDA terms.[44] As for single-name derivative contracts, the loss amount is cash-settled on the basis of a loss in market value of a specific reference bond, mentioned in the contractual terms of the securitisation transaction.[45] The loss-given-default (LGD) is usually determined via a dealer poll within a fixed time period upon loss occurrence, removing the uncertainty about the workout period and final recovery proceeds from the structure.[46]

Settlement payments resulting from the derivative transactions are then based on losses determined at a particular point in time only, and are therefore detached from actual cash-inflows of the collateral claims. The risk that the settlement payment does not meet the cash-flows actually lost is entirely borne by the originator.

In addition to the standardisation of loss determination, as explained for synthetic CBOs, and with reservations incurred by the lack of a market-priced reference bonds applicable to synthetic CLOs, the credit constraint of a fully-funded SPV becomes irrelevant. In the senior/subordinated direct note issuance structure depicted in figure 2.2, which does not rely on an intermediary SPV, all premium- or coupon claims are direct obligations of the originating bank. With respect to originator compensation for first-loss retention, excess spread is generated in the same manner as for true-sale structures, such that the above argument applies equivalently.

Structures using SPVs are generally set up such that cash-flow shortages are ruled out. Moreover, as opposed to true-sale CDOs, the contract specifications of synthetic transactions normally grant an extraordinary cancellation right in case of non-payments of scheduled premia or coupons.

The mechanism guaranteeing cash-flow sufficiency of the SPV for fulfillment of the tranche investors' claims works in a similar way as the creation of excess spread.

The two synthetic risk transfer alternatives, the full-portfolio transfer via the SPV that is easiest performed under single-name CDSs and the partial risk transfer using a single mezzanine or mezzanine/junior portfolio default swap between the originator and the

---

[43] Some transactions allow for tranche principal appreciation in case of late recovery payments, see Standard & Poor's (2003), p. 30 for this alternative. This feature has for instance been used in part of the Promise-transactions.

[44] See International Swaps and Derivatives Association (2003), art. VII for cash settlement.

[45] Physical delivery of a defaulted claim by the originator to the SPV in exchange for a non-default value is inconvenient for synthetic CBOs due to the reinvestment requirement for recovery proceeds.

[46] If not specified otherwise, the ISDA terms allow for a period of five business days for loss calculation, see International Swaps and Derivatives Association (2003) section 7.8, which accommodates the quarterly coupon periods of CDOs.

SPV, differ with respect to the premium inflow to the SPV.

Consider the structure where the entire portfolio default risk is swapped to the SPV, depicted in figure 2.3: In this case, where single-name risk pricing applies, the structural condition (2.9) between single-name CDS premia s_i and tranche premia holds perfectly analogously to the true-sale alternative. Cash-flow sufficiency follows from the weak positivity of excess spread.

Partial risk transfer under a portfolio default swap, as depicted in 2.4, requires a different approach: In this case, a constant nominal premium s_{SPV} is determined at origination. At every future coupon date, it is applicable to the non-defaulted principal of the portfolio default swap. For the partial transfer structure, cash-flow sufficiency requires that the portfolio default swap premium amount paid to the SPV by the originator equals or exceeds the premium outflows to tranche protection sellers. Both amounts are calculated on the basis of the sum of all tranche principals that are issued via the SPV. Thus, at issuance, the lower bound on the constant portfolio default swap premium rate s_{SPV} payable by the originator to the SPV is obtained as the weighted average premium $\mathcal{S}_{tr\,by\,SPV}(0)$ of the tranches issued by the SPV, generally a number of mezzanine tranches for the partial risk transfer structure:

$$s_{SPV} = \mathcal{S}_{tr\,by\,SPV}(0) = \frac{\sum_{tr\,by\,SPV} s_{tr} P_{tr}(0)}{\sum_{tr\,by\,SPV} P_{tr}(0)}. \tag{2.11}$$

Upon loss allocation, tranche principals are reduced according to the basic loss allocation rule (2.3), which affects both the total premium amount payable to the SPV by the originator and premia payable to the protection sellers by the SPV. On the side of the issued tranches, however, this reduces the accrual basis for the most subordinate tranche, bearing the highest premium claim, whereas on the side of the portfolio default swap between originator and SPV, the lower average premium is applied to the reduced principal. Even for the liming case, when setting s_{SPV} to its lower bound,

$$s_{SPV} \geq \mathcal{S}_{tr\,by\,SPV}(t^{pay}) \tag{2.12}$$

holds during the tenor, with equality prior to loss occurrence in the reference portfolio. Cash-flow sufficiency and the absence of liquidity risk are therefore guaranteed, despite the limited liability of the SPV.

The market usance of premium accrual on the basis of start-of-period principals is innocuous for synthetic structures, given that it also applies to the portfolio default swap between originator and SPV. The same assertion holds for the adjustment of tranche principals upon loss occurrence. These contractual elements determining payment obligations to the CDO protection sellers translate to the originator under the portfolio default swap, thus finally rendering the credit constraint of the SPV non-binding with regard to SPV insolvency risk.

The interpretation of a judiciously-structured CDO as a synthetic CBO largely facilitates formal analysis, given that the single-name loss definition is in line with the CDO issuance conditions. As a consequence, the desirable properties of the structure have recently been recognised by the rating agencies, as an analysis of SPV insolvency risk becomes redundant.[47]

Furthermore, the mitigation of interest and exchange rate risk that is accomplished by tailor-made swap agreements with default-dependent nominals in true-sale structures plays an almost negligible role: These risks are primarily retained by the issuer, and only the loss realisation upon reference asset default is still affected by these market risk factors. The same is true for maturity mismatches between the reference bonds and the synthetic structure, because neither a claim valuation at maturity is required, nor is the actual redemption cash-flow of relevance.

To summarise, the institutional differences between traditional and synthetic securitisation highlight the requirements that are to be fulfilled by a any type of CDO structure such that it provides effective portfolio credit risk transfer. Therefore, the formal analysis to be performed relies on the transfer of default risk only, using market-valued reference claims. European securitisation currently uses synthetic risk transfer to a large extent, such that pure risk transfer appears to dominate the need for liquidity creation. However, the picture for Germany may be expected to change: The 'True-Sale Initiative', currently being established by six German commercial banks, shall provide a platform for funded securitisation, so that not only risk transfer can be performed, but also a refinance means for loan extension will become available. The degree of standardisation that is to be achieved through this joint effort makes the need for effective and transparent risk transfer mechanisms even more salient.[48]

---

47 See Standard & Poor's (2003) p. 30 and Yoshizawa (2003) (Moody's) p. 5.

48 See Kreditanstalt für Wiederaufbau (2003).

2.2.2 The counterparties' motivations

2.2.2.1 Perception of trading gains: 'arbitrage' CDOs

The practitioners' literature makes use of the term 'arbitrage CDO' in order to characterise true-sales that acquire claims in the market.[49] Hence, as opposed to the capital relief motive, arbitrage CDOs are initialised because of the opportunity for trading gains perceived by the originator.

On the asset side, the originator acquires claims which he perceives as underpriced relative to the inherent default riskiness. On the liability side, CDO issuance exploits a possible mismatch between portfolio loss risk pricing and actual loss exposure in the waterfall, with the consequence that the value of the premium stream of an issued tranche under consideration does not compensate appropriately for the value of losses assumed by the tranche investor.[50] Hence, mispricings on either side of the transaction would permit to lock in a net profit at origination if first-loss protection could be acquired at lower cost than the claim on excess spread income, that is generated through the life of the structure. However, both claims are not normally valued by the market, but rather retained by the originator. Therefore, the perception of an 'arbitrage' gain has a clear speculative component, the motive to engage in an arbitrage CDO thus stemming from the originator's opinion on favourable collateral performance, taking his risk preferences into account.

The 'arbitrage' mechanism based on the violation of value additivity among the asset and the liability side raises the question of the presence of arbitrage opportunities, both in the underlying debt market and with regard to the CDO waterfall:

With regard to underlying debt, one might presume that converging bond and single-name credit derivatives markets leave little scope for acquisition of investment grade exposure at inappropriately low cost. The practitioner's literature referring to the US true-sale market (see Bakalar, Herrmann, Tierney, and Folkerts-Landau (2000)) mentions high-yield and distressed debt to be susceptible to mispricings then exploited by securitisation. As price discovery for high-yield debt is normally less based on active trading of securities than subject to research efforts made by the acquiring originator, the problems resulting from asymmetric information on claim quality outlined in section 2.1.2 arise. First-loss retention, implemented by the repackaging process, does indeed remedy the low marketa-

---

49 See for example Schorin and Weinreich (1998) pp. 6-13 for the mechanics of cash-flow arbitrage CDOs and Bakalar, Herrmann, Tierney, and Folkerts-Landau (2000) for the development of the US market.

50 As the counterparties' judgements on 'appropriate' CDO pricing rely on a formal valuation model, the formulae underlying the 'arbitrage' relationships are established in Chapter 5.

bility of information-sensitive collateral assets. Hence, the 'arbitrage' generated through trading underpriced collateral should compensate the originator for the cost of information gathering, circumventing severe discounts incurred by asymmetric information on the asset quality.

With regard to the CDO capital structure, consider an investor's risk exposure in the transaction. Structuring banks satisfy specific clients' needs with regard to the risk level choice by offering tailor-made tranche solutions, for which a certain willingness to pay can be exploited. What appears yet more important, however, is that securitisation offers investors exposure to credit *portfolio* risk, an exposure type rarely accessible otherwise: As opposed to undiversified single-name debt of comparable quality, portfolio losses impair an investor's wealth gradually, meeting the needs of a variance-minimising investor. Moreover, the diversification effort of the originator aims at the elimination of purely idiosyncratic risk factors not priced by the market (see Jarrow, Lando, and Yu (2003) for the translation of APT into the credit risk context), such that credit portfolio derivatives provide a superior risk/return-profile when compared to single-name debt. Hence, the 'arbitrage' relies on market incompleteness, to the extent that investors cannot perform the structuring effort on their own at reasonable cost. As a consequence, not only true-sales, mentioned as the classical 'arbitrage' transactions in the cited references, but also the synthetic risk transfer alternatives achieve a cost-efficient credit portfolio exposure. As a consequence, synthetic transactions may also be driven by arbitrage considerations, generating a margin on over-priced issued tranches.

2.2.2.2 Capital relief: balance sheet-CDOs

2.2.2.2.1 Incentives More frequently than for pure arbitrage reasons, CDOs are initialised because the issuer intends to remove defaultable positions from his balance sheet. In the context of true-sales, the structures are referred to as balance sheet-CDOs. Synthetic securitisations as opposed to true-sales, clearly do not imply a shortening of the originator's balance sheet. Their subsumption under the term balance sheet-CDOs seems inappropriate in the literal sense. However, the incentives provided by the regulatory environment to originate securitisations are comparable for both constructions.

Balance sheet-CDOs have been attractive for commercial banks for several reasons. From an economic perspective, asset sales can be advantageous due to the generation of liquid funds available for new business, increasing the originator's return on equity through financial leverage. Furthermore, existing obligor concentrations, built up through a specialised lending business, can be reduced in order to improve the overall diversification of the bank portfolio. Concentration risk reduction is achieved both by an asset sale and the protection obtained by a synthetic structure.

The main incentive for banks to engage in securitisations, however, has been created by the regulatory capital requirements under the Basel I legislation.

Banks are required to back up outstanding positions towards corporate debtors with the full 8% equity charge, risk-weighted at 100%, regardless of the credit-worthiness of the debtors.[51] However, information about the credit quality of a defaultable corporate claim is in many cases available and verifiable, either by an assessment of an external rating agency or by an internal rating in the bank's scoring system. As information about the quality of a corporate claim can be credibly transmitted to market participants, corporate claims of recorded quality are marketable, in as much as large price discounts due to quality uncertainty are not incurred. The incentive for banks to securitise low-quality assets mentioned in section 2.1.2, has until present been alleviated, if not overcompensated, by the incentive to securitise high-quality debt induced by inadequately high capital requirements. The prevalent capital inadequacy explains why transactions with high-quality collateral pools are indeed observed. As an undesirable consequence of the current regulation, a quality deterioration in the remaining bank portfolio is expected to occur.

The quality-dependent risk-weights applicable to corporate claims to be introduced under the Basel II legislation will clearly alter the incentives for collateral selection, such that the average quality of securitised claims is expected to decrease.[52]

2.2.2.2.2 Regulatory recognition of credit risk transfer The Basel II regulation explicitly intends an alignment of the treatment of traditional and synthetic securitisations.[53]

The treatment of true-sale structures has found its way into German legislation by means of the Federal Financial Supervisory Authority (BaFin) 4/1997 circular. It specifies criteria for ABS-transactions that have to be fulfilled by true-sales, such that the credit risk transfer is recognised and the transferred claims are exempt from the regulatory capital requirements currently specified in Grundsatz I.[54] The resulting capital relief creates an incentive for the sale of the respective assets, even in the presence of the considerable transaction costs incurred for setting up a true-sale structure.

At present, retained or purchased synthetic CDO tranches are dealt with according to

---

51 See Deutsche Bundesbank (2001)(Grundsatz I), § 13 Abs. 3, Nr. 1.

52 This conclusion can be drawn from the results of Repullo and Suarez (2003).

53 See BCBS (2003), no. 501-505. No. 504 equates synthetic positions with their true-sale counterparts.

54 See BaFin (1997). The stated criteria guarantee that legally and economically, a 'clean break' of the securitised assets from the originator is achieved in order exclude recourse by the ABS/CDO-investors towards the originating bank.

the rules applying to single-name credit derivatives, as put down by the Federal Financial Supervisory Authority 10/1999 circular.[55]

Regulatory recognition of protection provided through credit derivatives takes the form of substitution of the risk weight of the reference asset by the risk weight of the counterparty.[56]

Unresolved questions are currently being dealt with on a case-by-case-basis along the lines discussed under the Basel II approach.[57] The current recognition practice of the German supervisory authorities (i.e. the Bundesbank and the Federal Financial Supervisory Authority, see KWG (1998) § 7 for competencies) is summarised as follows:

Full capital relief for the originator is obtained through the issuance of CLNs that fulfill the criteria of the 10/1999 circular with respect to the homogeneity of the specified reference asset and the defaultable claim held by the originator. The protection of the face value cash collateral against counterparty default risk is recognised. In case of note issuance via an SPV, a pledge of the collateral on behalf of the originator is required in order to circumvent the 100% risk weight applicable to the SPV as a corporate debtor.

Default protection through CDSs instead requires a regulatory equity charge according to the counterparty's risk weight. By entering the CDS with an OECD-bank, the originator therefore reduces the regulatory capital requirement from 100% for the securitised corporate claims to the risk weight applicable to the CDS counterparty, i.e. 20% in case of an OECD-bank. Whereas super-senior protection is still required to obtain capital relief, the ongoing discussion suggests that Basel II tends to recognise that almost all risk is transferred by mezzanine tranches.[58] For instance, risk-weights applicable to both externally and implicitly rated, retained tranches are put down in the third consultative paper. For tranches of investment grade quality backed by granular pools, they fall below the counterparty-dependent (i.e. mostly 20%) risk weight currently applicable to super-senior synthetic tranches and would also apply to highly-rated senior tranches repurchased from traditional securitisations.[59]

---

55 See BaFin (1999) for the regulatory treatment of single-name CDSs and CLNs.

56 See BaFin (1999), section 2.1.1.

57 The development of rules accommodating both the risk profiles of retained tranches and the recognition of protection through tranches issued as credit derivatives are major concerns in the BCBS (2001a) and BCBS (2001b) documents. An outline of the recognition practice within the still uncertain environment is given by Watzinger (2000) pp. 304-306 and Hüttemann (2000) pp. 320-322.

58 For the current status of the discussion of the treatment of securitisation within the standardised and internal ratings-based approach, see BCBS (2003), no. 505-606. For the consideration of retained senior risk, see BCBS (2001a), no. 81.

59 See BCBS (2003), no. 584 for rating-based risk weights and no. 587, 588 for implicit tranche rating assignments.

Currently, the application of a 0% risk weight on unfunded tranches can be achieved through the inclusion of a default-free financial institution, acting as intermediary between the originator and tranche issuance, as described in section 2.2.1.3. In Germany, this function is performed by the KfW for the accomplishment of German Mittelstand loan securitisation programmes. As its liabilities are guaranteed by the state, the portfolio risk transfer through the full-portfolio default swap entails full regulatory capital relief.[60]

Retained or repurchased junior tranches are fully deducted from regulatory capital, thus amounting to a capital requirement of 100% of the tranche principal, creating the incentive to limit the first-loss principal $P_{jun}(0)$ to a maximum of 8% of the pool volume, a 0% risk weight to the superior tranches assumed.[61] This requirement is stated explicitly by the third consultative paper: In the standardised approach, the 100% capital charge applicable to an investor retaining a tranche implicitly rated below investment grade induces the originator to minimise the retained junior loss piece.[62] The internal ratings-based approach sets the threshold for full capital deduction explicitly in relation to the tranche riskiness as conveyed by the capital requirement of the reference portfolio.[63]

2.2.3 Risk factors: cash-flow and market-value CDOs

Most true-sale and synthetic structures are classified as cash-flow CDOs. The collateral pool or reference portfolio composition, respectively, remains static throughout the entire tenor. This has the implication that the tranche investors bear the pure default risk of the reference claims and are immune against spread changes due to changes in creditworthiness of the reference assets. A dependence on credit risk-related market variables is limited to a possible need for reinvestment of recovery proceeds and the redemption payments of matured collateral in true-sale structures. Market-value CDOs by contrast, are characterised by a collateral pool whose funded or unfunded claims are purchased at origination, regularly marked-to market and may be substituted.[64] Representing a small market share only, they are set up as arbitrage transactions, not permitting capital relief, due to market-based claim acquisition. Spread changes due to changes in obligor

---

60 See KfWG (2003) § 1a.

61 See BCBS (2001a) pp. 16-17 and BCBS (2001b) p. 20.

62 See BCBS (2003), no. 530.

63 See BCBS (2003), no. 570 and no. 575-577.

64 See Bakalar, Herrmann, Tierney, and Folkerts-Landau (2000), pp. 13-18 for a description of the market and risks of funded market-value CDOs. Synthetic market-value CDOs, the youngest instrument mentioned in this contribution, combine the flexibility to react upon unfavourable pool performance with the facilitation of risk transfer through derivatives, Tavakoli (2001), p. 240 and Humphries (2002), p. 11.

credit quality are transferred to tranche investors, whose positions may realise gains due to favourable collateral performance. As the adjustment of the pool composition is at the discretion of a collateral manager, those structures are generally subject to future asset selection by the agent, possibly altering the tranches' risk profiles. For these reasons and due to their relative insignificance, market-value CDOs are not considered further.

2.3 Literature review: modelling underlying portfolio credit risk

2.3.1 Model requirements for CDO valuation

The analysis and valuation of CDO tranche risk requires information both on the underlying default loss risk and the structural elements of the capital structure – i.e. tranche dimensioning and credit enhancements. Whereas the loss allocation mechanism is directly recovered from a transaction's sales information, a characterisation of stochastic loss occurrence requires the specification of an underlying default risk model.

Credit portfolio risk modelling combines two tasks: Firstly, the overall portfolio quality, formally captured by a number of borrower-specific solvency variables, determines the overall degree of portfolio riskiness, i.e. the expected value of losses.[65] Secondly, deviations of losses from the expected outcome, caused by factors that alter the quality of several borrowers, must be jointly modelled by an appropriate dependence structure.

A special requirement of a credit portfolio model with derivative valuation in view, is its capacity to be calibrated to price information of traded securities, conveying the market's assessment of underlying default risk.

This sets the starting point for a brief literature review, summarising the main directions of literature on defaultable claims pricing. Beginning with single-obligor default risk modelling, the extension to credit portfolio risk is being. I conclude by a short account on the current state of the art of multi-name derivatives pricing.

2.3.2 Modelling single-name default risk

The credit quality, and thus, the overall default risk level of a portfolio is given by the individual borrowers' credit-worthiness. Single-obligor default risk models find a broad classification in firm value or structural models and intensity or reduced-form models. The

---

[65] With respect to the notion of riskiness as a loss expectation, I adhere to the definition made in footnote 10.

first approach along the lines of Merton (1974) explains the prices of securities, including debt, issued by a firm by an underlying fundamental variable, referred to as the 'asset value'.

The central element of the structural model class is the explanation of default event occurrence: once the asset value falls below a given barrier, payment obligations towards the creditors cannot be fulfilled and bankruptcy is declared. Whereas in the work of Merton (1974), excess indebtedness is disclosed at maturity only, Black and Cox (1976) model interim bankruptcy as a first-passage time, where the asset value hits an exogenously specified default barrier. Longstaff and Schwartz (1995) extend the firm-value approach by the introduction of stochastic riskless interest rates and provide the theoretical foundation for the observation made by Duffee (1998) that interest rates and credit spreads exhibit negative correlation. The firm value framework has been extended to incorporate endogenous default decisions, either with respect to the capital structure optimisation in the presence of bankruptcy costs and tax shields (Leland (1994)) or strategic behaviour of agents (Anderson and Sundaresan (1996)).

Reduced-form models make no assumptions about the fundamental mechanism making a corporate claim default. Instead, default-related variables such as default probabilities or default event times are related to default-risky claim valuation. The approach of Jarrow and Turnbull (1995) implies default probabilities from the prices of risky debt. Lando (1998) captures the time structure of default riskiness by modelling default events as first arrival times of Poisson processes. The variation of a debtor's credit-worthiness as reflected by the spread is modelled by a stochastic intensity, the default mechanism thus being referred to as a doubly-stochastic Poisson process. Duffie and Singleton (1999a) generalise the intensity-based modelling framework further by establishing conditions under which contingent claims valuation can be performed by modelling the 'risk-neutral mean-loss rate'[66], i.e. the random instantaneous default loss expectation expressed as a proportion of the pre-default market value. Notwithstanding its inability to relate default risk to its fundamental causes, the reduced-form model class is particularly suitable for comparatively straightforward empirical implementation. Its explanatory power has been tested by Duffie and Singleton (1997) on the counterparty risk inherent in interest swaps, the contract type that is best captured by the recovery assumptions of the model. The model type is applied to US corporate debt in the works of Duffee (1999) and Driessen (2002) and to sovereign debt by Düllmann and Windfuhr (1999) and Geyer, Kossmeier, and Pichler (2003).

The model class to be selected for the CDO pricing issue would be required to explain risk premia of corporate debt observed in the market. Empirical validation of structural

---

66 Duffie and Singleton (1999a), p. 688.

models is hampered by the large number of parameters that enter valuation formulae of defaultable debt and have to be operationalised for estimation. Empirical evidence on both firm-value models with exogenous and endogenous barriers shows that the explanatory power of spreads of debt of different quality is still weak.[67] Reduced-form modelling, by contrast, makes riskless interest rate models available for defaultable claims valuation, including methods for parameter estimation. Affine models of one or several state variables, encompassing the short-rate models of Vasicek (1977) and Cox, Ingersoll, and Ross (1985), provide closed-form solutions of expected values determining the arbitrage-free bond prices, whose general properties have been examined by Duffie and Kan (1996). Conditional on the parameter set, both riskless and defaultable zero-bond yields for a given maturity class are affine functions of the factor realisation, which makes parameter estimation using term structure data appealing. The references given above use affine models, mostly with the assessment of their explanatory power in view. In the present work, I adopt the standard affine framework, estimating the model on the basis of defaultable corporate term structure information. CDO tranche prices, or spreads, respectively, do not only depend on the overall portfolio quality, but also on the full loss distribution. The latter is explained by dependencies among the individual solvency variables, making an extension of the basic affine model to the portfolio context necessary.

2.3.3 Modelling default dependencies

Recent literature has developed a large number of models with respect to the measurement, management, and capital allocation to portfolio credit risk. Whereas portfolio loss forecasting with capital allocation in mind relies on historical estimates of default probabilities, loss severity, and dependencies, arbitrage-based derivatives pricing requires the derivation of those quantities from market data.

As for single-obligor models, approaches to credit portfolio risk can be classified according to their structural richness. Starting with the CreditMetrics-model proposed by Gupton, Finger, and Bhatia (1997), the structural firm-value approach has been extended to what Frey and McNeil (2001) refer to as latent-variable models.[68] This model class inherits the assumption of normally-distributed asset returns from the single-obligor context. Dependencies between the current states of solvency of debtors are captured by a correlation matrix of asset value returns. A parsimonious approach to asset correlation

---

[67] See Wei and Guo (1997) for evidence on exogenous barrier models and Eom, Helwege, and Huang (2003) for an empirical comparison of both structural model types using US corporate bond data.

[68] See Gordy (2000) for a comparison of both models and Schönbucher (2000) for an instructive outline of the modelling approach.

modelling is achieved by linking individual asset returns using a single- or multi-index model. Unobserved asset values are modelled as latent variables, whose values are recovered from information on the individual borrowers' credit-worthiness. The notion of 'credit-worthiness' is linked to the forecasting context: The use of an asset-value model for capital allocation purposes, as for instance, envisaged under the Basel II internal ratings-based (IRB) approach, makes use of the historic default frequencies, as conveyed by agencies' letter ratings.[69] An extension of the approach to multi-name derivative pricing relies on spread information on single-name products. Especially designed to incorporate default event dependence through asset correlations, the estimation of asset correlations is the crucial point for the use of the model type. Research on asset correlations has for instance been conducted by Düllmann and Scheule (2003) on historical default frequencies with regulatory capital allocation in view. When applied to pricing multi-name derivatives, it should be taken into account that correlation risk may be priced, thus altering asset and default correlations.

Recent approaches circumvent the specification of the factor structure by modelling the dependence structure separately from the marginal distributions of single-obligor default risk levels, determining the variable of interest such as individual mean-loss rates or default event times. This so-called copula approach[70] will prove to be highly useful in order to extract implied dependencies from prices of basket products, as copula functions can be parsimoniously parameterised. For lack of the multi-name pricing data necessary for estimation of the dependence parameters, the empirical exploitation of the approach is still in its infancy.

The reduced-form modelling approach appears not to be constructed for portfolio modelling per se, as correlations are not addressed. However, the intermediary asset return dependence step performed explicitly or implicitly by structural models is not a necessary requirement for the specification of a dependence structure on obligor defaults. By linking solvency variables, i.e. intensities or mean-loss rates in the reduced-form framework, directly to an underlying factor structure, dependencies among those default-related variables are modelled in an accessible way. Referred to as 'mixture models' in the literature (Frey and McNeil (2001)), the doubly-stochastic Poisson default mechanism allows for non-zero default correlation through intensities whose joint evolution over time is explained by common or specific factors.

---

69 See BCBS (2003), no. 241.

70 The copula function is a mapping $C : [0,1]^n \rightarrow [0,1]$ that relates n standard uniform marginals to the multivariate probability distribution. The introduction of the Copula approach to credit portfolio modelling is attributed to Li (1999). Frey and McNeil (2001) characterise credit portfolio models by the copula capturing the dependence structure.

Reduced-form modelling has found entrance to portfolio analysis by the CreditRisk+ approach of Crédit Suisse First Boston (1997).[71] The number of portfolio default events is obtained as a Poisson mixture variable, relying on the assumption of perfectly granular subportfolios whose default risk is driven by the same systematic risk factors. Intensity-based portfolio loss modelling with derivative pricing in mind is performed by Duffie and Gârleanu (2001).

The lack of a structural element to joint default occurrence and the resort to a parsimonious factor structure actually facilitates estimation: The reduced-form model to be proposed can be directly calibrated to observed comovements in spread term structures.

2.3.4 Application to multi-name derivative pricing

Credit portfolio risk management applications mostly require forecasts of losses together with changes in portfolio market values for a given time horizon. The determination of premia of multi-name derivatives, by contrast, relies on the characterisation of the default event times of reference names, determining the time structure of settlement payments and future premium accrual.[72] A valuation model therefore characterises the joint distribution of default event times.

The recent, considerably heterogenous, contributions on multi-name derivative valuation can be subsumed under the derivatives type addressed and the modelling approach used, i.e. latent asset variable or reduced-form model type. The following outline gives a brief summary of prior research according to the mentioned criteria, motivating the choice of the reduced-form approach used in this contribution. In addition, I briefly review the approaches implemented in the literature, linked to the consideration of either true-sale or synthetic structures.

Note that despite the close similarities between basket CDSs and CDOs, a difference with respect to the factors affecting losses, and thus claim valuation must be taken into account. CDOs are credit-linked to large portfolios. Whereas macroeconomic and sector-related risk factors are of relevance to portfolio derivative valuation, purely idiosyncratic risk is largely diversified in highly granular portfolios. Borrower-specific risk factors are thus irrelevant to CDO-pricing and carry zero risk premia (see Jarrow, Lando, and Yu (2003) for the proof). Basket derivatives, by contrast, refer to a small number of names only. The imperfect diversification implies that borrower-specific risk factors, albeit not

[71] See Gordy (2000), pp. 121-124 for a summary of the probabilistic properties.

[72] With regard to the CDO pricing application, the dependence of relevant cash-flows on the default timing structure becomes evident by the loss allocation rule (2.3) and the payment consequences (2.6), (2.5) for true-sales and (2.10) for synthetics.

priced by the market, affect basket derivative payoffs.

The following implementations make use to some extent of the latent asset value approach: Pykhtin and Dev (2003) use a single-factor specification for the determination of tranche loss allocation. The study determines regulatory capital to be held by a financial institution against tranche loss risk. Their analysis aims at tranche loss rates instead of fair premia, such that default timing is not required to be taken into account. They measure the impact of borrower-specific factors for small reference portfolios on tranche riskiness, where the full diversification assumption conveniently applied to CDO analysis does not hold. Implicitly, they establish the link to basket analysis.

Furthermore, the asset-value approach is used for CLO-tranche pricing by Jobst (2002b), who performs a comparison of the asset value model with an extreme value approach applied to entire portfolio losses.

The copula approach, mostly specified to capture the distributional assumptions of the asset value model type, has gained recent attention due to its computational simplicity. A current research focus is the relationship between the chosen form and parametrisation of the copula generating the default event time dependency and resulting CDO tranche or basket derivative prices. References include Schmidt and Ward (2002), who address pricing and hedging of basket CDSs through single-name CDSs, and Boscher and Ward (2002), who implement a copula model for tranche loss allocation. With respect to the pricing of CDOs on the basis of given single-name spreads, Boscher and Ward (2002) suggest that usual mezzanine CDO tranches are rather insensitive to the asset correlation governing joint asset default – a result that will be confirmed by my contribution, despite the different approach to dependency modelling to be taken.

The implementations shown in the cited references have simulative character. The relevance of the dependence parameters for loss variation is examined, taking single-obligor marginal default probabilities as given. Evidence on estimation using market data is sparse, as the approach is not explicitly designed to recover dependence parameters from market time series.

The use of a reduced-form model for multi-name derivative pricing has been suggested by Duffie and Gârleanu (2001) and translated into CDO pricing relationships within a simulation approach. Their intensity-based model has the desirable property that default cumulation is obtained through intensity covariation, which, in turn is directly identified with reference obligor spread covariation. Hence, the convenient statistical properties of reduced-form models translate to the multi-issuer context, a main reason for the adoption of the model type for the study at hand. Default dependence is explained by a set of systematic risk factors, affecting all or a subset of the reference claims jointly, which can be extracted from single-name default risk pricing information.

My approach to specifying and estimating a factor structure finds two good matches in the recent literature. In addition to these, a detailed account of the more general literature addressing latent factor model estimation shall be given within the outline of the estimation approach to be taken. The reduced-form factor model used by Geyer, Kossmeier, and Pichler (2003) for the explanation of joint movements in European sovereign spreads corresponds to the parametrisation I too use for estimation. A noteworthy application of a similar model allowing for common and purely idiosyncratic effects is performed by Driessen (2002), who describes the evolution of a price sample of US corporate bonds. It is the only reference that links an estimated factor model to multi-name derivative pricing by an illustrative application to basket CDSs.

A final remark on cash-flow waterfall or loss allocation modelling in the literature is in order, as it is closely related to the implementation of risk transfer of the transactions under consideration.

The valuation study of Duffie and Gârleanu (2001) relies on careful modelling of cash-flows occurring within true-sale transactions, taking SPV liquidity constraints into account. Recent contributions, by contrast, as the exposition by Lehman Brothers (2003) or the numerical valuation study performed by Boscher and Ward (2002), draw the comparison with portfolio derivatives that refer to cumulated losses falling into the tranche-specific loss ranges. The mechanisms determining the cash-flows relevant to CDO tranche pricing outlined in the preceding sections suggest that the valuation of tranches of a carefully structured true-sale transaction not affected by SPV insolvency is equivalent to the loss transfer approach taken in the present study.

The formal model to be developed in the following chapters makes use of the following aspects covered in the given references: The underlying reduced-form loss model is based on the intensity approach of Duffie and Gârleanu (2001), including the common factor specification. As opposed to the true-sale transactions analysed by the authors, the valuation of synthetic CDO tranches subject to formal study is, to a large extent, insensitive against the precise cash-flow consequences of reference asset default, which is for instance shown by Boscher and Ward (2002). Hence, the well-known identification problem arising when estimating a Duffie and Singleton (1999a) reduced-form model from single-name spread data is of little relevance to the portfolio derivatives pricing task. The portfolio default model therefore relies on a mean-loss rate in the sense of Duffie and Singleton (1999a), pricing all claims within a subportfolio in the sense of the CreditRisk+ approach as functions of identical factors.

Chapter 3

Underlying Credit Risk: a Reduced-Form Factor Model

The following section summarises the reduced-form framework, used to price defaultable bonds in line with underlying loss expectations. Subsequently, the factor model is developed, pricing relationships exploited for estimation are given, and model implications relevant to derivative pricing are provided.

3.1 Defaultable bond pricing

The price of a default-free zero bond paying one unit of currency at maturity $T = t+\tau$ with certainty and the corresponding default-riskless yield to maturity $R_r(t,\tau)$ are determined by the expected evolution of the instantaneous ('short') stochastic default-riskless interest rate $f_r(t)$

$$D_r(t,\tau) = \mathbb{E}_t\left[\exp\left(-\int_t^T f_r(s)ds\right)\right]. \tag{3.1}$$

$$R_r(t,\tau) = -\frac{\ln D_r(t,\tau)}{\tau}. \tag{3.2}$$

Unless stated otherwise, all expectations are taken under a risk-neutral measure. To ensure absence of arbitrage, the existence of a probability measure is assumed such that security prices $D_{(\cdot)}(t,\tau)$ discounted by a riskless money market account with time-t-value

$$M(t) = \exp\left(\int_0^t f_r(s)ds\right) \tag{3.3}$$

are martingales:

$$\mathbb{E}_t\left[D_{(\cdot)}(t+\Delta t,\tau)M(t+\Delta t)^{-1}\right]=D_{(\cdot)}(t,\tau)M(t)^{-1}. \tag{3.4}$$

The price of a zero bond issued by a corporate entity promising the payment of one unit of currency at maturity T with issuer-specific yield to maturity $R_{corp}(t,\tau)$ is determined by the risk-neutral expectation over the evolution of the individual short interest rate of the corporate issuer considered

$$D_{corp}(t,\tau) = \mathbb{E}_t\left[\exp\left(-\int_t^T r_{corp}(s)ds\right)\right] \tag{3.5}$$

$$R_{corp}(t,\tau) = -\frac{\ln D_{corp}(t,\tau)}{\tau}. \tag{3.6}$$

The corporate zero bond yield exceeds the maturity-equivalent riskless spot rate by a quantity

$$S_{corp}(t,\tau) = R_{corp}(t,\tau) - R_r(t,\tau). \tag{3.7}$$

which will be denoted as the spot spread.[1] The spot spread of maturity τ is determined by the relative price discount of a corporate bond

$$S_{corp}(t,\tau) = -\frac{\ln\left(\frac{D_{corp}(t,\tau)}{D_r(t,\tau)}\right)}{\tau}. \tag{3.8}$$

Defining the short spread analogously to the short interest rate as the instantaneous yield difference

$$s_{corp}(t) = r_{corp}(t) - f_r(t), \tag{3.9}$$

corporate zero bonds are priced by the risk-neutral expectation over both riskless short rate and corporate spread evolution

$$D_{corp}(t,\tau) = \exp\left(-\mathbb{E}_t\left[\int_t^T \left(f_r(s) + s_{corp}(s)\right) ds\right]\right). \tag{3.10}$$

Corporate bonds may be subject to default prior to maturity T. The reduced-form frame-

[1] Spread positivity shall be assured by the stochastic properties of the state variables to be outlined subsequently.

work, established by Jarrow and Turnbull (1995), Lando (1998) and Duffie and Singleton (1999a) relates corporate spreads to expected values of random default event probabilities, or more generally, to expected values of bankruptcy costs incurred by default risk.

A defaultable zero bond with promised payment of one in time T, generating no cash-flows at or after the default event time Υ_{corp}, has a pre-default price of

$$\begin{aligned} D_{corp}(t,\tau) &= D_r(t,\tau)\mathbb{E}_t\left[\mathbf{1}_{\{\Upsilon_{corp}>T\}}\right] \\ &= D_r(t,\tau)\Pr{}_{\{\Upsilon_{corp}>T\}}(t). \end{aligned} \tag{3.11}$$

The reduced-form approach models default event times as unpredictable jump times of a generalised class of Poisson processes, referred to as doubly-stochastic or conditional Poisson processes, and also Cox-processes.[2] The following outline gives a characterisation of doubly-stochastic Poisson processes along the lines of Lando (1998).[3] The random survival probability $\Pr_{\{\Upsilon_{corp}>T\}}(t)$, equals the probability that a doubly-stochastic Poisson-distributed random variable $\#D$ with intensity parameter $h_{corp}(t)$ equals zero during a time interval $(T-t)$. The intensity $h_{corp}(t)$ is allowed to follow a random process. The default arrival intensity is defined as the instantaneous default probability at the respective – possibly future – time t

$$h_{corp}(t) : \lim_{\Delta t \to 0} \frac{1}{\Delta t} \Pr{}_{\{\Upsilon_{corp}\in(t,t+\Delta t)\}}(t) = h_{corp}(t). \tag{3.12}$$

Conditional on the intensity evolution during the time horizon $T-t$, the Poisson-distributed process

$$\Pr{}_{\{\#D=d|h_{corp}(s)\forall t\leq s\leq T\}}(t) = \frac{1}{d!}\left(\int_t^T h_{corp}(s)ds\right)^d \exp\left(-\int_t^T h_{corp}(s)ds\right) \tag{3.13}$$

evaluated at $d=0$ characterises the survival probability of a corporate bond during the contractual time to maturity

---

2 For a definition of the Poisson process, see Bielecki and Rutkowski (2002), p. 186.

3 The similarity between the properties of a Poisson process with deterministic, possibly time-varying, intensity, and the doubly-stochastic Poisson process when conditioning on the intensity path realisation is pointed out by Bielecki and Rutkowski (2002), pp. 192-193.

$$\begin{aligned}
\Pr{}_{\{\Upsilon_{corp}>T|h_{corp}(s)\forall t\leq s\leq T\}}(t) &= \\
\Pr{}_{\{\#D=0|h_{corp}(s)\forall t\leq s\leq T\}}(t) &= \exp\left(-\int_t^T h_{corp}(s)ds\right). \qquad (3.14)
\end{aligned}$$

For subsequent implementation, $h_{corp}(t)$ is assumed to be a function of a random state vector $h_{corp}(t) := h_{corp}(\mathbf{f}_s(t))$.[4] Taking the randomness of the intensity $h_{corp}(t)$ into account, the unconditional survival probability is determined by the expectation of $h_{corp}(s)\forall t \leq s \leq T$

$$\Pr{}_{\{\Upsilon_{corp}>T\}}(t) = \mathbb{E}_t\left[\exp\left(-\int_t^T h_{corp}(s)ds\right)\right]. \qquad (3.15)$$

The probabilistic assumptions allow for modelling of a default event time as the first arrival time of a Poisson-process $N_{corp}(t) \in \mathbb{N}$, with $N_{corp}(0) = 0$ and the increments $\Delta N_{corp}(t) = N_{corp}(T) - N_{corp}(t)$ for time periods $T-t$ being Poisson-distributed according to (3.13). Technically, the assumption that a debtor can only default once is assured by setting the intensity equal to zero upon default.

CDO pricing relies on a characterisation of random default event times, as settlement payments and exposure adjustments are due in Υ_{corp}. The doubly-stochastic Poisson default mechanism implies that default times are conditionally exponentially distributed. I will make use of the property pointed out by Lando (1998) that

$$\Upsilon_{corp} = \inf\left[t : H_{corp}(t) \geq E_{corp}[1]\right], \qquad (3.16)$$

where

$$H_{corp}(t) = \int_0^t h_{corp}(s)ds \qquad (3.17)$$

represents the default compensator such that the compensated process $N_{corp}(t) - H_{corp}(t)$ is a martingale and $E_{corp}[1]$ represents an exponentially-distributed random variable with an intensity parameter of one. [5]

With respect to defaultable claim pricing, substituting (3.15) into (3.11) and equating

---

4 The subscript s for the state vector indicates the corporate spread model as opposed to a default-free interest model.

5 See Lando (1998), pp. 101-102.

(3.10) and (3.11) shows that

$$s_{corp}(t) = h_{corp}(t). \tag{3.18}$$

From the equivalence of the short spread with the intensity of zero-recovery claims, it may be assumed that the state vector determining the default intensity evolution $h_{corp}(\mathbf{f}_s(t))$ explains equivalently price discounts of corporate bond prices as functions $s_{corp}(\mathbf{f}_s(t))$.

Extending the model to positive recovery is largely facilitated by the generalisation of the intensity framework to mean-loss rate modelling.[6] I therefore make use of the central result derived by Duffie and Singleton (1999a), that allows for modelling a 'mean-loss rate' from default risk only in the reduced-form framework outlined above. Assuming that upon default occurrence, the defaulted claim incurs a loss as a (possibly random) fraction with mean LGD of its pre-default market value $D^{-}_{corp}(t,\tau)$ and immediately recovers the remaining fraction (recovery of market value, RMV), the corporate short spread corresponds to the instantaneous mean-loss rate of the respective bond, to be denoted as $\overline{h}_{corp}(t)$:[7]

$$s_{corp}(t) = h_{corp}(t)LGD := \overline{h}_{corp}(t) \tag{3.19}$$

The multiplicative association entails that intensity and the mean LGD are substitutes for pricing defaultable bonds. Translation of the RMV assumption to coupon-paying bonds, both representing the debt contracts available in the market and the reference bonds in the portfolio, is performed under the zero bond decomposition. The dirty price of a coupon-paying bond $V_{corp}(t,\underline{\tau})$ is determined by a homogeneous term structure of defaultable discount factors $D_{corp}(t,\tau)$, a function of the riskless short rate and the short spread, or the instantaneous mean-loss rate, respectively. The discount factors apply to coupon or principal cash-flows $CF(\tau)$ at the respective payment dates, collected in a vector $\underline{\tau}= (\tau_1, ..., \tau_N)$:[8]

$$V_{corp}(t,\underline{\tau}) = \sum_{\tau=\tau_1}^{\tau_N} D_{corp}(t,\tau)\cdot CF(\tau). \tag{3.20}$$

6 The modelling technique has been derived for zero-recovery claims, as the distributional properties to be exploited within the subsequent simulation study rely on the zero-recovery case, where $h_{corp}(t)$ technically represents an intensity.

7 See Duffie and Singleton (1999a), p. 688.

8 See Duffie and Singleton (1999a), pp. 702-705. The RFV-assumption, by contrast, would apply higher discount factors to coupon payments than to the principal, valued at positive recovery.

This pricing relationship is to be exploited for the extraction of defaultable term structures and estimation of mean-loss rates from bond market data. The validity of mean-loss rate modelling for the portfolio derivatives pricing application shall be considered in section 5.1.3.2.2.

3.2 Factor model specification

3.2.1 Factor structure

The reduced-form framework allows a borrower-specific mean-loss rate $\overline{h}_{corp}(\mathbf{f}_s(t))$, to be driven by several factors. Factors are collected in a latent state vector. Adhering to the Duffie and Singleton (1999a)-framework, factors determine the random riskiness, as characterised by the term structure of risk-neutral survival probabilities $\Pr_{\{\Upsilon_{corp}>T\}}(t)$ and the mean LGD-rate of a defaultable corporate under consideration, whose claims are priced under the corresponding term structure of spot spreads (3.7) observed in the market.

The default risk evolution of several borrowers is expected to be interrelated due to systematic risk factors that affect all corporate borrowers or a subset of them simultaneously. I parameterise a dependence structure as follows, taking into account an economic meaning of the latent factors while keeping the model still tractable for estimation.[9]

Corporate reference claims are divided into classes $class = (risk, sec)$. Firstly, a reference claim is characterised by the level of default riskiness $risk$ of the borrower, which is assumed to be identified by the entity's agency rating at the origination date of the securitisation transaction. Secondly, the effects of industry concentrations in the reference portfolio shall be captured. Reference claims are therefore classified according to the borrower's sector affiliation *sec*.

Furthermore, it appears reasonable to allow for a factor affecting all reference claims jointly, such that systematic risk on the market-wide level is accounted for. In order to facilitate model estimation, I impose a simple additive structure on mean-loss rates or short spreads, respectively

$$\overline{h}_{corp}(t) := \overline{h}_{class}(t) = f_c(t) + f_{class}(t). \tag{3.21}$$

The factors driving the stochastic mean-loss rate evolution may all be considered as 'sys-

---

9 Modelling of systematic components requires simultaneous estimation of the respective factor processes. The fast increasing model size thus imposes restrictions on the richness of the model construction.

tematic', as they determine the risk level of several borrowers. Thus, in the general setup, neither of the modelled risk factors is diversified in a granular portfolio and is therefore of relevance for the CDO pricing task. The non-diversifiability suggests that factor risk is priced by the market (see Jarrow, Lando, and Yu (2003)). However, as the doubly-stochastic default mechanism still yields random default ocurrence conditional on $\overline{h}_{corp}(t)$, this implies that the final realisation of the default/survivial indicator $\mathbf{1}_{\{\Upsilon_{corp}>T\}}$ is idiosyncratic for every obligor. Despite the uniformity of mean-loss rate evolution within one class, the probability of two claims defaulting simultaneously in the continuous-time-limit is zero. Hence, the model setup implies independence of default times *within* the same class conditional on the realisations of the factors $f_c(t)$ and $f_{class}(t)$ and independence of default times *between* classes conditional on the realisation of factor $f_c(t)$.[10]

Concerning the distributional assumptions on class-specific factors, it is assumed that the sector specification does not rely on additional information. Therefore, only factors applying to the reference assets of distinct risk levels as identified by the agency ratings shall differ in distribution. Factors applying to assets of different sectors, but of identical riskiness are assumed to be i.i.d. This assumption allows for straightforward model extension to a flexible factor structure, taking sector-related concentration risk into account.

With respect to defaultable bond pricing, the factor model structure has the straightforward implication that all bonds within one class are priced under the same term structure. Defaultable discount factors $D_{corp}(t,\tau)$ thus evaluate to $D_{class}(t,\tau)$. Pricing under the same term structure applies to traded bonds valued at $V_{class}(t,\underline{T})$ and the pre-default values $V^-_{class}(\Upsilon_{corp},\underline{T})$, the event times remaining borrower-specific.

The latent factors are assumed to evolve stochastically over time, such that both spreads and mean-loss rates are random. With regard to estimation, the specification of an affine yield model for class-specific defaultable term structures appears desirable, such that a class-specific corporate zero bond yield of maturity τ is expressed as a linear combination of factors k

$$R_{class}(t,\tau) = \sum_k \left(A_k(\tau,\phi_k) + B_k(\tau,\phi_k) f_k(t)\right), \tag{3.22}$$

ϕ_k denoting a set of parameters governing the time series-behaviour of factor $f_k(t)$.

Duffie and Kan (1996) establish the drift $\mu(f_k(t))$ and variance function $\sigma^2(f_k(t))$ of a

10 Conditional independence is for instance characterised by Frey and McNeil (2001) and Bielecki and Rutkowski (2002), p. 268: When conditioning on the realisation of a factor common to the claims under consideration, the joint survival probability equals the product survival probability.

generalised Wiener diffusion process

$$df_k(t) = \mu(f_k(t))dt + \sigma(f_k(t))dW_k(t) \tag{3.23}$$

to be affine functions of the factors as a necessary and sufficient condition for zero bond prices to be exponential-affine in the factors.(3.22) follows by (3.6). For the sake of default-free and defaultable bond pricing, the riskless short rate shall be included by the state vector $\mathbf{f}(t) = (f_r(t), \mathbf{f}_s(t))$.

For the purpose of pricing CDO tranches as derivatives on the latent factors, a factor process specification under a risk-neutral measure is required:

I adopt the stochastic differential equation (SDE) introduced by Cox, Ingersoll, and Ross (1985) (CIR), as it combines affine pricing rules with stochastic properties particularly suitable for spread modelling.

The transition behaviour of every factor $f_k(t)$ is described under a risk-neutral measure by the SDE

$$df_k(t) = \kappa_k\left(\theta_k - f_k(t)\right)dt + \sigma_k\sqrt{f_k(t)}dW_k(t). \tag{3.24}$$

The process specification implies reversion to the long-run risk-neutral factor mean θ_k at an annual rate κ_k together with level-dependent process volatility and a reflecting barrier at zero. This property is desirable for default modelling, as negative intensity realisations, i.e negative default probabilities, are precluded. Factor orthogonality is assumed, such that the Wiener processes $W_k(t)$ are pairwise uncorrelated.

The factor process under the risk-neutral measure (3.24) is derived from the factor process whose time series would be empirically observed under the physical measure

$$df_k(t) = \kappa_k^*\left(\theta_k^* - f_k(t)\right)dt + \sigma_k\sqrt{f_k(t)}dW_k^*(t). \tag{3.25}$$

Parametrisation of the market price of factor risk as a function of the current factor realisation

$$\Lambda_k = \lambda_k\frac{\sqrt{f_k(t)}}{\sigma_k}, \tag{3.26}$$

together with the drift transformation by Girsanov's theorem

$$dW_k(t) = dW_k^*(t) + \Lambda_k dt \tag{3.27}$$

yields (3.24). The risk-neutral reversion speed κ_k and the risk-neutral unconditional factor mean θ_k are obtained as

$$\begin{aligned}\kappa_k &= \kappa_k^* + \lambda_k \\ \theta_k &= \frac{\theta_k^* \kappa_k^*}{\kappa_k}.\end{aligned} \tag{3.28}$$

Estimation and loss forecasting shall rely on the conditional factor probability distribution, which is noncentral χ^2, where the degrees of freedom and the noncentrality parameters are functions of the process parameters and the period length, see Appendix A.

3.2.2 Corporate spreads as observable functions of factors

The latent factors $\mathbf{f}_s(t)$ generating the dependence structure between mean-loss rates are unobservable. However, prices of securities that are derivatives on the factors are observed in the market: Defaultable securities of issuers of the respective risk/sector classes map unobserved factor realisations into prices.

From the decomposition (3.11) and the assumption of factor orthogonality, defaultable bond prices are treated as factor derivatives by setting $D_{class}(t,\tau) := D_{corp}(t,\tau,\mathbf{f}(t))$.[11]

Derivation of the pricing partial differential equation (PDE) for defaultable corporate bonds takes the expected instantaneous loss in market value of size $\lim_{\Delta t \to 0} \frac{1}{\Delta t} \mathbb{E}_t [\Delta N_{corp}(t)] \cdot D_{class}(t,\tau)$ with the consideration of a short time increment. It follows from absence of arbitrage that the expected instantaneous return from the underlying diffusion processes $\mathcal{D}D_{class}(t,\tau)$ net of expected default loss from jump risk to equal the instantaneous riskless rate, stated as

$$\mathcal{D}D_{class}(t,\tau) - \lim_{\Delta t \to 0} \frac{1}{\Delta t} \mathbb{E}_t [\Delta N_{corp}(t)] \cdot D_{class}(t,\tau) - f_r(t) D_{class}(t,\tau) = 0. \tag{3.29}$$

The instantaneous mean-loss rate, applied to the current defaultable zero-bond market value straightforwardly substitutes to

$$\lim_{\Delta t \to 0} \frac{1}{\Delta t} \mathbb{E}_t [\Delta N_{corp}(t)] = f_c(t) + f_{class}(t). \tag{3.30}$$

It follows that defaultable bond spreads compensate exactly for the expected instanta-

---

[11] With regard to the translation of the mean-loss rate model to the state-space setting, see Duffie and Singleton (1999a), pp. 697-698.

neous loss in market value. Hence, prices must fulfill

$$\mathcal{D}D_{class}(t,\tau) - (f_r(t) + f_c(t) + f_{class}(t))\, D_{class}(t,\tau) = 0, \tag{3.31}$$

subject to the boundary conditions

$$\begin{aligned} D_r(T,0) &= 1 \\ D_{class}(T,0) &= 1 \\ \Pr{}_{\{\Upsilon_{corp}>T\}}(T) &= 1, \end{aligned} \tag{3.32}$$

i.e. at maturity $t = T$, the expected value of default loss equals zero and any bond, riskless or defaultable, trades at face value.

Note that the defaultable zero bond price $D_{class}(t,\tau)$ solving equation (3.31), put down for the zero recovery case, shows to be invariant against the intensity/LGD-decomposition: Assume that upon a jump event, i.e. $\Delta N_{corp}(t) = 1$, a fractional market value loss of the mean amount $LGD \cdot D_{class}(t,\tau)$ occurs at a correspondingly higher intensity $\frac{h_{class}(t)}{LGD} = \frac{f_c(t)+f_{class}(t)}{LGD}$, holding the mean-loss rate $\overline{h}_{corp}(t)$ constant. The multiplicative association between the instantaneous jump probability and the loss amount causes the *LGD*-multiplier to be cancelled out in the pricing equation.

The expected price change $\mathcal{D}D_{class}(t,\tau)$ from the diffusion processes conditional on survival is obtained by Ito's lemma applied to risky bond prices as derivatives on three orthogonal CIR-factors, specified under the risk-neutral measure

$$\begin{aligned} \mathcal{D}D_{class}(t,\tau) &= \frac{\partial D_{class}(t,\tau)}{\partial t} \\ &+ \sum_{k=r,c,class} \left[[\kappa_k(\theta_k - f_k(t))] \frac{\partial D_{class}(t,\tau)}{\partial f_k(t)} + \frac{1}{2}\sigma_k^2 f_k(t) \frac{\partial^2 D_{class}(t,\tau)}{\partial f_k(t)^2} \right]. \end{aligned} \tag{3.33}$$

In case of the assumed CIR-factor transitional behaviour, closed-form solutions to the pricing equations are available, with the general affine pricing methodology relying on the work of Duffie and Kan (1996).

The affine characterisation of the model requires zero bond prices, and therefore, expected values of losses as conveyed by the price discount $\frac{D_{class}(t,\tau)}{D_r(t,\tau)}$ determining spot spreads for positive maturities by equation (3.8), to be exponential-affine in the state variables:[12]

$$D_{class}(t,\tau) = \exp\left(\sum_{k=r,c,class} \left(a_k(\tau,\phi_k) - b_k(\tau,\phi_k) f_k(t)\right)\right) \tag{3.34}$$

The time-invariant vector ϕ with elements $\phi_k = (\kappa_k^*, \theta_k^*, \sigma_k, \lambda_k)$ collects the parameters driving the unobserved factor dynamics and the market prices of factor risk parameters, both determining the risk-neutral parameters entering valuation formulae. Substituting the partial derivatives in (3.33) by their affine specifications, the maturity-dependent functions $a_k(\tau,\psi_k), b_k(\tau,\phi_k)$ solve the pricing PDE if the following ordinary differential equations are satisfied by every factor k

$$\begin{aligned} \frac{\partial b_k(\tau,\phi_k)}{\partial \tau} + \kappa_k b_k(\tau,\phi_k) + \frac{1}{2}\sigma_k^2 b_k^2(\tau,\phi_k) - 1 &= 0 \\ \frac{\partial a_k(\tau,\phi_k)}{\partial \tau} + \kappa_k \theta_k b_k(\tau,\phi_k) &= 0. \end{aligned} \tag{3.35}$$

Boundary conditions are $a_k(0,\phi_k) = 0$, $b_k(0,\phi_k) = 0$. The closed-form solutions for functions $a_k(0,\phi_k), b_k(0,\phi_k)$ are given in Appendix A.

The exponential-affine characterisation of defaultable bond prices has the desirable implication that risky zero bond spot rates are affine in the underlying factors:

$$R_{class}(t,\tau) = \sum_{k=r,c,class} \left(A_k(\tau,\phi_k) + B_k(\tau,\phi_k) f_k(t)\right), \tag{3.36}$$

with functions $A_k(\tau,\phi_k) = -\frac{1}{\tau} a_k(\tau,\phi_k)$ and $B_k(\tau,\phi_k) = \frac{1}{\tau} b_k(\tau,\phi_k)$, such that the initial requirement (3.22) on the factor structure to be exploited for estimation is fulfilled.

For estimation, I split up risky spot rates into the maturity-equivalent riskless rate and the two components related to default risk compensation

$$R_{class}(t,\tau) = R_r(t,\tau) + C(t,\tau) + Class(t,\tau), \tag{3.37}$$

each component representing an affine function of the relevant factor and

$$S_{class}(t,\tau) = C(t,\tau) + Class(t,\tau) \tag{3.38}$$

for observable spot spreads.

---

12 See Duffie and Kan (1996) pp. 383-384 for a general solution of the affine yield-factor model class.

3.2.3 Model implications: term structures of volatilities and term structures of correlations

A first model specification check would rely on the first moment of observed variables, i.e. riskless spot rates and spot spreads of selected maturity classes. This is subsequently achieved by a statistical analysis of yield and spread residuals when affine model term structures are compared with their observed counterparts. A second requirement draws on the second moments of observed quantities: the variation of the term structures of riskless spot rates and spot spreads is required to be explained by the model. As all factors are systematic, their risk is not diversified in the portfolio context. Hence, model validation will subsequently inquire to what extent the time-series variation of observed variables is in line with the model-implied time structures of volatilities, to be defined below. Moreover, in view of the model application to defaultable claims portfolios, a vital model part is the correlation structure between mean-loss rates, and hence, expected values of losses over long horizons, of different reference assets. I therefore extend the term structure analysis to cross-moments of observed market variables, i.e. the spot spreads of borrowers of different classes. A correlation structure between spot spreads $S_u(t,\tau)$ and $S_v(t,\tau)$ of classes $class = u, v$ is defined by the parameter vectors ϕ_c, ϕ_u and ϕ_v :

Defining the unconditional pairwise instantaneous correlation between the short spreads of two classes as

$$\lim_{t\to\infty} Corr^*(s_u(t), s_v(t)) = \frac{Cov^*(s_u(t), s_v(t))}{StdDev^*(s_u(t))StdDev^*(s_v(t))} \tag{3.39}$$

$$= \frac{Var^*(f_c(t))}{\left[Var^*(f_c(t)) + Var^*(f_u(t))\right]^{1/2}\left[Var^*(f_c(t)) + Var^*(f_v(t))\right]^{1/2}}$$

yields

$$\lim_{t\to\infty} Corr^*(s_u(t), s_v(t)) = \frac{\frac{\theta_c^*\sigma_c^2}{2\kappa_c^*}}{\left[\left(\frac{\theta_c^*\sigma_c^2}{2\kappa_c^*} + \frac{\theta_u^*\sigma_u^2}{2\kappa_u^*}\right)\left(\frac{\theta_c^*\sigma_c^2}{2\kappa_c^*} + \frac{\theta_v^*\sigma_v^2}{2\kappa_v^*}\right)\right]^{1/2}} \tag{3.40}$$

for the unconditional factor variances

$$\lim_{t\to\infty} Var^*(f_k(t)) = \frac{\theta_k^*\sigma_k^2}{2\kappa_k^*} \tag{3.41}$$

of the stationary distribution of the CIR-processes.

The asterisk identifies moments taken under the physical measure. Note that when working under the risk-neutral measure, i.e. within the CDO-valuation context, the unconditional moments implied by the risk-neutral process parameters θ_k and κ_k are of interest. Defined analogously, these differ from the second moments under the physical measure in the case of CIR square-root processes.

For spot rates or spreads, respectively, volatilities and correlations are characterised by term structures that are determined by the affine functional relationship between factors and defaultable spot rates.

The unconditional factor variances translate to the variances of spot rates and spreads as

$$\begin{aligned} \lim_{t\to\infty} Var^*(R_r(t,\tau)) &= B_r^2(\tau,\phi_r)\frac{\theta_r^*\sigma_r^2}{2\kappa_r^*} \\ \lim_{t\to\infty} Var^*(S_{class}(t,\tau)) &= B_c^2(\tau,\phi_c)\frac{\theta_c^*\sigma_c^2}{2\kappa_c^*} + B_{class}^2(\tau,\phi_{class})\frac{\theta_{class}^*\sigma_{class}^2}{2\kappa_{class}^*}. \end{aligned} \tag{3.42}$$

Due to the maturity-dependence of the unconditional variance of the observable variables, the square-root of this relationship will be referred to as a 'term structure of volatility'.

The instantaneous short spread correlations translate to the correlations between spot spreads of different risk classes as

$$\begin{aligned} &\lim_{t\to\infty} Corr^*(S_u(t,\tau),S_v(t,\tau)) \\ &= \frac{B_c^2(\tau,\phi_c)\frac{\theta_c^*\sigma_c^2}{2\kappa_c^*}}{\left[\left(B_c^2(\tau,\phi_c)\frac{\theta_c^*\sigma_c^2}{2\kappa_c^*} + B_u^2(\tau,\phi_u)\frac{\theta_u^*\sigma_u^2}{2\kappa_u^*}\right)\left(B_c^2(\tau,\phi_c)\frac{\theta_c^*\sigma_c^2}{2\kappa_c^*} + B_v^2(\tau,\phi_v)\frac{\theta_v^*\sigma_v^2}{2\kappa_v^*}\right)\right]^{1/2}}. \end{aligned} \tag{3.43}$$

This relationship will subsequently be denoted as a 'term structure of correlation'.

Chapter 4

Model Estimation

4.1 Outline of the estimation approach

Latent factors can be recovered from security prices, or corresponding spreads $S_{class}(t, \tau)$, respectively. Data requirements are imposed by the model structure and extend to the cross-sectional and time series dimension.

In the first instance, model dependence through systematic factors is observed in the market: The co-evolution of single-name spreads conveys the dependence information relevant to portfolio derivative pricing, hence establishing the need for time series data with observation periods t. Moreover, the use of time-series information does not only permit the estimation of market price of risk parameters λ_k, but is expected to improve the identification of factor volatility parameters κ_k^* (or κ_k, together with λ_k) and σ_k, that are rarely identified separately from just the term structure equations.

Cross-sectional data requirements are firstly imposed by the factor model structure, as concentration groups are identified by the *class*-assignments of corporate debtors: Pricing information on all factors that are common to all or a *class* in a portfolio is required, whereas idiosyncratic risk is irrelevant to the portfolio valuation problem. Issuer-specific bond pricing errors may therefore be discarded, expectations then normalised to zero.

The functional dependence of spreads on maturity τ can be exploited by the use of term structure information, such that default and factor risk perceptions for different time horizons enter the estimation setup as a second piece of cross-sectional information.

Regarding the choice of a reference market, single-name risk premia are in principle observed both in the corporate bond market and the single-name credit derivatives market. A short discussion shall highlight the suitability of either market to reflect the relevant information of 'appropriate' default risk pricing. I first review data availability in both markets. I then look into the relevance of differences of contract liquidity in both possible reference markets for the CDO pricing application, taking the different securitisation types into account.

The availability of underlying bond or CDS data must be considered in the view of sample transactions: Suitable CDO issuance information was available for 2001, which requires time series coverage prior to 2001 in the reference market.[1]

Consider the credit derivatives market first: The smaller number of corporate names traded in the CDS market poses a minor problem to factor identification, as replication on a class-specific level is all that is required. Therefore, the cross-sectional requirement on obligor coverage is fulfilled by the derivatives market. Time-series information is available from mid 2001 onwards, however, but it is still suffering from infrequent premium changes and only covering a small number of maturity classes. Shortness of the price series does not pose difficulties on the determination of an average spread, i.e. mean risk level in the model context. However, suitability of CDS data for dependence model estimation is impaired by little spread variation observed before September 2001.

In the bond market, issuance activity by European corporates has been high, as large volumes have been placed in succession of the EMU currency accord. I find that a large number of recent issues are indeed available, covering the desired reference debtors over a broad maturity range. Price quality, with regard to frequent quote updates, has been satisfactory since mid 2000, such that the autumn 2001 spread widening is mitigated by a longer period exhibiting stable spread behaviour. Due to longer time-series coverage, bond data does not only permit a more reliable estimation of the dependence model, but also appears more appropriate to capture medium to long-term forecast horizons.

With regard to market liquidity, by contrast, one would generally claim CDS pricing information to be preferable to bond information, due to possible illiquidity discounts in the case of restricted trading in corporate bonds. Conversely, CDS premia constitute neither entirely unbiased estimators for default risk compensation, as delivery options of physically-settled transactions and possible counterparty default risk tend to reduce observed premia.[2] Expected values of losses derived from bond spreads over virtually default-riskless government debt thus constitute a conservative estimate for default riskiness, as opposed to CDS premia that tend to understate underlying default risk. The focus of bond sample selection on recent issues, assuring an overall low age of the bonds,

---

1 A discussion of the suitability of the different securitisation types for empirical investigation is performed in Chapter 7. Availability concerns with regard to European securitisation suggest the focus on synthetic transactions, the need for the coverage of the reference entities' risk by market-priced assets draws the attention to CBOs.

2 The discount is increasing in the default correlation between the reference entity and the protection-selling counterparty, determining the probability of a joint default event in which settlement payments are not fulfilled.

causes the mean illiquidity bias to be a minor problem, when compared to the lack of time series data in the young credit derivatives market.

Finally, consider the markets to which the parties involved in a CDO transaction are exposed, which causes the choice of the reference market for factor estimation to not be clear-cut: Tranche investors clearly act as protection sellers, only being impaired in case of loss occurrence. However, in the case of CLN issuance, funding is provided by investors against the exchange of tailor-made structured notes. Given that illiquidity premia in the single-name bond market exist, CDO spreads may be susceptible to illiquidity premia at a even higher extent, as secondary trading opportunities for CDO tranches are a lot more restricted. Illiquidity premia compensating for restricted trading in CDO tranches, however, should be refinanced through the reference pool: Even in case of a synthetic securitisation, the originator finally attempts to hedge an on-balance-sheet debt portfolio. Thus, he is entitled to regular premium inflows, possibly yielding illiquidity premium in addition to default risk compensation. Alternatively, if not held since issuance, illiquid bonds can be purchased at a discount in the secondary market. Both for true-sales and synthetics, funds for both default and illiquidity risk are available for CDO investor compensation, as the originator's stake in the transaction is determined by the bond portfolio cash-flows.

The approach taken for factor estimation on the basis of corporate bond prices is summarised as follows:

In a first step, I extract implied term structures of defaultable and riskless spot rates. Estimation is largely facilitated by the use of hypothetical zero bond data. As borrower-specific pricing differences are irrelevant to granular-portfolio CDO pricing, the aggregation of information, such that risk level-specific zero bond term structures enter the estimation setup, entails little loss in generality.

The estimated spot rates and spreads exhibit a panel data structure, both meeting the time series and cross-sectional data requirements stated above. The method to be implemented for estimation permits both simultaneous estimation of the full parameter vector ϕ using time-series of risk-level dependent defaultable term structure data, and the extraction of a latent factor time series realisation.

A comparative-static model analysis with respect to the number of factors governing the default model and parameter estimates shall be performed in Chapter 5, such that both the CDO valuation model to be developed can be implemented and the large number of model parameters can be expanded around the obtained estimates.

4.2 Bond data for corporate spread estimation

The selection of the issuers to be considered for bond sample selection has been based on a review of CDO issuance information, which has been partly broken down to single entities.[3] A casual comparison shows that the European investment grade corporate debt market is covered to a large extent by borrowers whose risk is being securitised.

The selected corporate bond panel for spread estimation contains Euro-denominated bonds issued by entities from the Eurozone and non-EMU member states, the UK taking the largest proportion. The prices of 334 bonds issued by 105 firms are available, and all bonds have been rated investment grade by Moody's or, subsidiarily, by Standard & Poor's at the beginning of the 18 months sample period, or obtained an investment grade rating during the first half year of the sample period. All bonds are specified as straight bonds paying yearly coupons evenly. Odd first or last coupons are allowed and accounted for in the respective cash-flow series, but sinking fund bonds and bonds with any derivative features, such as call or put provisions or rating-sensitive coupons are excluded. With respect to prioritisation in the case of bankruptcy, the choice is limited to senior unsecured obligations.

Concerning the riskless interest rate model, German government debt (Bundesanleihen) is regarded to be priced under the riskless term structure $R_r(t, \tau)$ for the Eurozone. The riskless government sample comprises 56 bonds with yearly coupon periods.

In both the riskless and corporate segment, weekly clean prices as quoted on Wednesdays from 5/7/00 to 19/12/01 are used, accrued interest is added on an actual/actual basis. Choosing a narrower sampling interval would not be useful due to infrequent trading in corporate bonds. Pricing information of the corporate sample has been obtained from Datastream.[4] All bond specifications and rating histories are obtained from Bloomberg. Both price series and specifications of the Bundesanleihen are obtained from the German Capital Markets Database at Mannheim University.

The sample properties together with the specification of *class*-assignments required for factor model estimation are described as follows.

For spread structure estimation, the assignment of classes to reference claims is performed according to the risk-level, as identified by the agency rating. Paucity of data precludes an additional partition of classes according to the issuers' sectors affiliation

---

[3] For further reference pool description, see Chapter 7.

[4] The pricing information provided consists of price quotes from traders or exchange prices. Redundant price quotes (effectively filling time-series gaps) that did not change for one week were dropped. Outliers were identified on the basis of yields to maturity and 208 (of 17568) corporate price observations with highly abnormal yields that were apparently not due to rating changes were dropped.

while guaranteeing a sufficient number of price observations at every week, to assure a reliable estimation in the light of sample heterogeneity. Therefore, the classes assigned to corporate bonds for estimation capture the risk level only. For implementation, the class indices $class := risk = 1, 2, 3$ refer to the letter ratings Aaa/Aa, A, and Baa as classification devices, respectively.

In the view of rating migrations, one must make a choice as to whether bonds are allocated to new classes upon rating changes, or whether the class-composition remains unaltered. This is driven by the specific application at hand: The observed time series should represent a sample of spread realisations that may occur during the tenor of a static reference portfolio. Hence, model estimation aims at capturing the entire spread volatility during the sample period. A class-adjustment upon rating transition would not capture mean spread level changes associated with rating transitions, thus underestimating the variation in credit quality changes during the CDO tenor. Therefore, bonds are attributed to static classes only at the beginning of the rather short estimation period.

An overview of the bonds' characteristics is given in table 4.1.

Both in the riskless and corporate segments, short maturities are covered by a small number of old bonds. Pricing information for short maturities thus appears to be less reliable and is treated separately for estimation. Long maturities are well represented in both the riskless and the corporate sample. The discrepancy in nominal coupon size between governments and corporates is a consequence of the age of the issues: Whereas the high par coupon requirements on bonds issued during the early 1990s affect mainly the government sample, the corporate sample largely covers issues from the subsequent lower interest environment in the aftermath of the EMU currency accord. Issuance timing is (partly) reflected in the differences in median maturity.

The corporate bond sample, initially fully rated investment grade, encountered significant downgrading, as can be seen from the bonds' migration behaviour shown in table 4.2. The downgrade has been accompanied by an overall spread widening, amounting to an increase of about 36 to 49 basispoints for the median yield spread against government debt for different risk classes.[5] The Marconi restructuring event caused two bonds to lose their investment grade rating in September 2001. However, as the company has not filed bankruptcy, the downgrade from A3 has occurred gradually and a Ba-rating has been maintained through the estimation period. Albeit accompanied by a strong spread increase, in the modelling context, the credit event would probably not constitute a Poisson jump defining a default event in the model sense. Technically, one would presume that a positive Marconi intensity exists during the sample period, such that

---

[5] A comprehensive time series analysis of spreads shall be performed for spread structures to be estimated, as maturity and coupon effects are precisely controlled for.

	Start date	End date	Total period
German Bundesanleihen			
Valid prices	53	40	3523
Maturity[years]	2.82 (0.39/9.00)	2.05 (0.36/7.57)	2.50 (0.28/8.53)
Coupon[%]	6.50 (3.15/8.80)	6.38 (4.12/8.00)	6.50 (3.75/8.50)
Yield to maturity[%]	5.02 (4.55/5.17)	3.84 (3.49/4.56)	4.54 (3.56/5.17)
Aaa/Aa corporate class (risk=1)			
Valid prices	88	91	6751
Maturity[years]	4.66 (1.05/10.30)	3.98 (0.95/9.15)	4.28 (0.56/9.77)
Coupon[%]	5.75 (3.50/9.00)	5.75 (3.63/8.34)	5.75 (3.50/9.00)
Yield to maturity[%]	5.62 (5.15/6.27)	4.84 (4.84/6.14)	5.23 (4.06/6.22)
Median yield spread[%]	0.60	1.00	0.69
A corporate class (risk=2)			
Valid prices	83	112	7294
Maturity[years]	5.31 (1.20/9.73)	4.61 (0.86/8.84)	4.83 (1.17/9.33)
Coupon[%]	5.63 (3.64/7.74)	5.75 (3.75/7.06)	5.63 (3.63/7.13)
Yield to maturity[%]	5.87 (5.27/6.42)	5.05 (3.98/6.43)	5.46 (4.41/6.46)
Median yield spread[%]	0.85	1.21	0.92
Baa corporate class (risk=3)			
Valid prices	57	74	4569
Maturity[years]	5.96 (1.93/9.02)	4.53 (0.86/7.49)	4.86 (1.00/8.55)
Coupon[%]	5.75 (4.50/7.50)	5.88 (4.58/7.09)	5.88 (4.50/7.40)
Yield to maturity[%]	6.06 (5.32/6.77)	5.37 (4.41/6.96)	5.74 (4.59/6.85)
Median yield spread[%]	1.04	1.53	1.20

Table 4.1: **Corporate and government bond sample overview.**
Median (5%-quantile/95%-quantile) of contract specifications of German Bundesanleihen and Euro-denominated default-risky bonds issued by European corporates are given. Corporate classes are formed according to the level of riskiness as given by issuer's rating at the start of the estimation period.

the rating change-induced spread increase constitutes a regular event in the investment grade bond market, captured by the diffusion factors. In order to avoid a selection bias with respect to the set of events that may happen during the tenor of a CDO, Marconi price observations enter estimation, except for some severe outliers that would destabilise the numerical fitting procedure. A a result, one may expect the class two-yield spreads, encompassing Marconi, to encounter a stronger increase than the class three-spreads, not affected by a comparable event, in autumn 2001.

A disaggregation of the migration events in the sample among sectors shows that sector heterogeneity is present with respect to the observed evolution of riskiness. I apply the major level of the FTSE (2002) industry classification scheme on each issuer: basic industries, consumer goods (cyclical & noncyclical), services (cyclical & noncyclical), financial companies, and utilities.

Quality deterioration has been worst for noncyclical services: the 44 bonds of this sector encountered 50 downgrade events, but no upgrades. Rating deterioration has been due

	# bonds	Aa to A	Baa to A	A to Baa	Baa to Ba	Net
Entire sample	334	53	4	45	2	-96
Industry breakdown						
Basic	74	6	0	1	0	-7
Services, cyclical	12	0	0	0	0	0
Services, noncylical	44	19	0	29	2	-50
Consumer, cyclical	66	0	0	12	0	-12
Consumer, noncyclical	41	0	0	3	0	-3
Financials	63	24	0	0	0	-24
Utilities	34	4	4	0	0	0

Table 4.2: **Corporate rating migrations during sample period.**
The last column indicates the difference between up- and downgrade events.

to the distress in the telecommunications sector, which accounts for 38 out of 44 bonds issued by noncyclical services. This is followed by 24 downgrades on bonds issued mainly by banks and a few insurance companies (subsumed as the financial sector), that lost their Aa-rating. In the remaining sectors, downgrading activity was less severe.

4.3 Obtaining implied corporate spreads

4.3.1 Default-free and defaultable term structure estimation

A zero bond yield curve is derived for each corporate risk level or the riskless Bundesanleihen $class = r, risk$ at every observation date. Implied term structures of riskless rates $R_r(t,\tau)$ and defaultable spot rates of the three specified risk levels $R_{class}(t,\tau), class = risk$ and the associated spreads $S_{class}(t,\tau)$ as affine functions of the latent factors, as specified by (3.37) are obtained by interpolation.

I apply a smoothing procedure on hypothetical default-riskless and corporate zero bond spot rates, using the methodology of Nelson and Siegel (1987). Risk-based term structure estimation using a parsimoniously parameterised interpolation function is particularly appealing given the information requirements of the factor model: Estimated rates are less susceptible to possibly notable individual pricing errors, which would be the case if a spline function were used. As only the mean evolution of the classes under consideration is of interest for the large portfolio application, over-fitting due to individual mispricings in certain maturity buckets would be misleading, so larger unexplained errors are instead deliberately taken into account.

It is assumed that coupon bond prices $V_i(t, class, \underline{\tau})$, are explained by the riskless and corporate zero structures, where i denotes a price observation which may be part of any *class*. The implied term structures are treated as maturity-specific observations of the riskless rate $R_r(t,\tau)$ or the sum $R_{class}(t,\tau) = R_r(t,\tau) + C(t,\tau) + Class(t,\tau)$, where the components $C(t,\tau) + Class(t,\tau)$ are jointly observed as implied spread curves.

Using the zero bond decomposition for the riskless and corporate market price observations $V_i(t, class, \underline{\tau})$, each payment is discounted with the appropriate riskless or risky spot rate $R_{class}(t,\tau)$ of a zero bond with maturity τ applying to the respective riskless or corporate class

$$V_i(t, class, \underline{\tau}) = \sum_{\tau=\tau_1}^{\tau_N} e^{-R_{class}(t,\tau)\tau} \cdot CF_i(\tau - t) + \varepsilon_i(t, class, \underline{\tau}), \tag{4.1}$$

$\varepsilon_i(t, class, \underline{\tau})$ denotes the observation error of an individual coupon bond price when the bond is priced at the appropriate term structure of discount rates $R_{class}(t,\tau)$, determining the theoretical price $\widehat{V}_i(t, class, \underline{\tau})$. Market prices $V_i(t, class, \underline{\tau})$ are therefore explained by a regression, regressors being represented by the coupon- or principal payments $CF_i(\tau - t)$ occurring at payment dates $\underline{\tau}$, including odd first and last coupons in the corporate sector. In order to derive a smooth term structure, a parametrisation $R_{class}(t,\tau) = R_{class}(\beta_{class}(t),\tau)$ of the yield/maturity relationship is required, where the entries of the parameter vector $\beta_{class}(t)$ are specific for every week t and every $class = r, risk$.

The simple functional form for zero bond yields proposed by Nelson and Siegel (1987), is given by

$$\begin{aligned} R_{class}(\beta_{class}(t),\tau) &= \beta^0_{class}(t) + \left(\beta^1_{class}(t) + \beta^2_{class}(t)\right) \cdot \frac{1 - \exp(-\frac{\tau}{\beta^3_{class}(t)})}{\frac{\tau}{\beta^3_{class}(t)}} \\ &\quad -\beta^2_{class}(t) \cdot \exp(-\frac{\tau}{\beta^3_{class}(t)}). \end{aligned} \tag{4.2}$$

The interpolation function has the properties that the short rate and yield for maturities approaching infinity are directly related to the parameters

$$\begin{aligned} \lim_{\tau \to 0} R_{class}(\beta_{class}(t),\tau) &= \beta^0_{class}(t) + \beta^1_{class}(t) \\ \lim_{\tau \to \infty} R_{class}(\beta_{class}(t),\tau) &= \beta^0_{class}(t), \end{aligned} \tag{4.3}$$

such that $-\beta^1_{class}(t)$ is interpreted as the term spread. The parameter $\beta^2_{class}(t)$ determines whether the term structure displays an upward ($\beta^2_{class}(t) > 0$) or downward ($\beta^2_{class}(t) < 0$) hump in the short-term to medium segment, together with the parameter $\beta^3_{class}(t)$, which characterises the curvature.

The parametric identification of the intercept is convenient for the intended application: Pricing information of short maturities is to a large extent conveyed by bonds with short remaining maturity. However, due to low liquidity of old bonds, short maturity bond prices are expected to be rather unreliable with respect to an appropriate pricing of default risk. Furthermore, only a small number of very short term corporate bonds is available, which causes the estimation to be numerically unstable for short maturities. The weak identification of the short end is a consequence of the low sensitivity of the theoretical price $V_i(t, class, \underline{T})$ of a change in short-term discount factors. Based on those considerations, the intercepts are fixed as the median yields of bonds with remaining maturities of less than one year, updated quarterly, by imposing (4.3) to hold as a substitution constraint. The actual size of the intercept is of little relevance for factor model estimation, as implied zero bond yields of maturities exceeding two years only shall enter the dynamic estimation setup.[6] I find that the flexibility of the Nelson/Siegel functional form in the short maturity range together with the stabilisation at zero maturity provides a reasonable fit to the yield information conveyed by medium to long maturity bonds, yielding moderately humped term structures.

Imposing the short rate restriction to hold, the free parameters $\beta^0_{class}(t), \beta^2_{class}(t)$, $\beta^3_{class}(t)$ are estimated by solving nonlinear least squares problems of the form

$$\hat{\beta}_{class}(t) = \arg\min \sum_{i \in class} \left[V_i(t, class, \underline{T}) - \hat{V}_i(t, class, \underline{T})\right]^2 \tag{4.4}$$

for every $class = r, risk$ at every observation date, with $\hat{V}_i(t, class, \underline{T})$ priced at the relevant Nelson/Siegel term structure in accordance with 4.1.

The obtained estimates $\hat{\beta}_{class}(t)$ characterise the evolution of the implied term structures during the estimation period, such that riskless and corporate zero bond spot rates are generated by the parametric form (4.2). Summary statistics on the obtained parameter estimates characterising the hypothetical zero bond spot rates are reported in table 4.3.

The location statistics on the $\beta^0_{class}(t)$-estimates convey that the relationship between the risk level and average defaultable yields is monotonic, which also holds for nearly every single observation period, despite the lack of class-adjustments upon rating changes. The statistics on the slope parameters $\beta^1_{class}(t)$ convey that corporate yield curves are consis-

---

6 It shall be noted that in theory, yields of bonds close to redemption would be the closest proxy for riskless and defaultable short rates. Data reliability of old bonds, however, is unsatisfactory due to infrequent trading, presumed illiquidity and a small number of issues. As estimated Nelson/Siegel-functions rarely reflect short-term information appropriately, the precise approximation of the short end and the lower updating frequency is harmless to medium and long-term yields, as long as a smooth term structure is preserved.

	Risk-free				Risk=1			
	$\beta_r^0(t)$	$\beta_r^1(t)$	$\beta_r^2(t)$	$\beta_r^3(t)$	$\beta_1^0(t)$	$\beta_1^1(t)$	$\beta_1^2(t)$	$\beta_1^3(t)$
Mean	0.0545	-0.0066	-0.0234	2.0506	0.0613	-0.0091	-0.0388	0.9355
Median	0.0537	-0.0059	-0.0273	1.4999	0.0616	-0.0090	-0.0368	0.8676
5%-quantile	0.0501	-0.0146	-0.0564	0.3174	0.0570	-0.0114	-0.0814	0.3555
95%-quantile	0.0635	-0.0017	0.0083	4.0107	0.0643	-0.0069	-0.0116	1.6919

	Risk=2				Risk=3			
	$\beta_2^0(t)$	$\beta_2^1(t)$	$\beta_2^2(t)$	$\beta_2^3(t)$	$\beta_3^0(t)$	$\beta_3^1(t)$	$\beta_3^2(t)$	$\beta_3^3(t)$
Mean	0.0665	-0.0167	-0.5953	0.8235	0.0672	-0.0176	-0.0294	1.2091
Median	0.0654	-0.0154	-0.0833	0.3473	0.0663	-0.0169	-0.0212	0.7692
5%-quantile	0.0621	-0.0243	-2.5715	0.0112	0.0595	-0.0273	-0.0519	0.2391
95%-quantile	0.0743	-0.0122	-0.0079	2.7147	0.0771	-0.0099	0.0000	2.9967

Table 4.3: **Parameter estimates of Nelson/Siegel term structures.**
Hypothetical zero bond spot rates of different risk levels are obtained by a nonlinear regression of riskless and corporate coupon bond prices on maturities of contractual payments imposing the Nelson/Siegel-functional form on the zero curves.

tently steeper than the riskless counterpart, yielding strongly increasing spread curves. Figure 4.2 below gives an illustration of the shapes of the term structures of corporate spreads, to be then discussed.

4.3.2 Statistical analysis of term structures

A statistical analysis of the term structures of riskless rates $R_r(t,\tau)$ and corporate spreads $S_{class}(t,\tau)$ does not only highlight the cross-sectional and time-series properties of observed market variables, but also gives insight into the presence of a common component.

Figure 4.1 shows the evolution of the implied spot spreads $S_{class}(t,\tau)$ for the $\tau = 2,4,6,8,10$ constant maturity classes, formed conditional on the rating in July 2000.

The evolution reflects the deterioration of credit quality and the increase in yield spreads of coupon bonds during the estimation period.

A summary of the time series properties of the implied riskless spot rates and spot spreads is given in table 4.4. Mean spot spreads of all maturities are increasing with the risk level of the class, which shows that on average, the market performs the same ordinal ranking of default risk as the agencies. Moreover, initial rating assignments exhibit predictive power throughout the estimation period: Despite the lack of class adjustments upon severe downgrading, the monotony of the yield/rating relationship is maintained for most observation dates, the overlap in autumn 2001 due to the Marconi spread-widening in class two.

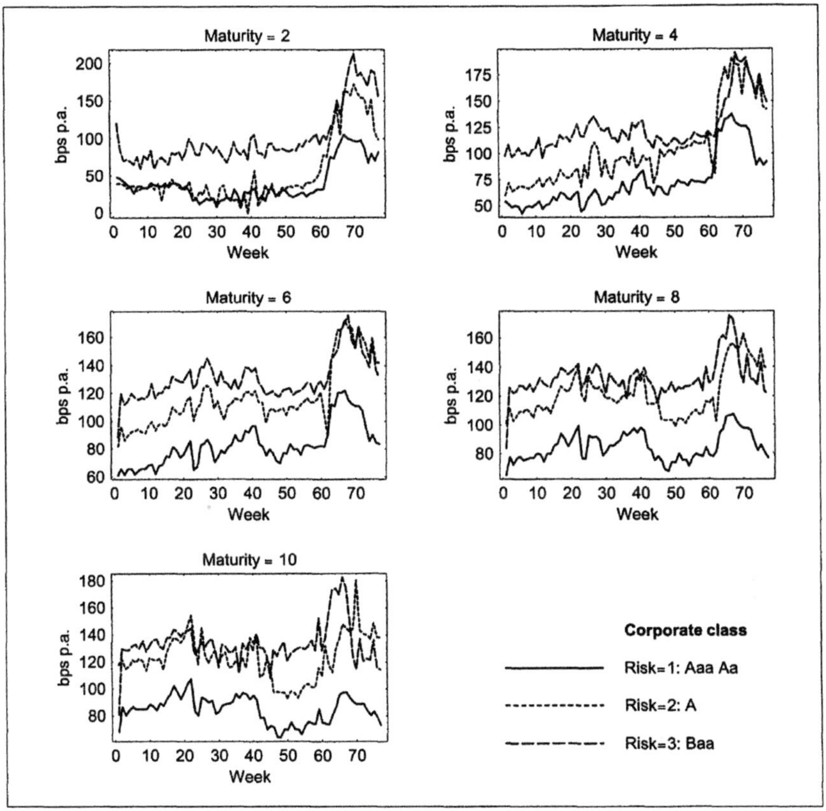

Figure 4.1: **Corporate spread term structure evolution.**

Zero bond spot spreads as implied by prices of bonds issued by European investment grade corporates are obtained for 2,4,6,8, and 10 year constant maturity classes. Spreads are calculated as the difference between the implied corporate zero bond spot rates of the relevant risk level and the riskless zero bond spot rates of the equivalent maturity. The sample period (weeks 1-77) starts on 5 July 2000 and ends on 19 December 2001.

	Term structures[%]			Term spreads[%]			DF-test	Autocorrelation			Autocorr. 1st diff.	
	Mean	Std dev.	Skew	Mean	Min	Max		Lag=1	Lag=2	Lag=10	Lag=1	Lag=2
$R_r(t,\tau)$												
2	4.424	0.604	-0.640*				-0.40	0.985	0.967	0.778	0.060	-0.033
4	4.556	0.460	-0.261				-2.08	0.974	0.948	0.724	-0.064	-0.052
6	4.709	0.331	-0.158	0.499	-0.141	1.337	-3.53	0.961	0.925	0.630	-0.066	-0.033
8	4.831	0.252	-0.348				-5.26	0.939	0.890	0.483	-0.110	0.005
10	4.923	0.210	-0.612*				-7.33	0.910	0.845	0.305	-0.146	0.048
$S_1(t,\tau)$												
2	0.398	0.255	1.315**				-2.40	0.951	0.914	0.461	-0.111	0.062
4	0.729	0.249	1.325**				-3.25	0.957	0.907	0.455	0.072	0.031
6	0.826	0.151	0.993**	0.447	-0.090	0.852	-7.30	0.916	0.831	0.203	0.010	-0.061
8	0.848	0.097	0.431				-14.48*	0.828	0.677	-0.208	-0.044	-0.138
10	0.845	0.100	-0.176				-14.34*	0.820	0.678	-0.038	-0.092	-0.161
$S_2(t,\tau)$												
2	0.531	0.454	1.518**				-4.39	0.936	0.918	0.479	-0.362	0.002
4	1.035	0.357	1.152**				-6.77	0.912	0.869	0.581	-0.259	-0.060
6	1.169	0.225	1.066**	0.702	-0.200	1.386	-7.83	0.904	0.842	0.451	-0.182	-0.055
8	1.215	0.161	0.831**				-8.09	0.895	0.827	0.200	-0.174	-0.060
10	1.233	0.166	0.356				-17.14*	0.771	0.687	0.114	-0.318	-0.154
$S_3(t,\tau)$												
2	1.003	0.374	1.612**				-4.08	0.934	0.886	0.439	-0.144	-0.070
4	1.244	0.237	1.534**				-5.28	0.931	0.883	0.350	-0.160	-0.007
6	1.306	0.145	0.908**	0.330	-0.987	0.775	-15.74*	0.839	0.755	0.120	-0.212	-0.076
8	1.326	0.127	0.650*				-28.91**	0.684	0.538	-0.094	-0.213	-0.056
10	1.332	0.151	0.775**				-29.73**	0.656	0.495	-0.179	-0.219	-0.004

Table 4.4: **Statistics on term structures of riskless interest rates and corporate spot spreads.**

Significance of skewness is indicated by ** at a 1%-level and by * at 5%-level, the two-sided test statistic being based on the asymptotic normality of the estimator with mean zero and variance $\frac{6}{T}$, $T = 77$ denoting the number of observations. The Dickey-Fuller test statistic ('DF-test') has been computed as $T(\widehat{\rho} - 1)$. The OLS regression includes a nonzero intercept. $H_0 : \widehat{\rho} = 1$ is rejected at a 5% confidence level if indicated by * and at a 1% confidence level if indicated by **. The term spread is computed as the difference between the ten-year and the two-year spot rate or spread.

The entire term structure of the risk class two spot spreads $S_2(t, \tau)$ however, is more volatile than the term structure of class three $S_3(t, \tau)$, hence indicating that volatility is not increasing in the default risk level.

Skewness is reported to provide an insight into the division of the probability mass applicable to observations near zero and to a long tail, which indicates high yield or spread observations occurring at a higher frequency than would be predicted by a Gaussian term structure model.[7] It is observed that spreads are significantly skewed to the right, with the empirical distributions becoming increasingly symmetrical for longer maturities, whereas riskless rates are almost symmetrically distributed, the third moments being on the whole not significantly different from zero.

Long term spreads and rates are less volatile than short term observations, which implies that market participants expect deviations of both types of market variables to be not persistent in the long run.

The Dickey-Fuller test statistics[8] indicate the absence of unit roots for spreads of long maturities, whereas for the highly volatile short-term spreads, the null hypothesis that spread processes are non-stationary is not rejected. Interest rate changes tend to be persistent, as the random walk hypothesis is not rejected for all maturities. Diminishing autocorrelation functions and the autocorrelational pattern of first differences, show however, that reversals of one-period changes are clearly present, hence giving evidence of a moderate mean reversion of spot rates and spreads of all classes.

The cross-sectional dimension is reflected by the shape of the estimated term structures. Example term structures for the low-spread environment in the first year of the sample period and of the high-spread environment of autumn 2001 are depicted in figure 4.2: Within the maturity range of two to ten years used for subsequent factor model estimation, spread term structures are mostly increasing. The spread widening in autumn 2001, however, causes all spread structures to exhibit a hump in the four years maturity range.

Both the monotonic increase within the estimation range and the hump yielding a maximum can be fitted by the affine solution of the CIR model. Some spread structures exhibit a minimum (not depicted), possibly falling below zero for the short-term maturities smaller than two years, which causes curves to be rather steep in the two-year maturity range.

---

7 For the significance test for skewness, see Campbell, Lo, and MacKinlay (1997), p. 17. The deviation from the Gaussian context indicates the appropriateness of CIR-factors for spread modelling: A linear combination of independent noncentrally χ^2–distributed random variables is noncentrally χ^2–distributed, see Jamshidian (1996), p. 95 together with Johnson and Kotz (1970), p. 135. See Appendix A for the transition density of CIR-factors.

8 The inclusion of a regression intercept is stipulated by the discretisation of the CIR-SDEs as AR(1)-processes with heteroscedastic disturbances. Critical values are -13.7 and -19.8 for the sample size, see Fuller (1976), p. 371, case 2 (nonzero intercept).

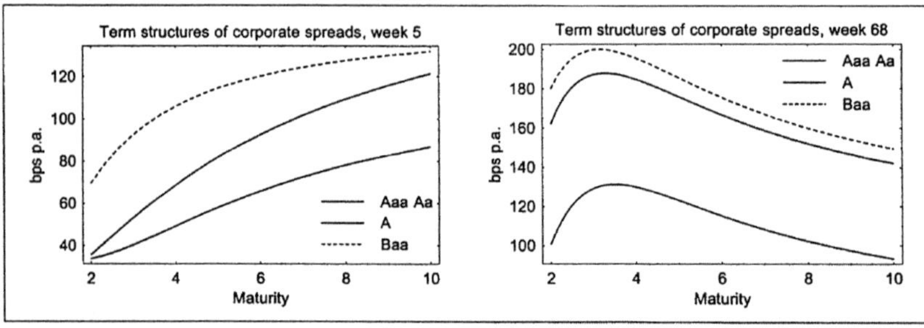

Figure 4.2: **Term structures of corporate spreads, low-spread and high-spread environment.**

Example term structures as obtained using the Nelson and Siegel (1987) estimation. The graph on the left-hand side plots corporate spread structures as of the 2 August 2000, exhibiting the typical shape observed during the low-spread environment in the first year of the sample period. The graph on the right-hand side depicts the term structures of 17 October 2001, exhibiting the typical shape observed during the high-spread environment of autumn 2001.

The steepness of term structures $R_r(t,\tau)$ and $S_{class}(t,\tau)$ is conveyed by the term spreads reported in table 4.4, calculated as the difference between the two year spot rate or spread and its ten year counterpart. The riskless term structure and the term structures of spot spreads of classes one and two are upward sloping in about 95% of the observation dates and in 90% for class three. Setting the slopes in relation to the levels of the respective term structures, by for instance, computing a ratio $\frac{Mean[S_{class}(t,10)-S_{class}(t,2)]}{Mean[S_{class}(t,2)]}$, reveals that relative term spreads of the corporate credit spread curves by far exceed those of the riskless term structure. Corporate spreads of long maturities therefore carry large term premia.

The presumed presence of a common factor affecting all positions in a reference portfolio must be reflected by the comovements of spot spreads $S_{class}(t,\tau)$ between the three corporate classes.

Dependencies among the evolution of the three spread structures indicate the presence of a market-wide risk factor, causing all spreads to move into the same direction. The estimation procedure to be used is based on observed levels, which should reflect the joint changes. Table 4.5 reports the pairwise relationships among term structures both for levels and first differences, which are significantly both positive and strong.

The strength of the linear relationship is measured by OLS. For regressions between spot spreads of the same maturity class, I choose the time series of the higher risk level to be the dependent variable. For the comparison of riskless rates with spreads, I choose the spot spread of the corresponding maturity to be the dependent variable. Correlation between spot spreads is strongest for short maturities and is also present in first differences

	Levels: correlation coefficient / linear regression coefficient					
τ	$S_1(t,\tau), S_2(t,\tau)$	$S_1(t,\tau), S_3(t,\tau)$	$S_2(t,\tau), S_3(t,\tau)$	$R_r(t,\tau), S_1(t,\tau)$	$R_r(t,\tau), S_2(t,\tau)$	$R_r(t,\tau), S_3(t,\tau)$
2	0.94 / 1.67**	0.85 / 1.25**	0.92 / 0.76**	-0.72 / -0.31**	-0.83 / -0.62**	-0.87 / -0.54**
4	0.93 / 1.33**	0.84 / 0.80**	0.89 / 0.59**	-0.89 / -0.48**	-0.89 / -0.69**	-0.83 / -0.42**
6	0.90 / 1.34**	0.88 / 0.84**	0.90 / 0.58**	-0.85 / -0.39**	-0.85 / -0.58**	-0.76 / -0.33**
8	0.80 / 1.32**	0.76 / 1.00**	0.62 / 0.49**	-0.63 / -0.24**	-0.73 / -0.47**	-0.45 / -0.22**
10	0.68 / 1.13**	0.40 / 0.60**	0.21 / 0.19	-0.32 / -0.15**	-0.56 / -0.44**	-0.10 / -0.07

	First differences: correlation coefficient / linear regression coefficient					
τ	$S_1(t,\tau), S_2(t,\tau)$	$S_1(t,\tau), S_3(t,\tau)$	$S_2(t,\tau), S_3(t,\tau)$	$R_r(t,\tau), S_1(t,\tau)$	$R_r(t,\tau), S_2(t,\tau)$	$R_r(t,\tau), S_3(t,\tau)$
2	0.39 / 0.81**	0.30 / 0.51**	0.48 / 0.40**	-0.48 / -0.20**	-0.35 / -0.23	-0.24 / -0.15
4	0.54 / 1.10**	0.58 / 0.70**	0.50 / 0.30**	-0.63 / -0.45**	-0.43 / -0.63**	-0.56 / -0.48**
6	0.64 / 1.01**	0.62 / 0.80**	0.58 / 0.48**	-0.63 / -0.42**	-0.49 / -0.52**	-0.58 / -0.50**
8	0.67 / 0.86**	0.58 / 0.98**	0.41 / 0.54**	-0.61 / -0.39**	-0.58 / -0.49**	-0.43 / -0.47**
10	0.42 / 0.79**	0.54 / 1.10**	0.14 / 0.15	-0.60 / -0.41**	-0.44 / -0.56**	-0.34 / -0.46**

Table 4.5: **Comovement of corporate spreads and relationship between spreads and riskless interest rates.**

Correlation coefficients between the time series of corresponding maturities and OLS-estimates of the coefficients of pairwise linear regressions are given. For regressions between spot spreads of the same maturity class, the time series of levels and first differences of the riskier class are chosen as the dependent variable. For the comparison of riskless rates with spreads, the spread level or first difference of the corresponding maturity is chosen as the dependent variable. ** indicate significance at 1%-level (t-test).

of the fitted series, as shown below. Furthermore, regression intercepts (not reported) are significantly positive, which suggests the modelling of class-specific additive factors accounting for mean differences.

The sharp increase of all spreads in autumn 2001 mainly affects observed correlation between spreads of short maturities. Correlations between the two year spreads decrease considerably to the order of 0.1 to 0.5 when the sample period is truncated on 5/9/2001.

Furthermore, all spreads exhibit negative correlation with riskless rates, which is in line both with theory, as explained by Longstaff and Schwartz (1995) in the context of a structural model in the Merton (1974) framework, and with existing empirical evidence in the US corporate bond market, as for instance, has been found by Longstaff and Schwartz (1995) and Duffee (1998) on US corporates, and by Düllmann, Uhrig-Homburg, and Windfuhr (2000) on DM-denominated defaultable foreign bonds. The relationship turns out to be strong, as spreads, the dependent variables, are considerably lower than riskless rates.

4.3.3 Error analysis: residual effects of liquidity proxies and sector affiliation

Table 4.6 gives summary statistics on pricing errors, computed as the deviations of market prices from the their theoretical counterparts priced at the estimated term structure, $\widehat{\varepsilon}_i(t, class, \underline{T}) = V_i(t, class, \underline{T}) - \widehat{V}_i(t, class, \underline{T})$, broken down for $class = r, risk$. To get an idea about the scale to which estimated pricing errors $\widehat{\varepsilon}_i(t, class, \underline{T})$ translate to differences on the return level, I calculate for each class, as explained in the annotations of table 4.6, a 'median' yield error based on the median characteristics with respect to coupon, maturity, and yield to maturity of the bonds contained in the class-specific samples, as displayed in the last column of table 4.1. Bond principals are normalised to 100[%].

The location parameters indicate that the Nelson/Siegel-interpolation underprices both German Bundesanleihen and European corporate bonds. The translation of pricing errors to yield deviations allows the assessment of the impact of systematic mispricings on spreads, used to obtain portfolio loss forecasts: Yield errors of the 'median' bond in the four samples reveal that the impact on spreads is smaller than ten basispoints for every sample. What is more important than the absolute size of the error measure is the fact that both for riskless and defaultable yields, it is in the same order of magnitude. Therefore, the bias present in all bond prices does not affect an analysis of spot spreads as the differences between risky and riskless rates.

A short excursus to individual mispricings is in order. It has been argued that bond- or reference obligor-specific price differences are perfectly diversifiable, and therefore irrele-

Residuals[%]	MAD	RMSE	Mean	Median	5%-qu.	95%-qu.	MYE
Bundesanleihen	0.221	0.308	0.196	0.164	-0.091	0.595	-6.6
Aaa/Aa corporates	1.310	2.147	0.111	0.218	-3.355	2.572	-5.5
A corporates	1.480	2.324	0.316	0.356	-2.763	3.484	-9.5
Baa corporates	1.583	2.398	0.097	0.292	-4.439	3.384	-7.8

Table 4.6: **Statistics on pricing errors of individual coupon bonds.**
The median yield error (MYE), given in basispoints, for the classes is calculated for a bond with the median maturity τ_N^{med} (with vector $\underline{\tau}^{med}$ collecting the corresponding payment dates) and coupon $CF_{class}^{med}(\tau - t)$ of the respective class as given in table 4.1. I choose the yield to maturity of the 'median' bond of each class $\widehat{ytm}_{class}$ to solve

$$V^{med}(class, \underline{\tau}^{med}) - \widehat{V}(class, \underline{\tau}^{med}) = \varepsilon^{med}(class, \underline{\tau}^{med}), \qquad (4.5)$$

where $\varepsilon^{med}(class, \underline{\tau}^{med})$ denotes the median pricing error, as given in column five.

$$V^{med}(class, \underline{\tau}^{med}) = \sum_{\tau=\tau_1^{med}}^{\tau_N^{med}} e^{-ytm_{class}^{med}\tau} \cdot CF_{class}^{med}(\tau - t) \qquad (4.6)$$

$$\widehat{V}(class, \underline{\tau}^{med}) = \sum_{\tau=\tau_1^{med}}^{\tau_N^{med}} e^{-\widehat{ytm}_{class}\tau} \cdot CF_{class}^{med}(\tau - t). \qquad (4.7)$$

ytm_{class}^{med} denotes the median yield to maturity of the considered class and $V^{med}(class, \underline{\tau}^{med})$ the hypothetical price of a bond characterised by all median characteristics. $ytm_{class}^{med} - \widehat{ytm}_{class}$ [bps] is given in the last column.

vant to CDO pricing, once normalised to zero. The MAD, RMSE, and quantile statistics show that pricing errors of corporate bonds are widely dispersed, which had been expected in view of market imperfections and rating transitions. Residual variation within the corporate sample is slightly increasing in the risk-level, a finding that parallels the study of Düllmann, Uhrig-Homburg, and Windfuhr (2000) on DM-denominated bonds. Whereas the MAD-statistic on German Bundesanleihen matches the measure reported by Düllmann, Uhrig-Homburg, and Windfuhr (2000) almost exactly, the MADs obtained for corporates exceed those reported by Düllmann, Uhrig-Homburg, and Windfuhr (2000) by about 50%. This finding is in line with higher sample heterogeneity, covering pricing information of diverse market segments, as opposed to the prior study relating to bonds listed on a single exchange. I therefore inquire to what extent residuals of the regression on risky yield curves convey information about two issues of interest: Firstly, possible liquidity differences within the corporate bond market shall be identified. The detection of a systematic relationship of price discounts with the variables serving as illiquidity proxies would permit to identify the magnitude of the spread component attributed to bond illiquidity. When translated to the portfolio derivatives pricing context, a rough assessment of the impact of the translation of underlying bond illiquidity to tranche pricing can be obtained. Secondly, the factor model for credit portfolio risk is constructed on the premise of sector-specific differences in default risk evolution. Although paucity of data precludes estimation for several sectors, the sector-specific effects are expected to show up in the residuals.

Directly liquidity-related information such as trading volumes or bid/ask-spreads is not available for the mainly OTC-traded corporate bonds. Instead, I adopt the approach of Sarig and Warga (1989), who explore the explanatory power of proxy variables that may convey information about illiquidity discounts of a specific price observation. Data is available for two proxies: the issue size, which should exhibit a positive relation towards the price deviations of the bond under consideration and the age of a bond, calculated as the difference of the observation and the issue date, which is expected to imply increasing price discounts.

Furthermore, it is conceivable that the amount of new price quotes obtained by Datastream is related to the trading intervals, a liquidity-related feature. I therefore include the number of price changes observed, normalised by the number of time series observations. The sample means of the liquidity-related covariates are EUR 546 mill. (issue size, with a sample minimum observation of EUR 15 mill. and a maximum of EUR 5000 mill.), 2.73 years (age) and 0.893 (price changes per week).

With respect to sector-specific differences, I hypothesise that industries considered as cyclical generally bear larger default risk premia than noncyclical ones. This can be motivated in a firm value setup along the lines of Merton (1974) by the put option character of debt, whose value decreases with the presumed higher volatility of the firm value of cyclical businesses. Empirically, this hypothesis has been examined by Longstaff and Schwartz (1995) for an US corporate sample, who find a positive relationship between the spread's sensitivity on industry-specific stock index changes and the spread level. Another finding, partly contradicting the cyclicity hypothesis, however, may be expected as a consequence of the severe observed downgrade activity in the noncyclical services (i.e. mainly telecommunications) and financial sectors during the sample period. I expect a considerable price discount on these bonds, as the subsequent downgrades are obviously not reflected in the initial letter rating. The basic-industries-dummy is included in the constant.

The residual regression is given in table 4.7, broken down for the various risk levels as identified by the bonds' letter ratings.

Neither of the presumed liquidity-related variables has the expected effects throughout all risk levels – the small effects are not even significant despite the large sample size and the coefficient of average weekly price changes does not display the expected sign for the entire corporate sample. For the European corporate bond sample at hand, any

Residuals corporates			Residuals Aaa/Aa-bonds		
R^2	0.115		R^2	0.324	
Variable	**Coeff.**	**Std err.**	**Variable**	**Coeff.**	**Std err.**
Constant	0.498**	0.129	Constant	-0.315	0.197
Issue size	0.241**	0.031	Issue size	0.111**	0.033
Age of issue	0.002	0.007	Age of issue	0.029**	0.008
Avg. price changes	-0.629**	0.130	Avg. price changes	0.833**	0.201
Sectors			**Sectors**		
Services, cyclical	-0.522**	0.089	Services, cyclical	-	-
Services, noncyc.	-1.563**	0.055	Services, noncyc.	-3.232**	0.071
Cons., cyclical	0.174**	0.048	Cons., cyclical	-2.231**	0.291
Cons., noncyc.	0.593**	0.057	Cons., noncyc.	0.317	0.180
Financials	0.777**	0.050	Financials	-0.110	0.057
Utilities	1.021**	0.058	Utilities	0.454**	0.075

Residuals A bonds			Residuals Baa bonds		
R^2	0.125		R^2	0.161	
Variable	**Coeff.**	**Std err.**	**Variable**	**Coeff.**	**Std err.**
Constant	0.297	0.306	Constant	-0.619**	0.212
Issue size	-0.037	0.061	Issue size	3.027**	0.141
Age of issue	-0.006	0.014	Age of issue	0.230**	0.021
Avg. price changes	-0.380	0.304	Avg. price changes	-1.818**	0.210
Sectors			**Sectors**		
Services, cyclical	0.959**	0.257	Services, cyclical	-0.207	0.108
Services, noncyc.	-0.690**	0.090	Services, noncyc.	-0.009	0.146
Cons., cyclical	0.366**	0.070	Cons., cyclical	0.291**	0.109
Cons., noncyc.	0.444**	0.108	Cons., noncyc.	1.086**	0.084
Financials	3.144**	0.124	Financials	1.307**	0.310
Utilities	0.990*	0.094	Utilities	2.139**	0.157

Table 4.7: **Explanation of pricing residuals by liquidity proxies and sector affiliation of the issuer.**

I investigate the relevance of the liquidity-related variables 'issue size' (billions EUR), 'age of issue' (years), and 'average weekly price changes' (a ratio between zero and one). With respect to sector affiliation, the basic industry dummy is included in the intercept. ** indicates significance at 1%-level, * indicates significance at 5%-level.

explanatory power of the age of an issue must be rejected, and the explanatory power of the issue size, displaying the wrong sign for A-corporates, is doubtful.

The remaining effect of unexplained time to maturity on errors is insignificant at the one-percent level and negligible when converted into yields, which indicates that the term structure-relevant information contained in coupon bond prices is adequately captured by the Nelson/Siegel curves.

The regression of residuals on sector dummies gives clear evidence of sector-specific price differences. As expected from the observed rating deterioration, the bonds issued by noncyclical services are significantly overpriced by the implied risky yield curves that reflect the mean spot rate evolution for the respective risk classes. This special case contradicts the hypothesis that industries considered as cyclical are generally riskier and therefore should trade at a price discount, but the result is in the present sample due to the telecommunications quality deterioration. In the consumption goods sector, it is observed that cyclical businesses of class one (Aaa/Aa) do indeed trade at a discount, which does not occur in conjunction with downgrade activity from Aa to A. However, based on the sample data, I must reject the hypothesis of discounts on cyclical businesses. Overall, a sector-specific pricing difference is evident between consumption good producers and service providers, regardless of cyclicity.

It is surprising that in spite of the considerable downgrades in the financial industry, bonds still, on average, trade at a price premium on all other bonds except utilities, and that the discount in class one, in which all downgrades occur, is small in comparison to the corresponding discounts in the services and consumer goods industries.

A conversion of the regression intercepts explained by sector dummies reveals that the sector-specific differences are substantial: Considering a bond paying a coupon of six percent and five years to maturity priced at par, the largest average pricing difference identified within the entire sample of 2.60% between services and utilities translates to a difference in yield to maturity of 60 bps. The analysis shows that the introduction of sector-specific factors into the valuation model is justified by the pricing differences observed in the corporate bond market. The shortness of the time series, however, precludes a further investigation of the sector-specific pattern, for instance, as to whether pricing differences are persistent, implying sector loss expectations differing in distribution, or whether the presumption of the factor model of i.i.d. sector-related factor processes of identical risk level is supported by the data.

4.4 Factor process estimation

4.4.1 Selection of estimation procedure

The estimation of the unobserved factor processes from the joint evolution of derived spread and riskless term structures requires the choice of a procedure that is capable of extracting the latent factor realisations. In a first step, estimation is facilitated by the fact that riskless rates and corporate spreads are observed separately, which permits the decomposition of the estimation of the factor model for corporate risky yields into a standard riskless term structure model estimation, and the estimation of the spread model. Both estimations are thus performed separately.

In the riskless sector, a factor proxy such as a short-term (i.e. one to three months) interest rate may standardly be used in order to estimate the time series behaviour of the factor under the physical measure.[9] Given the cross section of term structure observations, the risk-neutral parameters and thus, the market price of interest rate risk, are determined by the affine term structure equation.[10] The bias of the estimate is determined by the steepness of the yield curve. Chapman, Long, and Pearson (1999) show that the bias is small for relevant parameter sets.[11] Therefore, model estimation using a proxy such as a short-term money market rate together with the derived zero curve, would in principle be feasible for the riskless term structure model.

The estimation of the transitional behaviour of credit factors together with the market prices of factor risk parameters is exacerbated by the lack of identification of factors with an observed market variable. In addition, observed spot spreads are sums of two affine functions of the factors $f_c(t)$ and $f_{class}(t)$. The informational basis requires the use of an estimation method that implies the unobserved factor evolution from observed spot spreads. In the term structure estimation literature, several approaches have been proposed for latent factor setups, which differ with respect to the following criteria:[12]

The error structure of observations. The theoretical affine term structure equation

---

9 See Chan, Karolyi, Longstaff, and Saunders (1992) for an empirical comparison of affine single-factor models with respect to the explanation of the time series of the one-month treasury bill yield.

10 Note that the parametric form of the CIR term structure, as given in Appendix A only permits the identification of risk-neutral parameters κ_k and θ_k. The implied market price of risk parameter λ_k can only be backed out given the estimates κ_k^* and θ_k^* from the factor time series observed under the physical measure.

11 See Chapman, Long, and Pearson (1999), p. 779 for the pricing errors in long-term yields for specific parameter sets of affine models.

12 The two criteria to be discussed are not meant to be mutually exclusive: Any estimation approach must combine elements relating both to the error structure and to the distributional properties.

is clearly not fulfilled by every pricing observation to be explained by the model.

On one hand, one can assume that a number of yields or prices equal to the number of factors are precisely observed. Conditional on the parameter set ϕ, the relevant factor is characterised as the solution of a system of equations with dimensions equal to the number of factors. This inversion approach constitutes the basis for the work of Pearson and Sun (1994), who examine the method summarised below in a CIR-style factor model for riskless rates.

On the other hand, every observation may be treated as a 'noisy measurement' of the theoretical yield or spread. Measurement errors at different observation periods are i.i.d. with zero expectation and a covariance matrix $\mathbf{M}$. This specification permits the inclusion of information provided by the entire yield curve into the estimation. In this case, an exact inversion of selected yields is no longer feasible. Instead, a Kalman filter serves the purpose of forming a belief about current factor realisations. Once a term structure observation has been made, the belief minimising squared prediction errors is formed on the basis of the proportion between conditional factor variances, as determined by the parameter set ϕ^* governing processes under the physical measure, and the noise covariance $\mathbf{M}$.

The distributional properties exploited. The panel data structure yields two distributional implications that can be exploited for model estimation.

Firstly, assuming that factor realisations are known, either by inversion or by filtering, parameter estimates ϕ^* can be obtained by standard time series methods. Estimation is performed on the basis of the joint conditional density of factors, which is the density of the noncentral χ^2 distribution in the CIR case. As in the case of observable factors, the market price of risk parameters are obtained from the cross-sectional affine relationship. For the simplest setup, estimation is based only on factor time series data, which implies a strong identification of parameters under the physical measure, market price of risk parameters being obtained by the inversion of bond prices.[13] Pearson and Sun (1994) extend the approach to the inclusion of full term structure information, by converting the factor paths to discount factors for riskless interest rate model estimation, which is adapted by Düllmann and Windfuhr (1999) for the estimation of the transitional behaviour of the short spread of defaultable claims.

Secondly, again assuming that the factor realisation is known, the SDE of the factor evolution (3.25) together with the affine factor-yield relationship, permits the prediction of spread and yield term structures, conditional on the information available

[13] See de Jong (2000) for the restriction of the information set on time-series information.

in the previous period. Estimation is then performed on the basis of the prediction errors as the differences between observed rates and spreads and their model counterparts. This approach, by contrast, yields a strong identification of risk-neutral parameters that can be inferred from the cross-sectional affine term structure.

Parameter estimation from prediction errors of riskless spot rates in combination with a Kalman filter has been introduced by Pennachi (1991), examined for the CIR model by Duan and Simonato (1995) and applied to an intensity process by Duffee (1999). All cited references use maximum likelihood estimation. If both estimation approaches are feasible, parameter estimates can be derived using the product likelihood in order to maximise the information basis, and to yield a stronger identification of the market prices of factor risk, which has been implemented by Liu, Longstaff, and Mandell (2000) for a Gaussian spread and interest rate model. Alternatively, the separate solution of both maximisation problems, as performed by de Jong (2000) permits a test on the validity of the restrictions on the risk-neutral parameters imposed by the change of measure. Moreover, when working with Gaussian models, the two approaches coincide when selected diagonal elements of the covariance matrix $\mathbf{M}$ are restricted to zero, hence explaining those yields or spreads without error, which is equivalent to exact inversion.

For the contribution at hand, I chose to estimate the model by a Kalman filter-based quasi maximum likelihood method (KF-QML) based on the prediction error distribution in the cross section of observed riskless spot rates and spreads of the three risk levels. This choice is based on the fact that given the large model size and the dependence of every spread observation on two factors, an exact inversion of the term structures hardly seems feasible. The large computational burden is due to the fact that the numerical maximisation algorithm would require one inversion step at every observation period for every trial parameter vector. The Kalman filter instead makes a linear projection of observed spot spreads on factors, which is computationally less intensive. The achieved complexity reduction incurred by the likelihood construction from the cross section comes at the cost of a weak identification of the parameters governing the factor processes under the physical measure κ_k^* and $\theta^*{}_k$ and thus, the market price of risk parameters, given the estimated risk-neutral parameters κ_k and θ_k. As the valuation problem for CDOs as derivatives on the factors only requires risk-neutral process specifications, the limitations of the chosen method are not considered to be too restrictive.

The Kalman filter recursion requires the information provided by first two conditional moments of the factor transition distribution. In case of a Gaussian model, this captures the full distributional information on factor transitions. In the non-Gaussian case at hand, the linearised projection of observations on factors ignores the higher moments of the noncentral χ^2 distributions, although the level dependence of the factor variances is taken into account. The joint density of observation errors is then approximated as a quasi-likelihood, where the inherent deviation from the true likelihood is incurred by the inference on the factor realisation.

The implemented KF-QML method has been used by Duan and Simonato (1995) on non-Gaussian interest rate models and Duffee (1999) for yield spreads of individual corporate bonds. Recent contributions by Driessen (2002) and Geyer, Kossmeier, and Pichler (2003) extend the estimation literature by interlinking several observation sets using common factors, giving rise to simultaneous estimation: Driessen (2002) complements the Duffee (1999)-approach by the introduction of a market-wide factor. The approach taken by Geyer, Kossmeier, and Pichler (2003) parallels the study at hand, as a set of spread term structures of European sovereign debt against German Bundesanleihen is interlinked by a common factor.

For estimation of the factor model, I select a set of riskless spot rates and corporate spot spreads with constant maturities of 2,4,6,8,10 years for the three classes, representing the risk level as implied by the Nelson/Siegel interpolations during the estimation period to represent the term structures.[14] In order to provide consistency with the literature on filtering, these estimated yields and spreads will subsequently be referred to as 'observables'. All observables are treated as noisy measurements of the theoretical affine functions of the state vector as implied by the CIR model. I impose the noise covariance matrices $\mathbf{M}_r(5x5)$ for the single-factor riskless term structure model and $\mathbf{M}_s(15x15)$ for the factor model explaining corporate spreads to be diagonal, where the variances of measurement noise are expected to be small due to the smoothness of the interpolation function.

The following section translates the factor model into a state-space setup, on whose basis parameter estimation is performed. The Kalman filter recursion requires the formulation of two system equations. The transition equation is stipulated by the factor dynamics and captures the time series behaviour of the model. The measurement equation captures the cross-sectional model properties as defined by the affine term structure equation. The implementation of the Kalman filter algorithm is outlined in Appendix B, building on the general procedure discussed by Harvey (1989).

14 As spread curves are steep, an inclusion of the entire maturity spectrum is desirable in order to avoid a bias toward the represented maturity range. The selection of the two-year maturity class causes spread curves to have considerable curvature at the short end.

4.4.2 The factor model in state-space form

4.4.2.1 Transition equation

I collect the factors, or state variables, explaining riskless rates and corporate spreads of all classes, in a vector $\mathbf{f}(t)$, which will be referred to as the state vector. The intertemporal behaviour of the latent state vector is assumed to be determined by the first two conditional moments of the CIR-processes governing the factors' dynamics under the physical measure. The intertemporal behaviour of the $(5x1)$-state vector $\mathbf{f}(t)$ is governed by the parameters determining the factor behaviour under the physical measure. These are defined as outlined in Chapter 3 and collected in a vector ϕ^* with elements $\phi_k^* = (\kappa_k^*, \theta_k^*, \sigma_k)$, excluding the market price of risk parameters.

Following the exposition of Harvey (1989), the transition equation for a factor system governed by parameters ϕ^* and 5-dimensional white noise $\eta(t, \mathbf{\Sigma}(\phi^*))$ with covariance matrix $\mathbf{\Sigma}(\phi^*)$

$$\mathbf{f}(t + \Delta t) = \mathbf{T}(\phi^*)\mathbf{f}(t) + \eta(t, \mathbf{\Sigma}(\phi^*)) \tag{4.8}$$

takes a particularly simple form, implied by the conditional factor expectations and variances of the factors, as determined by the continuous-time dynamics of the CIR model.[15] As factor increments exclusively depend on the current factor level, hence implying orthogonality among all factors, the deterministic transition matrix, $\mathbf{T}(\phi^*)$ is diagonal, with the conditional expectations of the respective state variables for the next discrete observation interval with length $\Delta t = 1/52$ as diagonal elements $\mathbf{T}_{ii}(\phi^*)$:

$$\mathbf{T}_{ii}(\phi^*) = \mathbb{E}\left[f_k(t + \Delta t)\,|f_k(t)\right] = \left(1 - e^{-\kappa_k^* \Delta t}\right)\theta_k^* + e^{-\kappa_k^* \Delta t} f_k(t). \tag{4.9}$$

Analogously, the covariance matrix $\mathbf{\Sigma}(\phi^*)$ is diagonal with the factors' conditional transition variances for the discrete sampling interval as elements $\mathbf{\Sigma}_{ii}(\phi^*)$:

$$\begin{aligned} \mathbf{\Sigma}_{ii}(\phi^*) &= Var\left[f_k(t + \Delta t)\,|f_k(t)\right] \\ &= \frac{\sigma_k^2}{2\kappa_k^*}\left(1 - e^{-\kappa_k^* \Delta t}\right)^2 \theta_k^* + \frac{\sigma_k^2}{\kappa_k^*}\left(e^{-\kappa_k^* \Delta t} - e^{-2\kappa_k^* \Delta t}\right) f_k(t). \end{aligned} \tag{4.10}$$

[15] See Cox, Ingersoll, and Ross (1985), p. 392 for the conditional moments.

4.4.2.2 Measurement equations

The subsequent formulation of the measurement equations accounts for the fact that the riskless term structure model is estimated separately. Observables are the riskless spot rates and corporate spreads of maturities $\underline{\tau} = (\tau_1, ..., \tau_5) = (2, 4, 6, 8, 10)$. For the state-space setup, I collect the observable variables in two vectors $\mathbf{R}_r(t) = (R_r(t, \tau))$ and $\mathbf{S}(t) = (S_{class}(t, \tau))$, with maturities $\underline{\tau} = (\tau_1, ..., \tau_5)$ and risk levels $class = 1, 2, 3$ for the spot spreads. With regard to separate estimation, the state vector $\mathbf{f}(t)$ is partitioned into $f_r(t)$ and $\mathbf{f}_s(t) = (f_c(t), f_1(t), f_2(t), f_3(t))'$ and the parameter vector ϕ into ϕ_r and $\phi_s = (\phi_c, \phi_1, \phi_2, \phi_3)$. The Kalman filter does not require assumptions about the structure of measurement errors in the observed yields and spreads. However, due to the large number of parameters to be estimated from the spot spread data, I impose the covariance matrices of measurement noise $\mathbf{M}_r$ and $\mathbf{M}_s$ to be diagonal with elements $m_r(\tau_1), ..., m_r(\tau_5)$ and $m_1(\tau_1), ..., m_1(\tau_5), m_2(\tau_1), ..., m_2(\tau_5), m_3(\tau_1), ..., m_3(\tau_5)$ for the respective spread classes. The measurement noise $\varepsilon_r(t)'$ and $\varepsilon_s(t)'$ is represented by independently $N(0,1)$–distributed random vectors.

The measurement equations for the Kalman filter setup reflect the functional dependence of the CIR model-implied spot rates and spot spreads on the state variables, as given by (3.36)

$$\mathbf{R}_r(t, \phi_r) = \mathbf{A}_r(\phi_r) + \mathbf{B}_r(\phi_r) f_r(t) + \mathbf{M}_r \varepsilon_r(t)' \tag{4.11}$$
$$\mathbf{S}(t, \phi_s) = \mathbf{A}_s(\phi_s) + \mathbf{B}_s(t, \phi_s) \mathbf{f}_s(t) + \mathbf{M}_s \varepsilon_s(t)'. \tag{4.12}$$

For the model specification at hand, the arrays are given as

$$\mathbf{A}_r(\phi_r) = (A_r(\tau_1, \phi_r), ..., A_r(\tau_5, \phi_r))' \tag{4.13}$$
$$\mathbf{B}_r(\phi_r) = (B_r(\tau_1, \phi_r), ..., B_r(\tau_5, \phi_r))' \tag{4.14}$$

such that the short rate factor $f_r(t)$ is mapped to five riskless spot rates and

$$\underset{(15x1)}{\mathbf{A}_s(\phi_s)} = (A_c(\tau_1, \phi_c) + A_1(\tau_1, \phi_1), ..., A_c(\tau_5, \phi_c) + A_1(\tau_5, \phi_1), \tag{4.15}$$
$$A_c(\tau_1, \phi_c) + A_2(\tau_1, \phi_2), ..., A_c(\tau_5, \phi_c) + A_2(\tau_5, \phi_2),$$
$$A_c(\tau_1, \phi_c) + A_3(\tau_1, \phi_3), ..., A_c(\tau_5, \phi_c) + A_3(\tau_5, \phi_3))'$$

$$\underset{(15x4)}{\mathbf{B}_s(\phi_s)} = \begin{pmatrix} B_c(\tau_1,\phi_c) & B_1(\tau_1,\ \phi_1) & 0 & 0 \\ \dots & \dots & 0 & 0 \\ B_c(\tau_5,\phi_c) & B_1(\tau_5,\phi_1) & 0 & 0 \\ B_c(\tau_1,\phi_c) & 0 & B_2(\tau_1,\phi_2) & 0 \\ \dots & 0 & \dots & 0 \\ B_c(\tau_5,\phi_c) & 0 & B_2(\tau_5,\phi_2) & 0 \\ B_c(\tau_1,\phi_c) & 0 & 0 & B_3(\tau_1,\phi_3) \\ \dots & 0 & 0 & \dots \\ B_c(\tau_5,\phi_c) & 0 & 0 & B_3(\tau_5,\phi_3) \end{pmatrix} \tag{4.16}$$

such that four factors $\mathbf{f}_s(t)$ are mapped to 15 spot spreads at every observation period.

4.4.3 Parameter estimation

4.4.3.1 Likelihood construction

Both the transition and the measurement equation are linear in the state vector. This allows for the application of a linear Kalman filter for observed riskless spot rates and spot spreads, using the standard recursion described for instance by Harvey (1989), summarised in Appendix B.

The prediction error structure of observables generated by the filter algorithm is used to perform a quasi-ML-estimation of the parameter vectors ϕ_r and ϕ_s.

Let $\mathbf{v}_r(t)$ and $\mathbf{v}_s(t)$ denote the vectors of prediction errors of the filter algorithm and $\mathbf{V}_r(t)$ and $\mathbf{V}_s(t)$ the respective prediction errors' covariance matrices. The initial expectations and variances of the state variables are set equal to the unconditional moments of the respective CIR-processes, i.e. $\mathbb{E}[f_k(t)] = \theta_k^*$ and $Var[f_k(t)] = \frac{\theta_k^* \sigma_k^2}{2\kappa_k^*}$.

The Kalman filter algorithm generates factor estimates as linear projections of observed variables $\mathbf{R}_\tau(t,\phi_r)$ or $\mathbf{S}(t,\phi_s)$, respectively, into the state vector, according to the measurement equations (4.11) and (4.12), solving a least-squares problem on prediction errors $\mathbf{v}_r(t)$ or $\mathbf{v}_s(t)$, respectively, for a linearised model. The error-minimising regression coefficient is obtained as the proportion of the conditional factor variances and variances of observed variables, adjusting the prediction made on the basis of the transition equation (4.8) by a linear function of the prediction error incurred. The linearisation has the undesirable implication that negative factor updates may occur for the discrete observation intervals. Negative state variables however, are precluded by the CIR model and must be suppressed for estimation. For the estimation problems at hand, negative updates are actually obtained in the model part referring to corporate spreads due to the low mean spread level combined with high volatility. For the relevant observation periods, no update is made of the corresponding entry k of the state vector $\mathbf{f}_s(t)$, and the entries of its covariance matrix related to k, i.e. I set

$$\mathbb{E}[f_k(t)\,|\mathbf{S}\,(t)] = \mathbb{E}[f_k(t)\,|\mathbf{S}\,(t-1)], \tag{4.17}$$

$$Cov[f_k(t), f_l(t)\,|\mathbf{S}\,(t)] = Cov[f_k(t), f_l(t)\,|\mathbf{S}\,(t-1)] \text{ for } k, l = c, 1, 2, 3. \tag{4.18}$$

Taking into account the first two moments of the prediction error distribution, I maximise the following Quasi-log-likelihood functions (apart from a constant) with respect to parameter vectors ϕ_r and ϕ_s, state vectors $f_r(t)$ and $\mathbf{f}_s(t)$ and the variances of the spot rates' and spreads' measurement noise $\mathbf{M}_r$ and $\mathbf{M}_s$:

$$\mathcal{L}^r(f_r(t), \phi_r, \mathbf{M}_r) = -0.5 \sum_{t=1}^{T} \left(\ln|\mathbf{V}_r(t)| + \mathbf{v}_r'(t)\mathbf{V}_r^{-1}(t)\mathbf{v}_r(t)\right) \tag{4.19}$$

$$\mathcal{L}^s(\mathbf{f}_s(t), \phi_s, \mathbf{M}_s) = -0.5 \sum_{t=1}^{T} \left(\ln|\mathbf{V}_s(t)| + \mathbf{v}_s'(t)\mathbf{V}_s^{-1}(t)\mathbf{v}_s(t)\right). \tag{4.20}$$

Overall, the riskless interest model requires estimation of four model parameters, five measurement noise variances, and the factor path comprising 77 weeks. This path is however, firmly restricted by the transition equation, exploiting the information set provided by 385 interest rates. Analogously, spread model estimation produces 16 model parameters, 15 noise variances, and four factor paths comprising 77 weeks each, with the latter again restricted by the time-series behaviour imposed by the model. Spread model estimation relies on 1540 spread observations.

4.4.3.2 Technical notes on implementation

Some technical remarks on the solution of the maximisation problems and statistical inference are in order: Negative factor estimates must be precluded for model estimation, which can either be achieved by the replacement of negative updates by zero, or by the entire suppression of the respective factor update.[16]

The choice has been made on the basis of the following considerations. In the case of an actual occurrence of negative updates, both alternatives have the inconvenience that standard gradient methods fail for maximisation.

---

16 It shall be noted that the problems incurred by state variable negativity only arise in the spread context. Riskless interest model estimation is straightforwardly performed using a gradient method.

Factor replacement by zero has the effect that gradient entries relating to λ_k are not well-defined, hence causing the respective parameters to be not identified, due to lack of time series information at the zero factor points. Update suppression, by contrast, implies points of discontinuity of the likelihood, as the information set changes once state variables reach the corner at zero. For both methods, the solution of the maximisation problem is therefore tedious.

The advantage of the chosen update suppression consists of the lower number of occurrences of negative factor updates.

A worse explanation of spreads incurred by discarding information provided by negative factor estimates has the desirable effect to penalise the likelihood for producing negative factor updates. The information provided by the negative update is discarded, lowering the joint density of observed errors. Thus, the assumption works like a restriction on parameter estimation, imposed to draw the optimisation algorithm away from parameter sets that imply a high probability of negative state variables. Experimentation with the alternative treatment shows that the undesirable case of negative updates is indeed avoided more frequently. A graphical representation of the extracted factor paths is included in the empirical CDO pricing analysis performed in Chapter 7, see figure 7.1. Flat segments of time series indicate that negative updates would have been obtained by linear filtering.

Due to the discontinuity inherent in the optimisation task, a 31-dimensional grid search is performed for the spread model by evaluating a large number of function values for random trial parameters in plausible ranges. I then apply a derivative-free optimisation algorithm[17] to starting values with high function values. For the corporate spread model, I start on maximisation of a restricted version, imposing equality on the parameters κ_k^* and σ_k of all factors, effectively explaining different factor levels and volatilities entirely by factor-specific θ_k^*-estimates. The maximiser of the restricted version is shocked within 50% and 150% of the parameter values, to obtain starting values for the maximisation of the full model. Convergence behaviour of $\mathcal{L}^s$ shows that the likelihood function has local maxima with parameter constellations leading to similar risk-neutral parameters. This is due to the small likelihood contribution of time series information. Local optima are characterised by unstable factor behaviour caused by the suppression of negative updates. In order to impose factor orthogonality as far as possible, correlations between the extracted common factor series and the series of the three class-specific factors have been restricted not to exceed 0.4.

A second inconvenience caused by the discontinuous nature of the problem is related to

---

[17] The simplex algorithm provided by the RATS software is robust against ill-defined gradients. It stops once a point of discontinuity in the objective function is reached and returns the maximisers.

statistical inference and parameter identification. Heteroscedasticity-consistent estimators of the asymptotic covariance of parameter vectors ϕ_r or ϕ_s, respectively, are obtained as White (1980)-estimators. The computation of standard errors of the parameter estimates requires derivatives of observables with respect to parameters, evaluated at the parameter estimates, to be well-defined. Due to the use of both time series and cross-sectional information, both marginal effects of parameter changes on factor path estimates, and estimated spot rates and spreads as functions of parameter estimates and state variables have to be taken into account. When approximating the relevant derivatives numerically, the possible discontinuity of the factor path has to be taken care of. I therefore make sure that the observation times with negative updates do not change in order to keep derivatives computable. If continuity were not being assured, infinite derivatives would be obtained and standard errors would become unreasonably small.

4.4.4 Results and implications

Parameter estimates and the estimated standard deviations of the measurement errors of term structures $\sqrt{m_r(\tau)}$ and $\sqrt{m_{class}(\tau)}$ are displayed in table 4.8.

Heteroscedasticity-consistent estimators of asymptotic standard errors of parameters are given in parentheses (see White (1980)). The close correspondence of the standard errors of the κ_k^* and λ_k-parameters is due to the weak identification of the market price of risk parameters, as the likelihood construction exploits five times more cross-sectional than time series information.

The parameter estimates determining the short spread evolution for the three corporate classes considered vary qualitatively from the parameters characterising the riskless short rate process, which is due to the relatively low level of observed spot spreads in combination with their volatile time series.

The factor processes explaining the observed spread evolution of the three risk levels under the physical measure imply short spreads that exhibit both an increasing unconditional expected value θ_k^* and an increasing unconditional standard deviation of the steady-state density (given in table 4.8) within the risk level of the class. Mean reversion is present both in the short rate process and in the factor processes explaining the corporate spreads. The reversion speed κ_k^* under the physical measure is considerably higher for all corporate spread factors. The strength of mean reversion, however, still involves high unconditional process volatilities for all factors, as the volatility coefficients σ_k are high for all spread factors. As a result, the unconditional process standard deviation is about one third of the unconditional mean for the short rate process, but twice the mean level for all corporate spread factors. High spread process volatility occurring in conjunction with low mean

	Factors				
Processes	$f_r(t)$	$f_c(t)$	$f_1(t)$	$f_2(t)$	$f_3(t)$
κ_k^*	0.4912	1.5023	2.0658	1.5435	1.5173
	(0.075)	(0.060)	(0.114)	(0.136)	(0.196)
θ_k^*	0.0373	0.0016	0.0012	0.0022	0.0039
	(0.00569)	(0.00006)	(0.00006)	(0.00019)	(0.00052)
σ_k	0.0705	0.1639	0.1569	0.1427	0.1961
	(0.002)	(0.002)	(0.002)	(0.002)	(0.003)
λ_k	-0.1498	-1.2335	-1.1848	-1.1202	-0.7459
	(0.075)	(0.060)	(0.117)	(0.135)	(0.197)
κ_k	0.3414	0.2688	0.8811	0.4234	0.7714
θ_k	0.0536	0.0088	0.0028	0.0080	0.0077
Std dev.					
phys.	0.0137	0.0037	0.0027	0.0038	0.0071
EMM	0.0198	0.0209	0.0063	0.0139	0.0139
Half life					
phys.	1.41	0.46	0.34	0.45	0.46
EMM	2.03	2.58	0.79	1.64	0.90

	Std dev. of noise for maturity $\tau[bps]$				
TS	**2**	**4**	**6**	**8**	**10**
$R_r(t,\tau)$	23.6	7.8	1.1	5.4	9.3
$S_1(t,\tau)$	20.6	9.6	4.7	0.3	3.9
$S_2(t,\tau)$	28.2	7.0	3.0	5.2	10.2
$S_3(t,\tau)$	13.5	6.9	4.5	13.1	18.4

Table 4.8: **Parameter estimates for the factor model and estimated standard deviations of measurement noise.**

Heteroscedasticity-consistent White-estimators of the asymptotic standard errors of estimates are given in parentheses. The upper table comprises process properties (unconditional standard variation and half life) obtained both under the physical and the risk-neutral measure.

levels causes processes not to satisfy the Feller condition ($2\kappa_k\theta_k \geq \sigma_k^2$) for state-variable positivity.[18] Hence, as opposed to interest rates, spread factors reach the reflecting barrier at zero with positive probability, when processes under both the empirical and the risk-neutral measure are considered.

The corporate spreads carry high term premia, compensating risk-averse individuals who invest in corporate securities with long maturities for the risk of factor change. The strongly negative estimates for λ_k are obtained due to the amount by which long-term spreads exceed their short-term counterparts, although the subsequent error analysis shows that

[18] See Cox, Ingersoll, and Ross (1985), p. 391.

the short end is still poorly explained by the factor model. On average, the class three-spread structure is by far the flattest (see table 4.4 depicting the average term spreads). A lower λ_3-estimate has been obtained accordingly.

High risk premia imply that the risk-neutral factor processes specified under the equivalent martingale measure, which are of relevance for the valuation of CDOs as derivatives on the factors, differ notably from their counterparts under the physical measure. The drift transformation alters the mean and volatility parameters θ_k and κ_k considerably, such that the half-lives of spread factor increments consistently falling below a half year extend notably upon the change of measure. When applied to portfolio loss forecasting, the slow decay of the common factor with a half life of more than 2.5 years causes shocks affecting all reference claims uniformly to be persistent over a long maturity horizon.

The change of measure has significant impact on the unconditional process variances, all of them determining the degree of concentration risk in a CDO reference portfolio. The common factor variance increase is most pronounced, such that risk-neutral mean-loss rates of different classes exhibit stronger comovements than their analogues described under the physical measure. Hence, again considering the portfolio derivatives pricing application, the change of measure entails a pronounced increase in the joint evolution of default riskiness of the claims.

The risk-neutral factor mean of class two θ_2, as implied by the parameter estimates, exceeds its class three-counterpart by three basispoints, which is not in line with the assumed higher risk level of class three-claims. Therefore, the risk-neutral steady-state behaviour of class two and class three-spreads contradicts the default risk level implied by the rating assessment. The numerical implementation of the model to be performed, however, shall be based on initial factor realisations that render this inconsistency virtually irrelevant.

The estimated parameters shall be set in relation to the results obtained in companion studies performed by Düllmann and Windfuhr (1999) and Geyer, Kossmeier, and Pichler (2003), where one- or multi-factor CIR models are estimated using spread term structure data: Both studies explain the dynamic evolution of implied zero bond yield curves of European sovereign spreads against the German government term structure. Government spreads are on average lower than those of corporates, which is in line with the on average higher credit quality, as conveyed by the issuer ratings. The steepness of the government spread structures derived by the authors within a smoothing step partly exceeds the steepness of the corporate spread structures, when set in relation to the mean level of spreads, expressed in relative terms as for instance suggested in section 4.3.2.

The estimation results that have been obtained by the authors for government debt are qualitatively rather similar to mine: High spread volatility parameters σ_k have been obtained throughout, albeit with a smaller reaction on the events in autumn 2001 in the study of Geyer, Kossmeier, and Pichler (2003). The time series of Düllmann and Windfuhr (1999) ends in 1999, hence not covering the spread widening of 2001.

Market prices of factor risk parameters λ_k are consistently high: The λ_k−estimate obtained by Düllmann and Windfuhr (1999) for a one-factor CIR model causes the risk-neutral short spread process to become close to nonstationary, due to κ_k approaching zero. Geyer, Kossmeier, and Pichler (2003), who test three two-factor CIR model specifications in order to quantify the impact of a common factor on European sovereign spreads, use a model specification identical to my corporate model.[19] Whereas the corporate results still imply factor processes that are well-behaved both under the empirical and the risk-neutral measure, the government debt parameter estimates obtained by Geyer, Kossmeier, and Pichler (2003) yield factor processes that are notably mean-averting , i.e. 'explosive', when pricing under the risk-neutral measure. Whilst clearly a valid result in the estimation context, mean-averting behaviour of all factor processes would become a severe problem when out-of sample loss forecasts should be obtained, especially in a portfolio derivatives pricing context, where factor variation is of high relevance.

The comparison of results indicates that the strong pricing of credit factor risk, as conveyed by high absolute values of λ_k, is indeed a stable phenomenon throughout the literature making use of the CIR model for spread explanation, which is rooted in the observation that long-term spreads notably exceed their short-term counterparts.

For the study at hand, the change of measure still preserves a desirable factor behaviour, although, both the expected values of single-issuer losses and the dependence structure are altered considerably.

Some out-of sample loss properties are directly implied by the parameter estimates and shall highlight the impact of factor risk pricing on risk-neutral loss expectations and mean-loss rate comovements.

Individual borrowers' mean-loss rates determine overall portfolio riskiness. The affine solution of the factor model then characterises the survival probabilities under both measures as follows: The expected value of default loss of a zero-bond with principal normalised to one can be inferred from market data as the difference $1 - \frac{D_{class}(t,T)}{D_r(t,T)}$, the ratio being an affine function in $f_c(t), f_{class}(t)$. The expected value of losses under the empirical measure is obtained by evaluation of the expectations for zero market prices of risk parameters λ_k and an observed factor realisation. Under the risk-neutral measure, the valuation formula (using non-zero λ_k or risk-neutral parameters κ_k, θ_k interchangeably) applies to a factor

19 See Geyer, Kossmeier, and Pichler (2003), p. 31 for parameter estimates of the 'global-local'-specification.

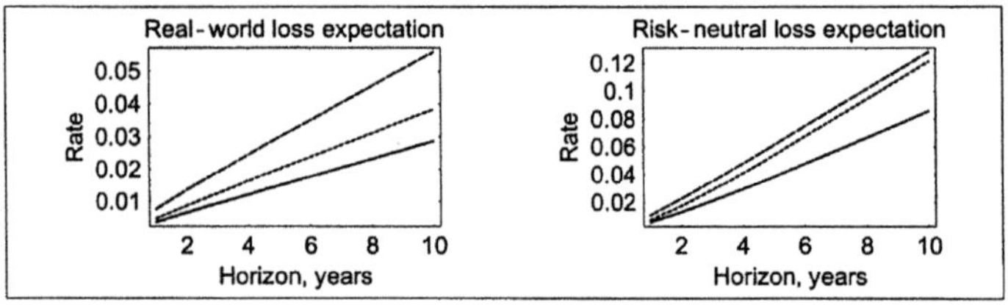

Figure 4.3: **Term structures of expected values of default losses.**
Expected losses are normalised to one unit of zero-bond principal. The solid lines relate to $risk = 1$. (Aaa/Aa), the short-dashed lines relate to $risk = 2$ (A), and the long-dashed lines relate to $risk = 3$ (Baa).

realisation whose probability distribution is specified under the risk-neutral measure. Due to high persistence of factors, the choice of the initial factor realisations is of high relevance to securities pricing. If not indicated otherwise, all expectations are subsequently evaluated at the averages of the estimated factor time-series as obtained from the update step of the Kalman filter recursion, amounting to (26 bps, 20 bps, 31 bps, 72 bps) for the common factor and the three class-specific factors, given in the order of increasing riskiness and, when required, to 3.92% for the riskless interest model. Figure 4.3 depicts the term structures of expected default losses of one unit of zero-bond principal. It is easily seen that the high pricing of credit factor risk causes long-term risk-neutral loss expectations to deviate notably from their real-world forecasts.

Considering the expected value of losses that occur in the context of a long-lived CDO reference portfolio, one may expect the derivative pricing results to be considerably affected by the pricing of credit factor risk.

For further analysis, it should be noted that term structures of expected values of default losses provide an insight into the information on bond rating performed by agencies: A rating assignment is normally identified with the historical default frequency. Together with an historical LGD estimate, an empirical loss rate for a given time horizon can be computed, the analogue to the model expectations illustrated on the left-hand side of figure 4.3. Hence, model results provide a market-based view of default risk of corporate bonds of the three rating classes when loss expectations are taken under the real-world measure.

Considering the full distribution of reference portfolio losses, a first assessment of the estimated model can be made for the two-borrower case: Within the doubly-stochastic Poisson default mechanism, dependencies among losses of different borrowers are created through covariation among mean-loss rates $\overline{h}_{class}(t)$. The estimation setup has restricted borrower classification only according to riskiness/rating. At this point, a first extension to the general model can be made, by allowing for additional borrower classification according to the industry. The assumption of factor orthogonality allows the quantification not only of the correlation between mean-loss rates among borrowers of different risk levels, but also among borrowers that have the same default risk level, but differ with respect to sector affiliation. Correlations among real-world short spreads are computed according to equation (3.40), they equal mean-loss rate correlations when factor processes are defined under the physical measure with parameter set ϕ^*. Mean-loss rate correlations under the EMM are computed by substitution of the parameter set ϕ. The model structure yields cross-moments of the steady-state densities of

$$\lim_{t \to \infty} Cov(\overline{h}_u(t), \overline{h}_v(t)) = \lim_{t \to \infty} Var(f_c(t)) \tag{4.21}$$

for two claims that belong to different classes u, v, either through different sector affiliation or risk level or both. The variances of the risk-neutral mean-loss rates are obtained as

$$\lim_{t \to \infty} Var(\overline{h}_{class}(t)) = \lim_{t \to \infty} Var(f_c(t)) + \lim_{t \to \infty} Var(f_{class}(t)) \tag{4.22}$$

$$\lim_{t \to \infty} Var(f_{class}(t)) = \lim_{t \to \infty} Var(f_{risk}(t)), \tag{4.23}$$

as specific factors of the same risk level that apply to different sectors are determined by i.i.d. processes. The relevant parameter sets are given by the risk-level specific estimates. The resulting steady-state correlations among the $\overline{h}_{class}(t)$ are obtained by substituting the above quantities into (3.40). The mean-loss rate correlations obtained from the parameter estimate given in table 4.8 under both measures are depicted in table 4.9.

	Expected loss rate correlation					
	Physical			**EMM**		
Risk	1	2	3	1	2	3
1	0.663	0.571	0.382	0.918	0.798	0.798
2		0.491	0.328		0.694	0.694
3			0.219			0.694

Table 4.9: **Pairwise correlations among class-specific mean-loss rates under the physical and the risk-neutral measure.**

As factor volatilities are altered by the change of measure, the correlation structure changes as well, such that all correlations experience a considerable increase. Thus, the change of measure does not only imply an increase in loss expectations, but the comovement between the borrower riskiness also strengthens, such that more probability mass applies both to joint survival outcomes, yielding lower than expected losses and to extreme losses caused by a large number of default events.

4.5 Explanatory power of the model

4.5.1 Explanation of individual term structures

The residual statistics summarised in table 4.10 permit an assessment of the explanatory power of the factor model with respect to the cross-sectional dimension of observables, as this is represented by the individual term structures of riskless spot rates and corporate spreads and their observed evolution through time.

For all observables, fitting errors and, correspondingly, the estimated standard deviations of measurement noise as depicted in the lower half of table 4.8 are particularly small for medium maturities: Riskless rates are almost exactly matched for the six year rate. With respect to spot spreads of classes one and two, considerable mispricings occur for short maturities: The CIR functional form evaluated for the parameter estimates allows for less curvature than the Nelson/Siegel term structure equation, overestimating spreads of short and long maturities, where mean errors at the long ends are still smaller than three basispoints, but considerably higher at the short ends of the spread curves.

The residual standard deviations given in the fourth column represent the sample quantities of the estimated measurement noise volatilities $\sqrt{m_r(\tau)}$ and $\sqrt{m_{class}(\tau)}$, given in table 4.8. The difference between the noise volatilities estimated by QML and the sample standard deviations is a consequence of non-zero residual sample means: The error volatilities inferred by the estimation approach are obtained under the presumption of zero-mean residuals, whereas the descriptive standard deviations are centred around the residual sample means given in the third column.[20]

With respect to time series behaviour, the explanatory power is similar: Judging from the autocorrelational pattern of residuals shown in table 4.10, the factor model explains a considerable part of serial correlation of those observed spot rates and spreads whose levels are well explained by the model. In case of riskless rates, the slow decay of residual autocorrelation in combination with the maturity-dependence of fitting errors gives a hint on the presence of a second factor related to the shape of the term structure not captured by the single-factor CIR model.

The model has been estimated using the information provided by the first two conditional

[20] Computation of the (non-centred) RMSE-measure for sample residuals yields a close approximation of the estimated measurement noise volatilities.

moments of the error structure generated by the KF-procedure, which itself relies on the first two moments of observed quantities, i.e. spot rates and spreads. An adequate model can therefore be expected to explain the unconditional observed moments of the observable variables as well. The fitting ability of the unconditional means is captured by the residual means, as discussed above. The second unconditional moments of the observables are represented by the term structures of volatilities, as defined in equation (3.42).[21]

Figure 4.4 compares the term structure of observed volatilities, i.e. the standard deviations of spot rates and spreads as reported in table 4.4, and the term structures of unconditional volatilities that would by forecasted by the factor model.

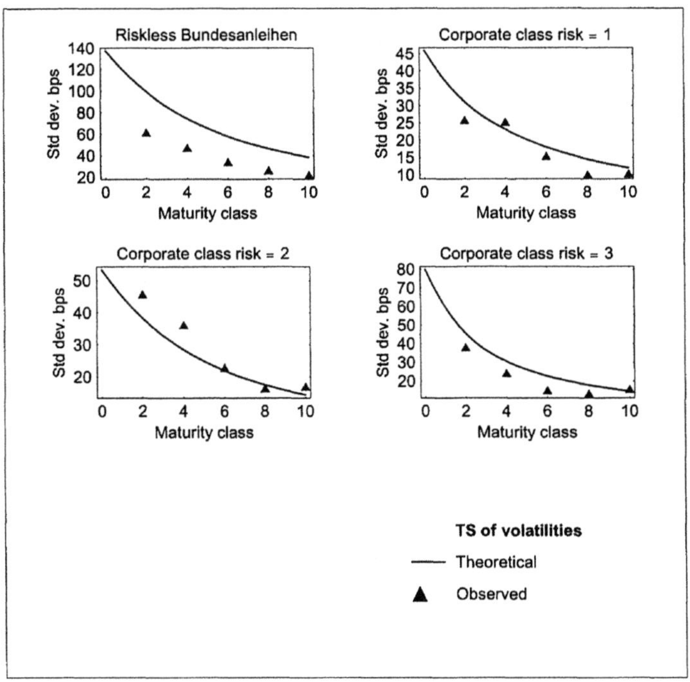

Figure 4.4: **Term structures of volatilities of riskless interest rates and corporate spreads of different risk levels.**

[21] The given comparison assumes that the observations are sampled from the rate and spread population whose transitional behaviour is governed by the unconditional factor dynamics.

Whereas the riskless model underestimates observed systematic spot rate volatility, the three term structures of systematic spread volatilities are remarkably well explained by the two factors affecting every class. However, as discussed above, this comes at the cost of inconsistency in the risk-neutral factor means of classes two and three.

4.5.2 Explanation of spread comovement

In the debt portfolio context, the model's ability to provide accurate forecasts of joint loss expectations is of central relevance. A comparison of the model-implied term structures of correlation, as have been defined in equation (3.43), with the empirically observed dependence, gives insight about the explanation of the comovements of corporate spread structures, which translates to the comovement of joint loss expectations of claims of the three risk levels.

Figure 4.5 shows that for all term structures of spreads, the observed correlation is matched for the eight years maturity class. Pairwise instantaneous correlations among the

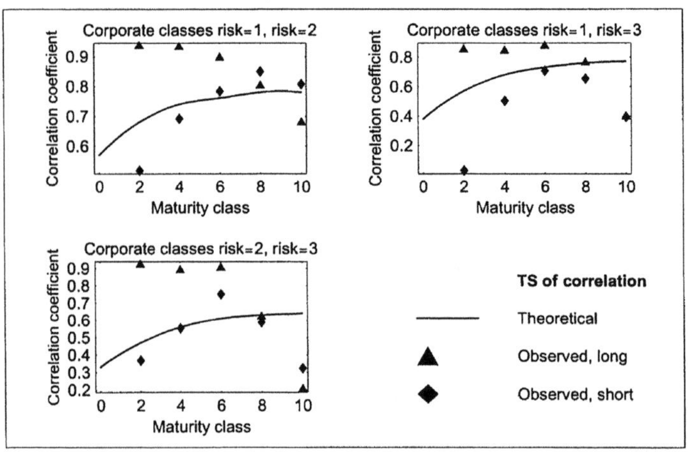

Figure 4.5: **Term structures of correlation between corporate spreads of different risk levels.**

three risk classes, as defined in (3.40), are between 0.3 and 0.6 and decreasing for classes bearing higher default risk, which is due to the higher unconditional process volatility of riskier class-specific factors.

The empirically observed decrease in dependence with maturity is not reflected by the model-implied correlation structure. Furthermore, the within-sample correlations between estimated class-specific factor series and their first differences, as displayed in table 4.11, are not always close to zero.

The graphical representation of the estimated factor series, obtained by the update step of the KF procedure (see figure 7.1), conveys that the strong interdependence between the class-specific factors of classes two and three is caused by the strong reaction of riskier corporate spreads (A, Baa) on the events in autumn 2001. The severe spread increase of class two and three bonds together with the moderate reaction of class one spreads is poorly explained by dependence on one additive common factor, which has uniform effect on all classes.

In order to assess the severity of this problem, I first determine the observed term structure of correlation for a shorter period ending on 5/9/01, which differs substantially from its full period counterpart. It is included in figure 4.5 and corresponds considerably better to the theoretical dependence. The observed high correlation between spot spreads of short maturities is entirely induced by a strong reaction to the events in September 2001. Secondly, the spread model is re-estimated for the shorter period displaying more homogeneous time series behaviour. Obtained parameter estimates, depicted table C.1 in the appendix are rather robust against the omission of this 'extreme' period, with the relevant exception that the class-specific factor $f_3(t)$ is less volatile. This is plausible given the strong increase of all class three-spreads in autumn 2001. These findings have the desirable implication that the estimation procedure and the assumed model type are robust to short term strong deviations from 'mean' time series behaviour, even for a sample period as short as one year. The drawback, however, is that the simple affine structure cannot capture both transitional and cross-sectional properties during the 'extreme' period whilst preserving factor uncorrelatedness by a suitable adjustment of parameter estimates.

A final analysis of residual correlation, as displayed in table 4.12, should reveal dependence between spot spreads and their changes that is neither explained by the factor model, nor captured in the comovements of factors.

With respect to the explanation of the joint spread level evolution, a comparison with table 4.5 shows that the very high correlation between the term structures of the three risk levels is largely explained by the factor model, except in the case for long term spread correlation among classes one and three. The explanation of the dependence of spread changes is weaker. The residual correlation coefficients between first differences are notably lower than among the observed spread series, although, a large proportion of dependence between spread changes is not explained.

4.6 Summary of results

The estimation approach exploits the perfect diversifiability of asset-specific risks in CDO reference portfolios, such that model estimation is based on common spread components of corporate bond prices. Given the availability of closed-form solutions for spot spreads when the transitional behaviour of latent factors is described by CIR square-root processes, parameter estimation from estimated zero bond curves appears desirable. Parsimoniously-parameterised yield curves are estimated both from riskless German Bundesanleihen and from defaultable investment grade corporate bond data of the three rating classes representing risk-levels in a reference portfolio. Evidence on the relevance of sector-related pricing differences is gained from individual bond pricing errors when maturity-dependence of prices is controlled for.

The KF-QML estimation procedure applied to spread and riskless yield curves exploits the panel data structure provided by the term structures. The chosen approach is advantageous, as parameters that govern inferred factor processes under the physical measure and market price of risk parameters are identified. In addition, the estimation of the common factor interlinking the dynamic evolution of the spread curves is facilitated.

Parameter estimates imply high pricing of spread factor change risk by market participants, such that all debt claims priced under the factor model carry high yield premia. The change of factor variation as a consequence of the change of measure causes the variance proportions among the factors to change considerably. With regard to the CDO valuation application, single-borrower mean-loss rates exhibit strong covariation throughout the time horizon.

The explanatory power of the factor model is considered as satisfactory. The two factor-stochastic applicable to every spread structure yields a good explanation of mean spot spreads of medium maturities, both with regard to the cross-sectional relationships implied by the term structure equation and with regard to the transitional properties. The restriction imposed by the homogeneous effect of the common factor on all term structures turns out not to be restrictive in the light of spread explanation. The dependence structure, by contrast, can be judged to be well explained only during the sample period ending before September 2001, characterised by stable spread behaviour. The sharp spread increase, especially for short maturity classes, is not entirely captured by the model, as the uniform effect of the common factor on the three risk levels appears overly restrictive.

The estimated factor dynamics shall be applied for portfolio loss forecasting, such that arbitrage-free premia of CDO tranches that refer to European investment grade corporate debt can be determined.

	Statistics on residuals[bps]						Autocorrelation		
	MAD	Mean	Std dev.	Median	5%-qu.	95%-qu.	Lag=1	Lag=2	Lag=10
$R_r(t,\tau)$									
2	17.44	11.59	14.30	9.61	-16.22	45.87	0.910	0.833	0.402
4	7.05	0.43	3.78	1.74	-12.72	11.49	0.930	0.865	0.486
6	0.23	-0.13	0.19	-0.12	-0.56	0.36	0.481	0.401	0.118
8	4.36	1.25	3.28	-0.51	-4.89	11.61	0.900	0.835	0.408
10	7.36	2.88	6.10	-0.10	-7.47	19.71	0.894	0.830	0.373
$S_1(t,\tau)$									
2	17.32	-14.69	16.22	-11.95	-39.00	9.34	0.712	0.574	0.067
4	8.34	-2.87	10.07	-4.88	-13.82	20.25	0.818	0.718	0.285
6	3.67	0.03	5.12	-0.78	-5.37	10.99	0.825	0.721	0.380
8	0.67	-0.61	2.18	0.02	-2.88	0.11	0.116	0.231	-0.055
10	3.29	-2.12	4.12	-1.49	-9.86	3.43	0.681	0.613	0.179
$S_2(t,\tau)$									
2	24.67	-23.11	16.90	-23.78	-48.28	1.09	0.453	0.212	0.174
4	6.35	-1.55	8.08	-0.73	-12.01	8.72	0.343	0.243	0.032
6	2.43	0.19	4.41	1.31	-3.77	3.37	0.106	0.137	0.005
8	4.43	-1.06	5.19	-1.78	-8.45	7.90	0.350	0.254	-0.032
10	8.23	-2.64	9.53	-3.95	-14.54	13.54	0.335	0.167	-0.078
$S_3(t,\tau)$									
2	10.21	-3.40	12.20	-5.10	-21.71	15.64	0.579	0.402	0.023
4	5.35	0.17	7.27	1.59	-13.45	10.48	0.741	0.602	-0.107
6	3.27	-0.14	5.41	0.92	-6.75	4.55	0.239	0.169	-0.183
8	8.67	-0.76	12.04	0.41	-19.18	19.24	0.729	0.531	-0.101
10	13.88	-1.25	18.72	-1.09	-28.97	34.40	0.807	0.629	-0.062

Table 4.10: **Statistics on residuals of the factor model.**

The location and dispersion statics indicate the goodness of fit to the term structures, and the autocorrelation coefficients give an indication of the time series explanation.

Levels	$f_r(t)$	$f_c(t)$	$f_1(t)$	$f_2(t)$	$f_3(t)$
$f_r(t)$	1	-0.677**	-0.279*	-0.738**	-0.416**
$f_c(t)$		1	0.242*	0.382**	-0.092
$f_1(t)$			1	0.226*	0.186
$f_2(t)$				1	0.748**
$f_3(t)$					1

First diff.	$f_r(t)$	$f_c(t)$	$f_1(t)$	$f_2(t)$	$f_3(t)$
$f_r(t)$	1	-0.406**	-0.075	-0.272*	-0.436**
$f_c(t)$		1	0.344**	0.110	-0.255*
$f_1(t)$			1	-0.326**	-0.207
$f_2(t)$				1	0.390**
$f_3(t)$					1

Table 4.11: **Within-sample correlations between estimated factor series.**
** indicates significance at 1%-level, * indicates significance at 5%-level.

	Levels		
τ	$S_1(t,\tau), S_2(t,\tau)$	$S_1(t,\tau), S_3(t,\tau)$	$S_2(t,\tau), S_3(t,\tau)$
2	0.201	-0.336	0.184
4	-0.120	-0.276	0.195
6	0.096	0.551	0.262
8	0.334	0.565	0.208
10	0.256	0.518	0.054

	First differences		
τ	$S_1(t,\tau), S_2(t,\tau)$	$S_1(t,\tau), S_3(t,\tau)$	$S_2(t,\tau), S_3(t,\tau)$
2	0.402	0.161	0.328
4	0.188	0.348	0.218
6	0.434	0.461	0.427
8	0.523	0.516	0.239
10	0.198	0.521	0.014

Table 4.12: **Residual correlation between term structures of corporate spot spreads.**

Chapter 5

CDOs: Valuation and Model Specification

5.1 A basic valuation model

5.1.1 CDO valuation: fair issuance premia

The valuation of the tranches of a securitisation transaction addresses the determination of two contract variables: the tranche spread or premium s_{tr}, payable periodically on the outstanding principal exposure $P_{tr}(t^{pay})$, and the current tranche value, given a contractual spread s_{tr}.

The determinants for CDO pricing are easiest explained for the case of synthetic securitisation: Consider the issuance mode of a particular CDO tranche, either as funded portfolio CLN, where settlement payments towards the originator are made from a cash-deposit, or as portfolio default swap, involving no riskless bond component.

Whereas in case of CDO issuance in the form of portfolio CLNs, the current value of a tranche depends on both the value of the principal funding serving as cash collateral and the value of the portfolio default swap component. According to the hedging practice of interest rate risk mentioned in the introductory Chapter 2, which transforms all fixed-coupon interest payments into a floating market rate, interest rate risk shall be regarded as completely eliminated, such that riskless cash collateral always trades at par plus accrued interest. This property allows us to disregard the funding component of any tranche when considering synthetic transactions. As has been argued in Chapter 2, true-sales with perfect hedge agreements also accommodate the valuation approach.

I hence examine the valuation of unfunded synthetic CDS tranches with time-t value $CDS_{tr}(t)$, exchanging a premium s_{tr} against portfolio loss protection, assuming absence of interest risk.

In the primary market for CDO tranches, the determination of premia s_{tr} is the task actually faced by the parties involved. As for any swap pricing problem, issuance premia are to be determined such that the contract is initialised at zero value, or, given the provision of funding, the tranche under consideration is issued at par. Subsequent secondary market prices for a tranche paying a fixed spread or premium s_{tr} can be computed conditional on the actual default history, taking the current default riskiness of the pool into account, as conveyed by the spreads of reference collateral.

The valuation problem shall first address the simplest loss allocation scheme: As was pointed out in the introductory Chapter 2, the direct issuance structure, termed a senior/subordinated portfolio derivative transaction and depicted in figure 2.2, provides an identification of cumulated portfolio loss ranges with tranche principals. Based on an in-depth investigation of the basis structure, the subsequent Chapter 6 shall measure the effect of credit enhancement provided by the accumulation of excess spread.

For the basic senior/subordinated portfolio default swap scheme, the valuation problem for issued tranches requires determination of annualised swap premia s_{tr}, such that the time-zero expectation evaluates to

$$\begin{aligned} s_{tr} : CDS_{tr}(0) &= 0 \qquad (5.1) \\ \mathbb{E}_0 \left[\sum_{t^{pay}} D_r(0, t^{pay}) \left[\left(s_{tr} \Delta t^{pay} - 1 \right) P_{tr}(t^{pay} - \Delta t^{pay}) + P_{tr}(t^{pay}) \right] \right] &= 0, \end{aligned}$$

causing the portfolio default swap to trade at zero value. Quarterly settlement payments occurring in $t^{pay} = \Delta t^{pay}, ..., T$ equal the principal reductions. The timing and the amount of payments are a function of the reference portfolio default event times Υ_{corp}, and the related loss amounts determined according to (2.3).

The above valuation equation can straightforwardly be decomposed into a loss allocation leg and a premium leg, which must have the same discounted expectation taken under the risk-neutral measure. Assuming the absence of counterparty risk the mode of senior and mezzanine issuance, either as funded CLNs or unfunded CDSs with premia payable in arrears, is irrelevant to the valuation task.

For the base case, a three-tranche structure shall be subject to analysis, comprising a large senior and a smaller mezzanine tranche issued against a premium for default risk transfer, and a retained junior tranche providing overcollateralisation to the issued tranches.

In the market, however, multi-mezzanine issuing is often observed. Given that the simple senior/subordinated basket structure applies, loss allocation of the tranche considered is a function of the tranche position and size only, as determined by $\underline{K}_{tr}, P_{tr}(0)$, directly identified with the portfolio loss range. Therefore, loss allocation and consequently, the fair issuance spread of a tranche under consideration is independent of the premium stream towards the remaining tranches, once the upper and lower thresholds of the tranche under considerations are held fixed.[1] Independence of loss allocation towards a particular tranche for the contract parameters of other tranches causes expected tranche loss allocation over the full capital structure to be additive.[2] Further slicing is therefore of little interest for the basic results.

It is interesting to see that additivity does not hold for nominal premia. Hence, multi-mezzanine slicing, as observed in the marketplace, yields a premium payment profile differing from the single-mezzanine structure considered as the base case: It shall be proven that the average premium rate payable on the entire mezzanine range at origination, weighted at the respective tranche principals

$$S_{mez}(0) = \frac{\sum_{mez=mez1}^{\#mez} s_{mez} P_{mez}(0)}{\sum_{mez=mez1}^{\#mez} P_{mez}(0)} \tag{5.2}$$

is monotonically increasing in the number of tranches $\#mez$. This is a straightforward consequence of the asymmetric loss allocation rule, reducing subordinate principals first. Consider two otherwise identical capital structures, comprising either one or two mezzanine tranches, $mez1$ and a subordinate $mez2$, such that $s_{mez2} > s_{mez1}$, where $\underline{K}_{mez} = \underline{K}_{mez2}$, $P_{mez}(0) = P_{mez1}(0) + P_{mez2}(0)$.

Additivity in expected discounted mezzanine loss allocation, determined by rule (2.3) is expressed as

$$\begin{aligned} & \mathbb{E}_0\left[\sum_{t^{pay}} D_r(0,t^{pay})\left(P_{mez}(t^{pay}-\Delta t^{pay}) - P_{mez}(t^{pay})\right)\right] \\ = \; & \mathbb{E}_0\left[\sum_{t^{pay}} D_r(0,t^{pay})\left(P_{mez2}(t^{pay}-\Delta t^{pay}) - P_{mez2}(t^{pay})\right.\right. \\ & \left.\left. + P_{mez1}(t^{pay}-\Delta t^{pay}) - P_{mez1}(t^{pay})\right)\right]. \end{aligned} \tag{5.3}$$

---

1 'Independence' is not meant in the statistical sense, as premia are clearly interlinked by reference to the same portfolio. Independence refers to the timing of contractual premium payments only, i.e. for example, the irrelevance of the decision between periodical premium/coupon payments on the current principal basis, upfront premium payment (amounting to discount-bond sale in the funded case), or retention to the pricing of other tranches.

2 The following chapter examines credit enhanced structures where these properties do not hold.

As the loss allocation legs of the two-mezzanine tranche swaps equal the loss leg of the single-mezzanine swap, premium legs must be valued equivalently as

$$\begin{aligned} &\mathbb{E}_0\left[\sum_{t^{pay}} D_r(0,t^{pay}) s_{mez}\Delta t^{pay} P_{mez}(t^{pay}-\Delta t^{pay})\right] \\ =\ &\mathbb{E}_0\left[\sum_{t^{pay}} D_r(0,t^{pay}) \left(s_{mez1}\Delta t^{pay} P_{mez1}(t^{pay}-\Delta t^{pay})\right.\right. \\ &\left.\left.+s_{mez2}\Delta t^{pay} P_{mez2}(t^{pay}-\Delta t^{pay})\right)\right]. \end{aligned} \tag{5.4}$$

Upon loss occurrence, in the two-mezzanine structure, $P_{mez2}(t^{pay}) < P_{mez1}(t^{pay})$ holds as long as $P_{mez1}(t^{pay}) > 0$. Otherwise, both tranches are reduced to zero principal. Hence,

$$\mathcal{S}_{mez}(0) = \frac{s_{mez1}P_{mez1}(0) + s_{mez2}P_{mez2}(0)}{P_{mez1}(0) + P_{mez2}(0)} > s_{mez} \tag{5.5}$$

must hold such that equivalence among premium legs (5.4) is fulfilled.

It should be stressed that this result relies on the sequence of dynamic loss allocation to tranches, causing the principal basis for spread payments to diminish in an asymmetric manner.[3] Stated here for mezzanine premia only, the result extends straightforwardly to the full capital structure: The periodical premium outflow at origination is increasing in the number of tranches, despite the irrelevance of slicing to expected loss allocation to issued tranches, including the cap of losses retained by the originator.

The degree of risk transfer is determined by the valuation of the positions held by the originator. Additivity of the gross values of the tranche swap legs implies that the premium specification of a junior tranche is irrelevant to the valuation of issued tranches. First-loss retention is valued as the loss leg

$$CDS_{jun}(0) = \mathbb{E}_0\left[\sum_{t^{pay}} D_r(0,t^{pay})\left[P_{jun}(t^{pay}) - P_{jun}(t^{pay}-\Delta t^{pay})\right]\right], \tag{5.6}$$

that falls below zero. As has been argued in the outline of the tranched loss transfer mechanism (see section 2.1.2), the payment of a regular coupon or premium for junior compensation cannot be effectuated from the cash-flows generated from the reference portfolio. Instead, the originator is compensated for first-loss retention by the residual

[3] For instance, premia that are paid upfront would not be affected by an asymmetric loss allocation mechanism.

claim on excess spread income, generated by the pool exceeding the mezzanine and senior premium payments

$$RC_{orig}(0) = \mathbb{E}_0 \left[\sum_{t^{pay}} D_r(0, t^{pay}) XS(t^{pay}) \right] \tag{5.7}$$

The period excess spread $XS(t^{pay})$ is determined by the weighted average spreads $\mathcal{S}_{pool}(t^{pay})$ and $\mathcal{S}_{tranches}(t^{pay})$ as defined in (2.7) and (2.8), applicable to the principals currently outstanding

$$XS(t^{pay}) = \mathcal{S}_{pool}(t^{pay}) P_{pool}(t^{pay}) - \mathcal{S}_{tranches}(t^{pay}) \sum_{tr=1}^{\#tr} P_{tr}(t^{pay}). \tag{5.8}$$

For the basis structure, not only superior tranche valuation is unaffected by the junior terms, but also the originator's net stake in the transaction is valued at zero, such that equality between the two risk-neutral expectations

$$RC_{orig}(0) = -CDS_{jun}(0) \tag{5.9}$$

is required to hold to assure absence of arbitrage, given that both the residual claim and the first-loss piece are priced according to (5.6) and (5.7). Every cash-flow that would accrue to the junior claimant during the life of the structure, like for instance a regular premium claim, reduces excess spread income and thus the residual claim by the same amount, leaving the value of his total position unaffected.[4]

A remark on the discretisation of loss allocation is in order: Condition (5.9) holds exactly if losses are allocated to the trancheholder precisely at the instant of occurrence, who, in turn, would only obtain a partial premium payment, reduced to the amount accrued up until default.[5] Consequently, immediate adjustment of the principal basis determining the next premium payment, would be required. For the setting examined, accommodating standard CDO terms, premia are calculated at discrete quarterly intervals on the basis of the start-of-period principals. As the accrual basis is larger or equal than in the continuous-time loss allocation setting, smaller premium rates are required than would be adequate in a setting with timely loss allocation. The expected present value of the savings on fair premia $\mathbb{E}_0 [PV(savings)]$ incurred by the payment of premia whose underlying bond has already defaulted during the preceding quarter increases the value of the residual

[4] Special junior terms as a basis for credit enhancement are subject to analysis in Chapter 6.

[5] The discussion of Duffie (1999) for single-name CDSs applies analogously.

claim, such that

$$RC_{orig}(0) = -CDS_{jun}(0) + \mathbb{E}_0\left[PV(savings)\right]. \tag{5.10}$$

Conveniently, the above relationship permits an approximate check on the correctness of calculations. Generally, $\mathbb{E}_0\left[PV(savings)\right]$ is expected to be small, as loss allocation occurs rather timely. Furthermore, the term must be identical for all structures providing identical loss protection for the reference portfolio. This assertion is of relevance for the study of credit enhancements to be performed in the following chapter, although the specification of the junior CDS and the generation of the residual claim may differ.

In addition to the valuation of issued tranches, the effectiveness of risk transfer securitisation is of interest in a supervisory context, aiming at bank portfolio value risk reduction. I therefore include the volatility of the originator's retained stake in the securitisation structure in the analysis, numerically computed as

$$StdDev_{orig}\left[\sum_{t^{pay}} D_r(0, t^{pay})\left(P_{jun}(t^{pay}) - P_{jun}(t^{pay} - \Delta t^{pay}) + XS(t^{pay})\right)\right]. \tag{5.11}$$

In addition, the comparison of different structural variants shall include the 5%-quantile of the above quantity, hence indicating the risk of severely bad outcomes affecting the originator.

Dispersion measures serve as criteria for the comparison of the effectiveness of different structures, characterised by various variants of credit enhancements. From a supervisory point of view, a volatility- or severe loss risk-minimising structure is preferable. However, it must be stressed that all statistics refer to the risk-neutral distribution of cash-flows applied to issued and retained tranches, hence rather characterising the risk profiles of the stakes in the transaction than giving volatility and downside risk-measures relying on the forecast distribution of real-world losses.

Value additivity among tranches causes fair premia to be characterised by independent single equations. Losses allocated to the junior piece are determined independently, whereas the value of the residual claim depends both on loss realisations and the premia of the superior tranches.

Due to the additivity of the tranche swap loss legs, I adhere to the three-tranche capital structure. The subsequent evaluation of the model is performed for various capital structures, differing with respect to tranche position and initial tranche size $P_{tr}(0)$. For both the senior and the junior tranche, the position is fixed. The size of the senior tranche $P_{sen}(0)$ determines the exposure of the protection seller to increasing riskiness. The size of the junior tranche $P_{jun}(0)$ determines the participation of the junior claimant in low-loss scenarios. Considering the initial mezzanine piece, it can be stated that when holding $\underline{K}_{mez}$ fixed, an extension of $P_{mez}(0)$ both reduces the expected value of mezzanine loss allocation and increases senior overcollateralisation.

Arbitrage-free CDO issuance premia depend on both the random default event times Υ_{corp} of the individual reference claims and on the severity of losses incurred by defaults. Premium determination shall be preceded by a discussion of the properties of underlying portfolio losses explained by the estimated factor model, assumptions and implementation issues.

5.1.2 Large portfolio loss properties

5.1.2.1 Characterisation of portfolio losses

The random outcome, the discounted loss $PV(loss)$ of a reference portfolio within a given time horizon T and default event times Υ_{corp}, is obtained as a mapping of the multivariate default time-/default loss-path into the value dimension

$$PV(loss) = \sum_{\Upsilon_{corp}} D_r(0, \Upsilon_{corp}) \sum_{corp} loss(\mathbf{f}(\Upsilon_{corp})), \tag{5.12}$$

where the random loss amount $loss(\mathbf{f}(\Upsilon_{corp}))$ of a defaulted reference entity is a function of the state vector as a consequence of the RMV-assumption or evaluates to zero in case of survival.

The discounted portfolio loss therefore denotes the present value of costs incurred by default risk, i.e. bankruptcy costs of the portfolio. The probability distribution of this random variable will henceforth be referred to as the 'loss distribution'. It aggregates the multidimensional information about the underlying variables relevant for contingent claims pricing, and therefore provides a means for the analysis of portfolios differing with respect to the default mechanism governed by the reduced-form factor model. For valuation purposes, the loss distribution is determined under the risk-neutral measure, i.e. factor processes according to (3.24) apply. The risk-neutral discounted expected value of losses has a natural interpretation: It equals the fair premium, payable upfront, if the entire portfolio default risk were swapped under a portfolio derivative.

Alternatively, if loss allocation to tranches is of interest rather than the aggregate portfolio outcome, undiscounted losses, evaluated at market values at default shall be referred to, if indicated.[6]

Undiscounted expected values of portfolio losses are obtained as a value-weighted average of single-name expected values of losses, as determined by the term structures depicted in figure 4.3 for one unit of defaultable zero-bond principal.

Whereas the location of the loss distribution is determined by the mean portfolio credit quality, CDO pricing relies on the entire shape of the distribution. For the portfolio loss problem at hand, any deviation of the loss variable from its mean shall be referred to as dispersion, including the asymmetry incurred by the Poisson mechanism and the fatter tails as a consequence of the systematic factor variation. The doubly-stochastic Poisson mechanism gives rise to two distinct model components determining loss dispersion.

Firstly, by construction, portfolio loss dispersion is governed by factor variation. All factors whose risk is not fully diversified reduce the benefits from reference portfolio granularity, increasing the probability mass applicable to the tails of the loss distribution. Thus, the variation of economy-wide and industry-specific factors is of relevance for derivative pricing. Purely borrower-specific factors are considered as fully diversified.

With respect to the factor model, the borrower class assignments $class = (risk, sec)$ specify the number of factors governing the default mechanism. Factors are orthogonal, thus loss dispersion is decreasing in the number of classes present in a portfolio. The class partition is chosen in accordance with the reference portfolio of interest.

Secondly, for the Poisson model, loss volatility is a function of the location of the distribution. As a consequence of default modelling by Cox-processes, both expectation and variance of the number of independent default events caused by the underlying Poisson processes are equal to the intensity parameters. Therefore, the mean factor level affects loss variation, even when factor volatilities are held constant.

The relevance of both class definition and parameter constellations to portfolio losses and CDO premia are examined from a comparative-static viewpoint, starting from the parameter estimates obtained from corporate spreads.

5.1.2.2 Specification: class assignments

The valuation setup requires the assignment of classes $class = (risk, sec)$ to the individual claims of the reference portfolio considered, with the total number of classes determining

---

[6] The appropriateness of the loss definition clearly depends on the modelling and valuation setup. Alternative definitions would either refer to principal losses, possibly taking recovery payments into account or just to undiscounted losses. Examples include Duffie and Gârleanu (2001), who report the number of defaults, corresponding to the defaulted principal, Boscher and Ward (2002) who refer to undiscounted loss amounts, reduced by positive recoveries and Lehman Brothers (2003), who take the view of expected losses of market value.

the dimensionality of the factor space. For the basic valuation model and the comparative-static model analysis, I assume the following distribution of claims among risk levels

#reference assets(risk=1, Aaa/Aa): 10

#reference assets(risk=2, A): 50

#reference assets(risk=3, Baa): 40.

Since single-obligor concentrations, i.e. large exposures towards particular borrowers, in CDO reference portfolios are mostly avoided, standardisation of reference principals to one percent of the 100 claims portfolio does not appear overly restrictive. The number of claims therefore corresponds to the nominal principal exposure.

Although the analysis is kept general at this point, the reference portfolio riskiness corresponds to the portfolio composition observed in the empirical valuation study to be performed in Chapter 7 and therefore represents the level of investment grade credit risk as it is traded in securitised form.

Due to a lack of sector-related estimation results, the impact of sector diversification on the loss distribution shall be measured by a comparative-static exercise. The severity of the sector identification problem is subsequently assessed with regard to the CDO pricing issue. I define the following reference portfolios, each of which is to be analysed by the estimated factor model:

Minimal Classes are formed according to risk levels only, i.e. $class = risk$, $risk = 1, 2, 3$.

Sectors Classes are formed according to the reference claims' risk level and sector affiliation $class = (risk, sec), risk = 1, 2, 3, sec = 1, 2, 3$. Within a particular risk level, claims are homogeneously subdivided into three sectors.

Maximal The mean-loss rates of individual reference claims are driven by a borrower-specific factor. This is implemented as the limiting case where every reference borrower represents his own sector, i.e. $class = (risk, sec), risk = 1, 2, 3, sec = 1, ...,$#reference assets.

The scenario *Minimal* corresponds to the aggregation made for the estimation approach, which has just been based on the spot spreads of risk levels, leaving sector- or issuer-specific effects as a residual pricing error. Implicitly, maximum positive dependence among stochastic mean-loss rate evolution among all borrowers exhibiting the identical initial risk level has been assumed.[7] The default mechanism in the *Minimal* portfolio is driven by

---

7 Note that within the intensity framework, maximum dependence is limited to loss rate identity.

four factors, determining three mean-loss rates $\overline{h}_{class}(t)$ and the term structures of spreads. However, the explanation of default risk by the risk level alone seems overly restrictive. The relevance of sector affiliation has become transparent through the detection of sector specific pricing deviations when corporate bonds of various sectors are valued at their risk level-specific mean yields, see section 4.3.3. The portfolio *Sectors* incorporates this finding with the assumption of a small number of sectors, where the default risk in the portfolio is driven by ten factors, determining nine distinct mean-loss rates, interlinked by one economy-wide factor. The *Sectors* scenario is most appropriate to capture concentration risk through the impact of class-specific factor variation on overall loss dispersion.

The upper bound of diversification that is attainable within the estimated factor model is implemented as the *Maximal* portfolio, whose default risk is driven by #reference assets+1 factors, with the number of distinct mean-loss rates being equal to the number of reference claims. For a perfectly granular portfolio, class-specific factor variation becomes irrelevant to loss dispersion.

The *Sectors* assumption shall represent the base case throughout the study. The extension to the limiting cases is subsequently made within a comparative-static analysis of factor space dimensionality. Lower and upper bounds on premia that are in line with the estimated factor processes are determined for the respective portfolio exhibiting none or maximal industry-related concentration risk.

5.1.2.3 Reference claim valuation

In order to translate the loss-of-market value assumption made for estimation to the forecasting context, the reference assets' contract parameters must be specified such that pre-default values can be computed. Little generality is lost by assuming that reference assets are straight coupon bonds that mature simultaneously at the end of the horizon. The predominant maturity for synthetic CDOs corresponds to five years (see Chapter 7), which is assumed to translate to reference assets.

Coupons are assumed to be paid quarterly, consistently with the usances in the credit derivatives market and the cash-flows related to synthetic structures. This simplifying assumption aligns coupon payment dates in the reference portfolio with the payment dates of the tranche claims. Therefore, cash-flow sufficiency is assured through the payments made not only under derivatives, but also by premium income derived from the reference portfolio, given that all premia are paid in arrears.

Equivalence between reference bonds and CDS conditions at origination is assured by setting the contractual coupon size such that bonds with prices $V_{class}(t, \underline{T})$ initially trade at par. The par coupon rate of a default-free or defaultable claim of a class c_{class} is determined by

$$\sum_{\tau=\tau_1}^{\tau_N} D_{class}(0,\tau) c_{class} \Delta t^{pay} + D_{class}(0,\tau_N) = 1. \tag{5.13}$$

The class-specific discount factors $D_{class}(0,\tau)$, applying to the quarterly coupon dates $\underline{\tau} = (\tau_1, ..., \tau_N), \tau_N = T$, are determined by the exponential-affine pricing rules of the factor model, evaluated at the initial values.[8]

With regard to initial factor values, I maintain the restriction imposed by the estimation setup: As the information set has been restricted just to bond risk levels, the factor processes of all reference assets with the same risk level at origination shall be initialised at the identical realisation of factor $f_{class} = f_{risk}$. This has the convenient implication that par coupons of reference claims, and thus, par spreads, depend just on the risk level, simplifying the identification of excess spread generated by a portfolio.

Based on the assumptions made so far, equation (5.8) evaluates to

$$\begin{aligned} XS(t^{pay}) &= \mathcal{S}_{pool}(t^{pay}) \cdot [\#(t^{pay}, risk=1) + \#(t^{pay}, risk=2) + \#(t^{pay}, risk=3)] \\ &\quad - \mathcal{S}_{tranches}(t^{pay}) \sum_{tr=1}^{\#tr} P_{tr}(t^{pay}), \end{aligned} \tag{5.14}$$

the weighted average $\mathcal{S}_{pool}(t^{pay})$ taking the three par spread levels into account and $\#(\cdot)$ denoting the number of the surviving assets in t^{pay} on the premise of homogeneous principals.

For loss forecasting, two different assumptions will be used: For the comparative-static analysis to be conducted in the first place, I maintain the assumption made for the illustration of maturity-dependent expected values of losses given in figure 4.3: Factors are initialised at the sample time-series averages. Hence, it is assumed that the factor

---

8 Alternatively to the factor model, one could in principle price the reference claims under the estimated Nelson/Siegel term structures at every point in time. My choice of the closed-form solution of the factor model assures that prices are exactly consistent with risk-neutral expectations. Furthermore, a comparative-static analysis on model parameters straightforwardly extends to reference claims pricing.

realisation at the origination date is known to the market participants.[9]

For the empirical pricing study to be conducted subsequently, it shall be assumed that market participants take the factor realisations at CDO origination into account, extracted from the term structure observations by Kalman filtering. I hence provide a comparison of fair CDO issuance premia on both premises: Reference to the comparative-static approach is provided by evaluating the model at the time-series averages, and the full information set at origination is taken into account by evaluating the model at the factor estimates.

Interest rate risk is absent in synthetic CDOs and should represent a minor risk factor in true-sales, if it is assumed that spread and short rate factors are independent. Expectations are formed according to the affine model solution, such that interest rate expectations do not interfere with default risk. Yet the discount function applying to cash-flows going to the protection seller is of relevance for CDO pricing, such that the model-based riskless term structure equations will enter valuation.

Claim valuation at default is performed according to the affine pricing function of the current factor realisations, yielding pre-default bond prices $V^{-}_{class}(t,\underline{T})$. As high default probabilities tend to occur in conjunction with a low market valuation of the respective class, claims have the expected market value falling below par at the instant preceding default, when uncorrelated interest rates, i.e. discount factors, are assumed.

The relevance of recovery risk to CDO pricing, i.e. the impact of a deterministic or possibly random LGD-rate on the portfolio loss distribution, which is not identified separately from market data, is to be quantified subsequently. The relevance of recovery risk, holding the mean-loss rate $\overline{h}_{class}(t)$ fixed, is first addressed within a short theoretical investigation. I then perform a simulation exercise on the LGD rate for the investment grade reference portfolio introduced before.

---

9 Alternatively, one may assume that an investor having no prior information on the credit/interest risk factors demands a risk premium on time-zero factor risk, such that expectations would be formed on the basis of the unconditional factor means of the risk-neutral processes. See Duffie and Gârleanu (2001) for the respective choice. Note that for the estimated parameter set, high persistence of initial values together with material factor risk pricing causes the start values to have considerable effect on CDO pricing, which is quantified below. The decision between the alternatives depends on the forecasting environment: The choice made by Duffie and Gârleanu (2001) for their comparative-static approach causes factor processes to exhibit the properties of the steady-state distributions (see equations (3.40) and related, applied to risk-neutral parameters). The selection of an initial state conforming with real-world factor realisations is clearly favourable within the context of empirical valuation results: All reference asset and CDO pricing relationships accommodate the retrospective approach applying both to model estimation (see Chapter 4) and CDO pricing comparisons (see Chapter 7), assuming the 'average' factor scenario.

5.1.2.4 Implementation of simulation

Both default event times Υ_{corp} and loss amounts $loss(\mathbf{f}(\Upsilon_{corp}))$ for an individual corporate are explained by the factor realisations – the first as the first-jump-time of a Poisson-process whose intensity is a function of the factors, the latter as the stochastic market value of a defaulted claim (multiplied by a possibly non-zero LGD).

The default mechanism is implemented by the simulation of class-specific compensators, suggested by Lando (1998) and Duffie and Singleton (1999b). The uniformity of the intensity evolution within one class translates into class-specific compensators. Default barriers, however, are claim specific, yielding default times that are independent when conditioning on the class-specific compensator. First-jump-times of a vector of dependent Poisson processes are generated by adaption of (3.16) to the respective specification of the factor model. The dependence among the Poisson processes is governed by the common and, in the scenarios *Minimal* and *Sectors*, by the class-specific factors. The following adaption of (3.16) accommodates the dependency concept of the doubly-stochastic Cox-process: Whereas dependency is created by identical mean-loss rates or spreads within one class, conditionally independent borrower-specific default event times Υ_{corp} are obtained by maintaining independence of default barriers $E_{corp}[1]$

$$\Upsilon_{corp} = \inf\left[t : H_{class}(t) \geq E_{corp}[1]\right]. \tag{5.15}$$

The compensator at a specific point in time t is obtained through discretisation of definition (3.17)

$$H_{class}(t) = \Delta t \cdot \sum_{s=1}^{t} h_{class}(s). \tag{5.16}$$

The period length is set equal to one week $\Delta t = 52^{-1}$. The determination of default occurrence would only require quarterly loss determination, but the dependence of the loss amount on the factor realisation at the default time makes a shorter time period desirable for accurate loss determination.

The factor path realisations are governed by the relevant CIR square-root processes (3.24) specified under the risk-neutral measure. For the square-root affine model class, the transitional behaviour of the state variables is characterised by a noncentral χ^2-distribution. Future factor levels at time $t + \Delta t$, conditional on the factor realisations at a given time t, are functions of noncentrally $\chi^2[df, n]$-distributed variables, with degrees of freedom df and noncentrality parameters depending on the current factor realisation, the interval length Δt and the respective parameter vector ϕ_k. The conditional factor probability distribution functions are given in Appendix A.[10] The algorithm used for the generation of noncentrally $\chi^2[df, n]$-distributed random variables builds on the characterisation of the $\chi^2[df, n]$-distribution as a mixture of a central $\chi^2[df]$ and a Poisson distribution determining the degrees of freedom, which are obtained using the inverse-CDF-method on $U[0, 1]$ variates.[11] The algorithm implemented, based on the work of Duan and Simonato (1995), is outlined in Appendix A.

Exponentially-distributed claim-specific default barriers $E_{corp}[1]$ are simulated by the application of the inverse exponential-CDF on $U[0, 1]$ variates, the latter being simulated as antithetic variables. Noise reduction appears desirable, as the default barriers clearly represent those variables that, per draw, have the highest impact on the default loss realisation. 10000 replications are simulated.

The CDO valuation problem is solved on the basis of discounted cash-flow expectations formed by the simulated loss path realisations. Tranche premia are determined by determining s_{tr} numerically, such that (5.1) is solved. The algorithm evaluates the cash-flows between the counterparties for every replication, searching for zero points of the values of tranche CDSs.

5.1.3 CDO valuation: results for the base case

5.1.3.1 Fair premia and tranche loss allocation

The tranche valuation results for the reference portfolio *Sectors*, obtained for estimated factor processes evaluated at the time-series factor averages, are depicted in table 5.1.

A comparable table shall be disclosed for every capital structure under consideration, i.e. hypothetical cash-flow waterfalls that differ with regard to credit enhancement, as examined in the subsequent chapter. For the base case with direct exposure to portfolio losses, the positions included are as follows: Every capital structure is characterised by the tranche principals $P_{tr}(0)$, of which the junior is increasing to the right, holding the mezzanine size constant, and vice versa downwards.

The variation of the tranche dimensions is motivated by what is indeed observed in the marketplace: Both for true-sales and for synthetics, the first-loss piece is mostly set such that mezzanine tranches receive at least a Baa or Ba agency rating. For synthetic

10 Prior experimentation has shown that the discretisation of the processes using the normal approximation with level-dependent factor variance suggested by the KF-based estimation procedure leads to poor convergence of default rates, even if negative factor realisations are allowed to contribute to the compensator $H_{class}(t)$.

11 For unit intensity, the inverse exponential CDF evaluates to $\Pr_{x<X} = -\ln(1-u)$, u being standard uniform.

	$P_{jun}(0) = 2$				$P_{jun}(0) = 3$				$P_{jun}(0) = 4$				$P_{jun}(0) = 6$			
			$E[PV(loss_{tr})]$				$E[PV(loss_{tr})]$				$E[PV(loss_{tr})]$				$E[PV(loss_{tr})]$	
Tranches	$P_{tr}(0)$	$s_{tr}[bps]$	Abs.	Rate[%]	$P_{tr}(0)$	$s_{tr}[bps]$	Abs.	Rate[%]	$P_{tr}(0)$	$s_{tr}[bps]$	Abs.	Rate[%]	$P_{tr}(0)$	$s_{tr}[bps]$	Abs.	Rate[%]
Senior	90	11.7	-0.47	0.52	89	9.7	-0.39	0.43	88	8.1	-0.32	0.36	86	5.6	-0.22	0.25
Mezzanine	8	832.8	-2.60	32.54	8	614.5	-2.01	25.06	8	455.7	-1.53	19.11	8	260.1	-0.90	11.24
Junior	2	0	-1.73	86.33	3	0	-2.41	80.21	4	0	-2.95	73.77	6	0	-3.68	61.36
Residual			1.86				2.54				3.09				3.82	
Std dev. orig.			0.44				0.68				1.04				1.72	
Senior	88	8.1	-0.32	0.36	87	6.8	-0.26	0.30	86	5.6	-0.22	0.25	84	3.9	-0.15	0.18
Mezzanine	10	688.1	-2.75	27.53	10	514.0	-2.13	21.29	10	384.9	-1.63	16.30	10	223.0	-0.97	9.68
Junior	2	0	-1.73	86.33	3	0	-2.41	80.21	4	0	-2.95	73.77	6	0	-3.68	61.36
Residual			1.86				2.54				3.09				3.82	
Std dev. orig.			0.42				0.69				1.05				1.73	
Senior	86	5.6	-0.22	0.25	85	4.7	-0.18	0.21	84	3.9	-0.15	0.18	82	2.7	-0.10	0.12
Mezzanine	12	584.7	-2.85	23.78	12	440.3	-2.21	18.43	12	331.8	-1.70	14.16	12	194.1	-1.01	8.46
Junior	2	0	-1.73	86.33	3	0	-2.41	80.21	4	0	-2.95	73.77	6	0	-3.68	61.36
Residual			1.86				2.54				3.09				3.82	
Std dev. orig.			0.41				0.70				1.06				1.73	

Table 5.1: **Tranche valuation in base case.**

The columns show the tranche dimensions, as conveyed by the initial principals $P_{tr}(0)$, annualised tranche premia $s_{tr}[bps]$, payable quarterly on the outstanding principal basis and the expected value of loss allocation of every stake $E[PV(loss_{tr})]$, including the value of the residual stake of the originator. The small discrepancy between the value of the junior first-loss position and the residual claim is a consequence of end-of-period loss allocation. Expected loss allocation is both expressed in absolute terms (Abs.) and normalised by $P_{tr}(0)$ (Rate[%]). The last row of every array includes the standard deviation of the originator's position as a symmetric measure of residual cash-flow uncertainty.

transactions referring to investment grade debt, it is observed that the market perceives junior support in the order of two percent as sufficient for the desired rating. Speculative grade debt securitisations, as for instance the German SME loan programmes, consistently exhibit larger equity pieces: Retentions exceeding eight percent of the portfolio nominal receive do not favourable regulatory capital treatment and are thus not observed.

The column $s_{tr}[bps]$ shows annualised premia payable for the senior and mezzanine tranche swaps on the time-varying principal basis. The last two columns of every array provide insight into the risk profile of the stakes: Tranche riskiness is conveyed by the expected value of loss allocation. The gross values of the settlement payments under the tranche CDS or retained losses of the junior tranche have been calculated. Expected discounted losses $E[PV(loss_{tr})]$ obtained under the risk-neutral probability measure are given in absolute and relative terms as the loss rates of the initial tranche sizes. The last row of every array includes the standard deviation of the originator's aggregate position as the symmetric measure of residual cash-flow uncertainty, computed by evaluating equation (5.11) for the simulated cash-flow series.

The dependence of senior tranche premia on the overcollateralisation ratio is illustrated in figure 5.1.

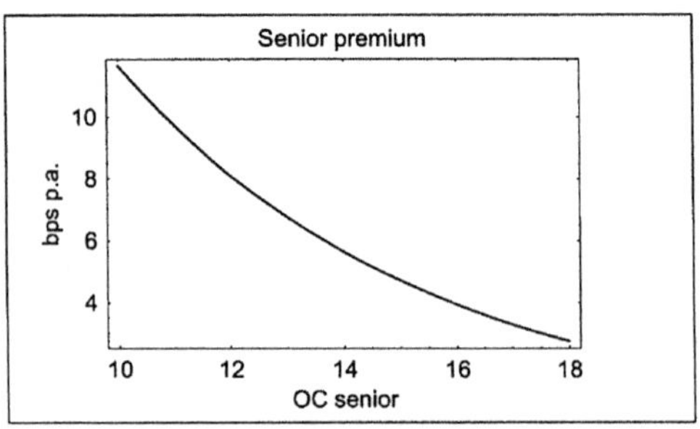

Figure 5.1: **Senior premium for base case as a function of tranche size/overcollateralisation (OC).**

The senior premium is clearly decreasing with the level of overcollateralisation provided by subordinate tranches, where the marginal effect diminishes with additional overcollateralisation. Senior tranches comprising 90% of the transaction nominal carry a five-year model premium of 12 bps p.a. The marginal effect of an overcollateralisation increase is notable, such that a premium reduction by more than one half is achieved by extending the overcollateralisation ratio by five percent of the transaction nominal, i.e. $P_{sen}(0) = 85$. A further increase of the senior tranche size beyond 90% of the transaction nominal is accompanied by a progressive senior premium increase.

The loss allocation rates reported in table 5.1 reveal that a senior tranche comprising 90% of the structure is not regarded as entirely riskless by the market: On expectation, it suffers a loss allocation of 0.52% of its nominal during a five-year horizon. Note, however, unlike almost-riskless single-name claims, the probability of loss allocation to senior tranches is still notable. For instance, the frequency of scenarios obtained over the course of the simulation that causes a senior tranche with 10% overcollateralisation to be impaired by losses during a five-year time horizon amounts to 10.29%. Clearly, the loss amount actually allocated to the senior counterparty, i.e. the analogy of the LGD in the single-name context, is very small relative to the entire tranche size. For the above example, the average LGD is in the order of 5% of the senior principal. The 'high-frequency/low-severity' nature of senior portfolio risk makes the entire position less volatile than high-quality single-name exposures. Albeit evaluated at net zero value, the risk profile may be appealing to investors due to the comparatively stable risk/return-relationship in different states of the world.

Figure 5.2 illustrates the two-dimensional dependence of the mezzanine premium on mezzanine position, as determined by the overcollateralisation provided by the junior loss piece and the mezzanine sizes as given by principals $P_{mez}(0) = 8, 10, 12$.

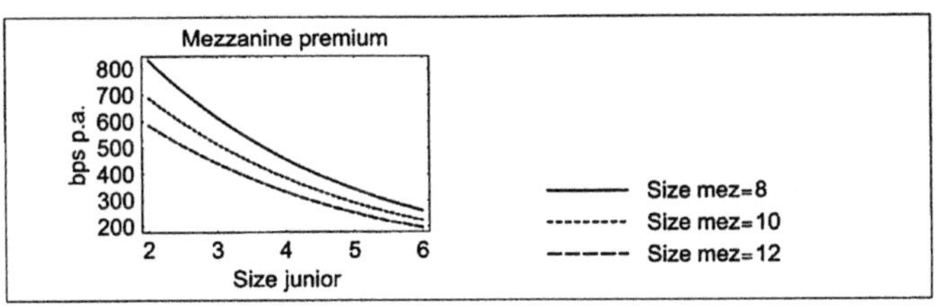

Figure 5.2: **Mezzanine premium for the base case as a function of tranche position and size.**

Mezzanine premia indicate that the risk-neutral distribution puts heavy probability mass on losses falling in the mezzanine range. According to average portfolio losses for a five-year horizon, such as those plotted in figure 4.3 as a function of maturity for the model estimates, expected mezzanine discounted loss allocation is in the range of 32.54% for the (90/8/2)-capital structure with a mezzanine tranche with earliest loss participation and smallest mezzanine size, and still 8.46% for the least risky (82/12/6)-scheme. In addition to high expected loss allocation risk, the amount of loss borne by the mezzanine tranche is highly volatile – the tranche LGD assumes all values between zero and one. Furthermore, premium accrual on the basis of the current tranche principal, which is heavily reduced in high-loss scenarios also declines, such that a mezzanine investor holds an extremely volatile position. For example (not depicted in the table), in the (90/8/2)-structure, the discounted mezzanine five-year CDS cash-flow has an absolute standard deviation of 2.76, higher than for a senior CDS tranche with 1.96 at by far a higher principal.

Loss allocation reported in the table shows that small junior tranches are almost entirely lost, and a junior tranche of size six still has an expected loss rate of 61.36%. Computation of the difference between the absolute value of the junior loss leg and the residual claim (see equation (5.10)) quantifies the savings of protection costs due to late loss allocation, amounting to 0.13.

Finally, the volatility of the consolidated originator's position, included in table 5.1, measures the hedge effect of credit risk securitisation: As expected, residual volatility is increasing in the junior tranche size. The impact of the partition of the securitised loss range between the mezzanine and senior tranche, on the originator's cash-flow volatility is, however, not unique.

5.1.3.2 Assessment of two identification problems

5.1.3.2.1 Factor space dimensionality The uncertainty resulting from the lack of identification of sector-related factors from the estimation part of the study at hand clearly introduces uncertainty into CDO tranche pricing. In order to assess the relevance of the contribution of independent risk factors to overall loss dispersion and CDO pricing, I compare loss distributions and arbitrage-free CDO issuance spreads for the three reference portfolios under consideration: CDO premia obtained for the portfolio *Sectors*, representing the base case scenario, are compared with the limiting cases *Minimal* and *Maximal*, together with the corresponding loss distributions. Except for the underlying reference portfolios, differing in factor space dimensionality, all other parameters remain unaltered, as defined for the base case.

Summary statistics on five-year losses and the cumulated loss amounts evaluated at market value to be allocated to the tranche waterfall are given in table 5.2. I include both discounted losses, conforming to my definition of derivative pricing at time-zero and undiscounted losses, computed as the sum of losses, evaluated at their time-Υ_{corp} market value.[12]

Quantiles indicate the probability mass applicable to low and extreme losses and range statistics are given as robust measures of dispersion. The estimated density functions of the three portfolio loss distributions are graphed in figure 5.3.

---

[12] Note that the expected value of the latter is obtained by the closed-form solutions of the factor model: Weighting the five-year expected values of losses of the three risk levels, depicted in figure 4.3, by the principal proportions of 10%, 50%, and 40% yields the undiscounted loss expectation, evaluating to 5.54 for the 100-claims portfolios.

	Reference portfolio					
	minimal		*sectors*		*maximal*	
	$PV(loss)$	$\sum loss(t)$	$PV(loss)$	$\sum loss(t)$	$PV(loss)$	$\sum loss(t)$
Mean	4.77	5.44	4.71	5.50	4.77	5.37
Std dev.	4.03	4.04	3.78	4.04	3.66	4.04
Quantiles						
5%	0.78	1.00	0.82	1.97	0.90	1.01
10%	0.90	1.02	1.69	1.01	1.74	1.97
90%	9.65	10.19	8.93	10.99	8.87	9.91
95%	12.58	13.87	12.04	14.61	11.54	12.88
Ranges						
95%-5%	11.80	12.87	11.22	13.64	10.64	11.87
90%-10%	8.75	9.17	7.95	9.98	7.18	7.95
75%-25%	4.46	3.99	3.54	5.02	3.37	3.87

Table 5.2: **Statistics on risk-neutral loss distributions: relevance of factor space dimensionality.**

Reference portfolios *Minimal*, *Sectors*, and *Maximal* differ in the number of orthogonal factors determining subportfolios with uniform loss expectations. As no positive-valued positions are involved, the negative sign of losses has been omitted. All figures refer to a portfolio nominal of 100.

Consider the quantile ranges: The interquartile range, referring to losses of positive, but moderate size, exhibits the strongest sensitivity against an extension of the number of classes, as implemented by the alteration of the reference portfolio. The same is true for zero-loss probabilities, as can be inferred from the intercepts of the loss densities depicted in figure 5.3. Quantiles and range statistics referring to the more extreme scenarios, by contrast, indicate that probabilities for severe losses are rather insensitive to the number of orthogonal factors affecting only a subset of reference claims. Correspondingly, the long tails of the loss density graphs are rather similar for the three portfolios. Furthermore, taking once again very bad outcomes into consideration, the tails indicate that the diversification effect is largely realised by the transition from the portfolio *Minimal* to *Sectors*. An investigation of simulation results shows that extreme loss scenarios are caused by high common factor values affecting all claims, regardless of the number of risk factors yielding additional diversification benefits. The *Minimal* portfolio still leaves scope for worse outcomes, where a high common factor path realisation occurs in conjunction with high realisations of the risk-level specific factors affecting up to half of the reference claims. This effect is largely mitigated for portfolio *Sectors* and precluded for portfolio *Maximal*.

Overall, the above analysis shows that the number of factors that affect even a large subset of reference claims only has minor impact on portfolio loss dispersion, given the estimated parameters. This is clearly a consequence of the large variance proportion of the common factor, dominating the impact of additional class-specific factors that are not

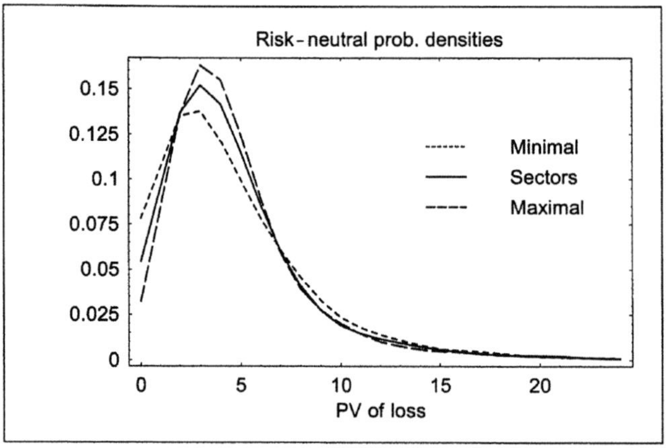

Figure 5.3: **Estimated risk-neutral loss density functions: relevance of factor space dimensionality.**

entirely diversified.

Notwithstanding the small impact of factor space dimensionality and subportfolio specification on overall loss dispersion, the severity of the lack of identification of sector-related information from corporate term structure information should be assessed in the light of the consequences for CDO valuation.

Senior tranche issuance premia of various capital structures for the three reference portfolios are shown in figures 5.4.

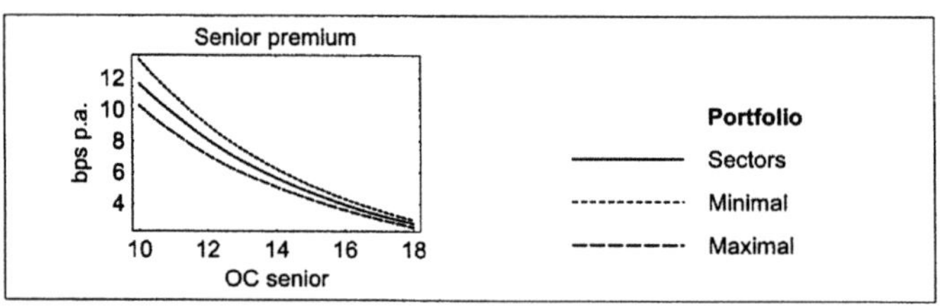

Figure 5.4: **Senior premium for base case: relevance of factor space dimensionality.**

The reaction of loss allocation to trancheholders and resulting issuance premia on factor space dimensionality can be interpreted in an option-theoretic context. A senior tranche bearing losses whose aggregate market values at default exceed the senior threshold $\underline{K}_{sen}$, which is depicted on the abscissa in figure 5.4, has the character of a long call position on the portfolio loss amount with a basis price of $\underline{K}_{sen}$. The decrease in loss dispersion achieved by additional class-specific factors implies a lower probability for high losses and thus a spread reduction. Taking funding into account, senior tranches of any size thus exhibit the characteristics of standard defaultable debt in the Merton (1974)-framework: The senior stake is replicated by a riskless bond and a short put position on the underlying reference portfolio value, the put option value sensitivity with regard to a change in underlying portfolio loss volatility being negative. Senior premia are therefore uniquely decreasing in the number of orthogonal factors. Furthermore, figure 5.4 shows that the invariance of extreme loss probabilities against the factor space dimensionality is mirrored in the senior tranche valuation: Whereas senior tranches receiving little support from junior and mezzanine, hence already being exposed to losses of moderate size, exhibit visible sensitivity towards the extension of the factor space, senior tranches that are exposed to extreme loss risk only are almost insensitive to the class specification.

The equity-like character of a junior tranche also becomes evident using the interpretation in the option-theoretic framework: As a first-loss position capped at $\underline{K}_{mez}$, it is comparable to a short put on portfolio losses, or to a long call on the underlying portfolio value. Hence, the junior stakeholder benefits from increasing underlying volatility. In the portfolio context, a decrease in loss dispersion implies smaller probabilities for losses near zero, such that the expected value of junior losses uniquely increases in the contribution of additional factors to portfolio diversification. Retained junior tranches lose value upon the introduction of additional diversified factors, which is shown in figure 5.5, comparing expected loss allocation to junior. In order to restore absence of arbitrage, the expected value of residual excess spread income must experience a corresponding increase.

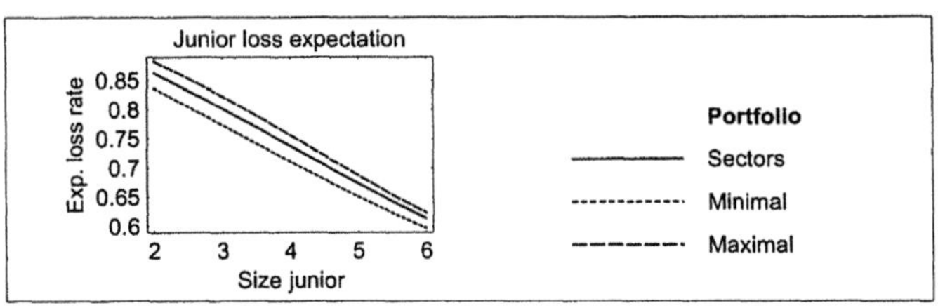

Figure 5.5: **Expected loss allocation to junior tranche: relevance of factor space dimensionality.**

For mezzanine tranches, by contrast, the effect of diversification on the premium is not expected to be unique: The mezzanine loss participation profile corresponds most closely to a bull spread, i.e. a participation in losses exceeding $\underline{K}_{mez}$, capped at $\underline{K}_{sen}$. The sensitivity of mezzanine premia therefore clearly depends both on position $\underline{K}_{mez}$ and size $P_{mez}(0)$ of the tranche under consideration within the capital structure: Mezzanine tranches receiving little overcollateralisation by the junior piece are expected to inherit the equity-like reaction of junior risk on an underlying volatility change. Accordingly, highly-overcollateralised mezzanine tranches and/or those with large principals, permitting a participation in the low-risk range, exhibit the debt-like sensitivity on underlying loss volatility. The precise values of the upper and lower thresholds, characterising a change in the sign of the sensitivity of mezzanine premia towards a diversification change, clearly depends on the precise shape of the loss distribution in the relevant range. The computation of mezzanine premia for the variety of capital structures under examination, depicted in figure 5.6, shows that the sensitivity of mezzanine premia on the factor space dimensionality may be very low: The premium of the *Risky*-mezzanine tranche, corresponding to the (90/8/2)-capital structure is virtually invariant to factor space dimensionality. The extension of both junior and mezzanine principals causes the sensitivity of the mezzanine premium with regard to the extension of the factor space dimensionality to rise to a difference between the upper and lower limit of 50 bps (between 223 bps and 173 bps) for the (82/12/6)-structure.

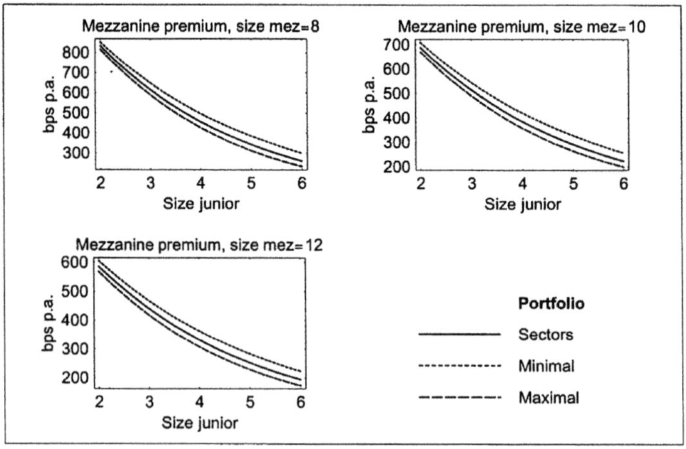

Figure 5.6: **Mezzanine premium for base case: relevance of factor space dimensionality.**

To summarise, figures 5.4 and 5.6 suggest that the lack of sector-specific factor identification has contrary effects on senior and mezzanine premia: The first are most sensitive against the factor space dimensionality when little overcollateralisation is provided, whereas the latter exhibit the highest sensitivity in the case of high overcollateralisation. Overall, the results show that although it is a fundamental problem for the determination of an appropriate dependence structure, the actual differences among bounds on premia obtained in the limiting cases are small. I conclude that model estimation based on a larger number of pre-specified factors, identified by the reference borrowers' industry affiliation, would have little impact on resulting CDO model premia. The restriction of the valuation study to a reference portfolio exhibiting sector-related, non-diversified concentration risk factors therefore entails little loss of generality.

5.1.3.2.2 Mean-loss rate decomposition of reference asset spreads The reduced-form framework of Duffie and Singleton (1999a), exploited for defaultable bond pricing outlined in section 3.1, states the substitutional relationship between intensity and LGD as a fraction of the pre-default value market value, hence only permitting the identification of the mean-loss rate $\overline{h}_{class}$ from single-name market spreads.

The question as to what extent the lack of separate identification of both mean-loss rate components affects the validity of CDO pricing results merits a short investigation.

The theoretical argument relies on a perfectly granular debt portfolio: As stated in the introductory chapter, perfect granularity characterises a portfolio with nominal exposures P_i to individual entities approaching zero and the number of entities I approaching infinity.

In order to investigate the relationship between the recovery assumption and portfolio losses, the following three cases shall be distinguished, all of them defining losses as a fraction of the pre-default market value to be allocated to CDO investors: (i) zero recovery (i.e. $LGD = 1$ with certainty), (ii) positive, but deterministic recovery (i.e. $\overline{LGD} < 1$), (iii) random recovery LGD_i of every entity i.

Consider the most general case (iii): If it is argued that individual borrower recovery uncertainty is a perfectly diversifiable risk factor, one would firstly claim that the market price of recovery risk equals zero.[13] With regard to the granular portfolio context, it follows that $\lim_{I \to \infty} \frac{1}{I} \sum_{i=1}^{I} LGD_i = \overline{LGD}$, such that portfolio loss properties correspond to case (ii) with deterministic positive recovery. Now consider case (ii): Default modelling by dependent Cox-processes captures two sources of randomness: Dependencies are exclusively modelled by random mean-loss rate covariation, whereas the realisations of individual default times are purely idiosyncratic. Therefore, the portfolio risk contribution of an individual reference asset is limited to the common components of the mean-loss rate applied to the exposure in market value. The partition of the mean-loss rate, by contrast, affects the outcome only conditional on loss occurrence, the latter being borrower-specific and therefore, fully diversified and irrelevant to the single-name portfolio risk contribution. Hence, the granular portfolio outcome in case (ii) gives way to the outcome in case

---

13 See Duffie (1999) for diversifiability of recovery risk and Driessen (2002) for empirical evidence of the pricing of jump risk in US corporate bonds.

(i).

The theoretical argument, establishing irrelevance of the mean-loss rate decomposition of reference asset spreads to granular portfolio derivatives pricing, suggests that the lack of LGD identification is of minor importance to CDO pricing. This raises two questions, as the fiction of perfect granularity cannot be fulfilled by real-world reference portfolios:

(i) What happens in non-granular portfolios?

(ii) How large is the error incurred by equating a CDO reference portfolio with the perfectly granular case, where equivalence of the three cases examined above holds?

The first question addresses the relevance of non-replacement of defaulted claims, affecting the outcome in non-granular portfolios as opposed to the granular case. Consider the dynamic default stochastic of two non-granular portfolios whose individual partitions trade at identical short spreads, equal to the mean-loss rates $\overline{h}_1 = \overline{h}_2$, but with $h_1 > h_2, LGD_1 < LGD_2$.

Equality of mean-loss rates causes the absolute loss amount that occurs during the first infinitesimal short time interval to have identical expected value. Comparison of the loss stochastic for future periods, however, shows that the expected value of losses of the lower-intensity portfolio actually exceeds future expected losses occurring in the higher-intensity portfolio: The large number of surviving claims in the low-intensity portfolio one leaves a larger population that shall be impaired at the mean-loss rate, hence $\mathbb{E}_0\left[PV(loss_1)\right] < \mathbb{E}_0\left[PV(loss_2)\right]$. The difference is increasing the time horizon and the mean-loss rate, and it is decreasing in the number of claims, all three variables causing a portfolio to deviate from perfect granularity. In addition to the impact of non-zero LGD on the expected value of losses, the assumption of positive LGD yields a higher degree of subdivision of individual risks than in the zero-recovery case, hence reducing loss dispersion in non-granular portfolios.

The second question is solved pragmatically by performing a comparative-static analysis for the base case, the five-year senior/subordinate capital structure referring to the *Sectors* portfolio. Figure 5.7 illustrates the response of the portfolio loss distribution to a variation of the LGD rate, adjusting intensities such that mean-loss rates remain unaltered.

As has been the case for the lack of sector identification examined before, the relevance of the difference should be assessed in the light of the CDO pricing task at hand.[14]

As this question and the subsequent comparative-static examination of contractual features and model parameters incur considerable computation burden, all comparative-static analysis shall be performed for two specific capital structures: I adopt the (90/8/2)-

[14] See Boscher and Ward (2002) for a similar analysis.

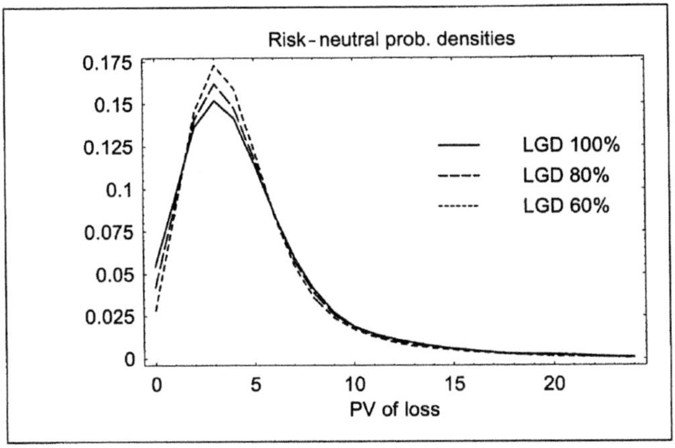

Figure 5.7: **Response of loss distribution to a change in the LGD, holding mean-loss rates constant.**

scheme, providing the smallest degree of overcollateralisation to both issued tranches, which will subsequently be referred to as *Risky*. Whereas the *Risky* scheme captures the proportions applicable to synthetic investment grade debt securitisations, the tranche dimensions (86/10/4) correspond to what it observed in the market for below-investment grade debt securitisations. Providing considerable overcollateralisation to issued tranches, it will be referred to as *Safe*.

The portfolio loss stochastic translates into *Risky* and *Safe* CDO issuance premia, as illustrated in figure 5.8.

Both illustrations reveal that the LGD identification problem has little impact on portfolio losses and CDO pricing. For high values of the 'true', yet unidentified, LGD, the possible error incurred by the assumption of unit LGD made for simplification is in the same order of magnitude as the uncertainty incurred by the lack of sector-specific factor identification.

A glance at historical estimates of recovery rates shows that especially for synthetic CBOs referring to European investment grade market-traded bonds, that shall be subject to empirical comparison in Chapter 7, high loss rates of the underlying debt do indeed apply: Hamilton (2002) reports that during the period between 1985 and 2001, 0.2% of European corporates having issues outstanding rated investment grade by Moody's defaulted on their obligations. For European senior unsecured bonds, Moody's reports an average recovery rate of 20.8% of the bonds' face values, which is much lower than in the US with 50%. It also falls below the rate of 45% suggested by the BCBS (2003)-proposal applicable on bank loans towards corporate debtors, the discrepancy towards bonds being

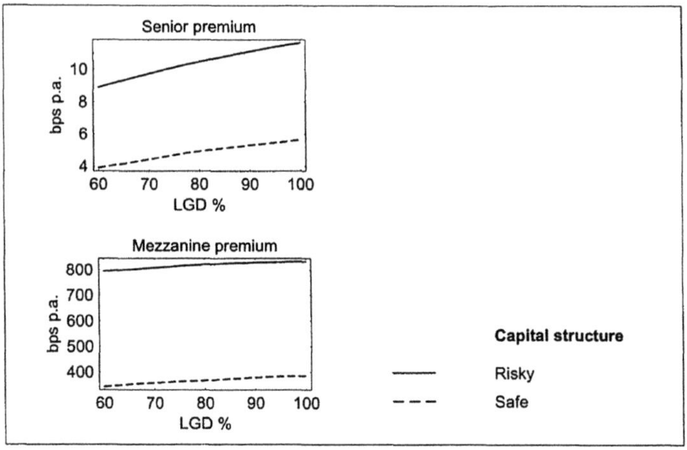

Figure 5.8: **Premia of CDO tranches as a function of the LGD, holding mean-loss rates constant.**

presumably due to priority rules in favour of bank loans in the bank-dominated continental financial systems.

The numerical results presented above permit the conclusion that the simplifying assumption of zero recovery is innocuous when dealing with European investment grade bond securitisation. Note, however, that the simplification to zero-recovery expected loss modelling applies to synthetic structures only, where loss allocation to trancheholders is de-linked from actual cash-flow occurrence of defaulted coupon bonds. As shown by the comparative analysis of the RMV and RFV assumptions performed by Duffie and Singleton (1999a), the suppression of the actual cash-flow sequence of coupon debt default has negligible impact on reference claim pricing, which holds true both for true-sales and synthetics. As has been argued above, true-sale CDOs are vulnerable to SPV insolvency risk, such that the precise cash-flow-timing structure is required to be modelled. This means that the ability to identify defaultable discount factors $D_{corp}(t,\tau)$ from the zero bond decomposition, using a unique defaultable term structure for coupon and principal cash-flows, is lost.

5.1.3.3 Impact of issuance timing: factor realisations at origination

The factor realisations at origination determine current reference claim riskiness. As the central tendency under the risk-neutral measure has shown itself to be rather weak, the factor realisations at origination, entering the valuation task as initial values, are expected to have considerable impact on CDO issuance spreads.

Again, the analysis is restricted to the two relevant capital structures *Risky* and *Safe*, introduced in the preceding section. The initial factor values are varied between zero and a common multiple of 1.4 applied to the values assumed so far, i.e. the averages of the estimated factor time series.

Five-year reference claim par spreads adjust to the credit market environment and are illustrated in table 5.3. The columns 'Minimum' and 'Maximum' refer to the factor realisations close to zero and the 1.4-fold factor increase, the centre column reports five-year par spreads evaluated at the factor time-series averages.

	Factor start value change		
	Minimum	**Average**	**Maximum**
risk=1	59.4	78.2	85.8
risk=2	83.0	110.2	121.2
risk=3	93.3	126.7	140.1
$S_{pool}(0)$	84.7	113.6	125.2

Table 5.3: **Reference asset par spreads as functions of initial factor values.**
The column 'Minimum' refers to the scenario with zero initial factor values, the column 'Maximum' refers to the scenario with a factor increase of 1.4-times the estimated factor series averages, the latter being depicted in the centre column. The weighted average spread of the base case reference portfolio is reported.

Figure 5.9 depicts premia for the *Risky* and *Safe* example transactions for different initial credit factor values, ranging from zero to a multiple of 1.4 of the estimated factor series averages.

The long half life of the initial factor deviations from the means, especially the one of the common factor amounting to 2.578 years, causes the timing of CDO origination to be of central relevance to fair issuance conditions. Origination in a low factor environment causes the *Risky* senior premium to drop to one half of its value when evaluated at the time-series averages, and even the *Safe* senior premium reduces to two basispoints. Mezzanine premia of both schemes reduce by the order of one half, when the initial factor level approaches zero. Overall, premia of the tranches considered turn out to be linear in the initial factor values within the examined range.

5.1.3.4 Impact of the tenor: term structures of CDO premia

CDOs are set up for different maturity ranges. The tenor of a true-sale is normally chosen to match the maturities of the collateral claims, hence, a cash-flow structure in the literal sense precludes collateral sale. Timing risk with respect to tranche redemption may

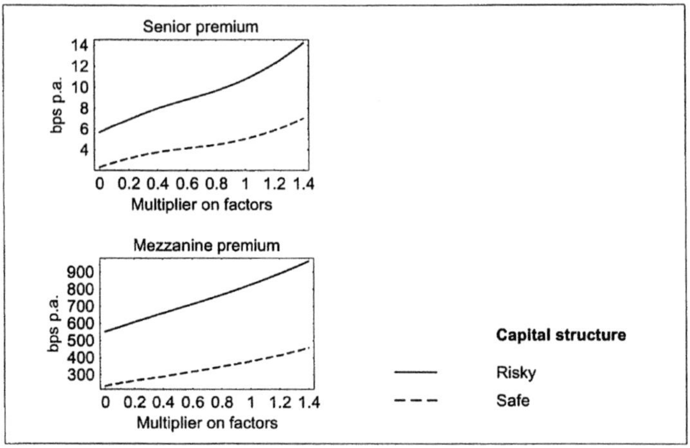

Figure 5.9: **Premia of CDO tranches as a function of the factor realisation at origination.**

be reduced by offering tranches differing in redemption schedules. Tranche maturities of synthetic CDOs, by contrast, are set arbitrarily in order to meet the originator's protection demand and the time horizon desired by a tranche investor. Synthetic CBOs referring to market-traded assets often align tranche maturities with common maturity classes in the credit derivatives markets. The five-year time horizon assumed for the base case therefore corresponds to what is observed for synthetic transactions.

An extension of the tenor of a transaction has two major consequences for tranche premia, both effects reinforcing each other, such that tenor is expected to have notable impact on CDO premia, but at diminishing marginal effect:

Primarily, the portfolio loss expectation is strictly monotonically increasing in maturity, however with diminishing marginal effect, as defaulted claims are not replaced. This directly translates to CDO loss expectations and issuance spreads when overcollateralisation levels are held constant.

In addition, CDO valuation is affected by the time structure of payments of both legs of the tranche swap: Whereas the loss allocation leg suffers from payments rather evenly until principal reduction to zero, the premium leg benefits from high premium rates applicable to large outstanding principals during early periods. Therefore, early premium payments have to make up for late losses, which allows for nominal premium growth falling below expected loss allocation growth, a consequence of discounting at positive interest rates. The effect is expected to be negligible for senior tranches, but becomes substantial for subordinate tranches bearing high nominal premia.

Both effects together suggest that the tranche premia are concave in the tenor of the transaction. The transactions *Risky* and *Safe* permit a quantification of the mentioned effects. Table 5.4 gives an illustration of the par spread curves of the reference assets, whose maturities are chosen to match the tenor of the transactions.

	Tenor of transaction		
	3 years	**5 years**	**10 years**
risk=1	70.3	78.2	87.6
risk=2	96.9	110.2	125.7
risk=3	119.7	126.7	135.2
$S_{pool}(0)$	103.3	113.6	125.7

Table 5.4: **Reference asset par spreads as functions of time to maturity.**
The weighted average spread of the base case reference portfolio is reported.

Figure 5.10 depicts the 'term structures' of fair issuance premia resulting from a variation in the tenor of the structure.

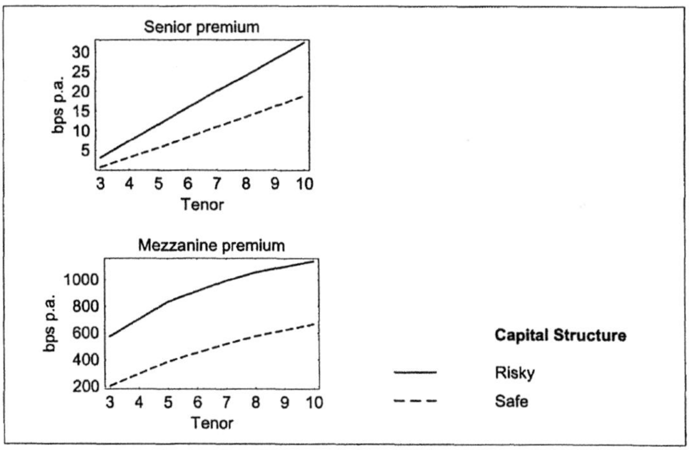

Figure 5.10: **Term structures of CDO premia.**
CDO tranche issuance premia are obtained as functions of the tenor of the transaction.

Senior premia indicate that severe loss probabilities increase pronouncedly with the time horizon, the increase turning out to be linear in the examined maturity range. Note that senior premia are highly sensitive against an extension of the time horizon: The notable increase in severe loss probabilities causes senior premia of both structures examined to triple when the tenor is extended from five to ten years. Mezzanine premia, by contrast, are less sensitive against an extension of the time horizon: The increase of the tenor from five to ten years yields a 1.4-fold mezzanine premium increase for the *Risky* mezzanine tranche and a 1.7-fold increase for the *Safe* mezzanine premium. As expected from non-replacement and premium accrual during early periods, the relationship is clearly concave and the sensitivity on tenor is higher for the *Risky* mezzanine tranche, receiving low overcollateralisation.

Tranche maturity is a contract parameter that is chosen by the counterparties, and the initial factor values studied above relate to the decision of the origination time. Both aspects may thus be considered as decision variables. The underlying loss stochastic, by contrast, is exogenous to the structuring effort, presumed that the reference portfolio is held fixed. Model specification is studied using the following comparative-static approach, which starts with the estimated case and relates the large number of possible parameter constellations to scenarios affecting reference claim valuation.

5.2 Comparative-static analysis of model parameters

In addition to the class assignments governing the risk resulting from industry-related concentration groups affecting overall loss dispersion, the portfolio characteristics are captured by the factor process parameters, estimated for investment grade reference assets. Due to the large number of parameters and the non-negligible computational burden, as a consequence of the need of an entire portfolio simulation per parameter constellation, I restrict the analysis to a few relevant cases. Variations in the parameter vector determine the levels of mean-loss rates and their covariation. The process parameters relate to the average credit quality, determining the expected value of portfolio losses, and to the mean-loss rate covariation, governing the dependence structure among default events. Hence, the parameter variation serves the purpose of assessing the impact of a change of overall portfolio loss characteristics on CDO tranche pricing.

A comprehensive study on loss distributions and tranche valuation is performed for the reference portfolio *Sectors*, mirroring a typical securitised bank portfolio exhibiting certain industry-related concentration risks. The assignment of risk-sector-related classes to the reference assets is held fixed, hence maintaining the factor structure of the base case *Sectors*. The parameter set is varied with respect to the following objectives:

The first exercise addresses the dependence model: The occurrence of severe losses is governed by loss rate covariation. Volatility parameters of both the common and class-related factors determine low- and severe loss events, affecting tranches in quite a different manner.

The second exercise relates to the average portfolio quality: I perform a variation of the factor means, determining single-name mean-loss rates. Aside from a mere investigation of process parameters, this exercise provides a rough appraisal of the impact of a possible bias of the estimate for default risk compensation, incurred from the choice of the market from which the model has been estimated.

The final comparative-static exercise relates to the valuation of credit factor risk by market participants. Factor risk valuation is of interest for two reasons: Firstly, factor risk pricing has a notable impact both on the expected values and on the volatilities of factors, determined under the risk-neutral probability measure. Secondly, insight is gained about the decomposition of CDO tranche premia into compensation for actual loss allocation risk and a premium for factor uncertainty.

In order to assure comparability of loss severity in the case of default, par coupons for the reference claims (5.13) are adjusted upon the parameter variation, the five-year horizon and factor initialisation at unconditional risk-neutral means being maintained.

5.2.1 Impact of factor volatilities and dependence structure

A change in volatilities of all factors in the *Sectors* portfolio alters the dependence structure among mean-loss rates, and thus, the dispersion of the portfolio loss distribution.

Concerning factor volatilities and the resulting dependence structure, two points of interest merit detailed consideration. Firstly, the central determinant of loss dispersion is the common factor volatility. I thus examine the impact of a change in the relevant factor volatility parameter on CDO valuation. Secondly, the effect of concentration risk prevailing in the *Sectors* portfolio considered implies that class-specific factor volatilities still contribute to portfolio loss dispersion, altering probabilities for losses of moderate severity.

Based on those considerations, I examine two scenarios characterised by a change in the common factor volatility, but differing with respect to the importance of class-specific volatility. The change in common factor variation is implemented through a change in σ_c.[15] In the first case, class-specific factor volatilities are left at their values as implied by the class-specific parameter estimates, such that mean-loss rates of all claims experience an identical volatility change. In the second case, class-specific volatility parameters σ_{class} are adjusted in order to hold mean-loss rate volatility constant at the level characterised

[15] A comparative-static analysis with respect to the reversion speed κ_c is omitted, as results are expected to differ only slightly from a volatility analysis based on σ_c.

by the parameter estimates (marked by the roofs):

$$\sigma_{class} = \sqrt{\left[\left(\frac{\hat{\theta}_c\hat{\sigma}_c^2}{2\hat{\kappa}_c} + \frac{\hat{\theta}_{class}\hat{\sigma}_{class}^2}{2\hat{\kappa}_{class}}\right) - \frac{\hat{\theta}_c\sigma_c^2}{2\hat{\kappa}_c}\right]\frac{2\hat{\kappa}_{class}}{\hat{\theta}_{class}}}. \tag{5.17}$$

Considering the first case, where specific factors are described by the estimated processes, the parameter σ_c is varied between 0.5 and 1.5 times its point estimate. In the second case, the analysis is restricted to a decrease in common factor volatility up to half of its estimated value, as the high estimated common factor variance proportion leaves little scope for an increase in mean-loss rate correlations when constant mean-loss rate volatilities are imposed.

With regard to single-name riskiness, term structures exhibit slight sensitivity towards a change in factor volatilities, which entails a small change in single-name par spreads (not reported).

Resulting tranche premia of the two subordination scenarios *Risky* and *Safe* are graphed in figures 5.11 and 5.12, respectively. The abscissa depicts the value of the common factor volatility parameter σ_c. However, it should be noted that for the scenario where mean-loss rates volatilities are held constant, class-specific volatilities are adjusted in the opposite direction, according to equation (5.17).

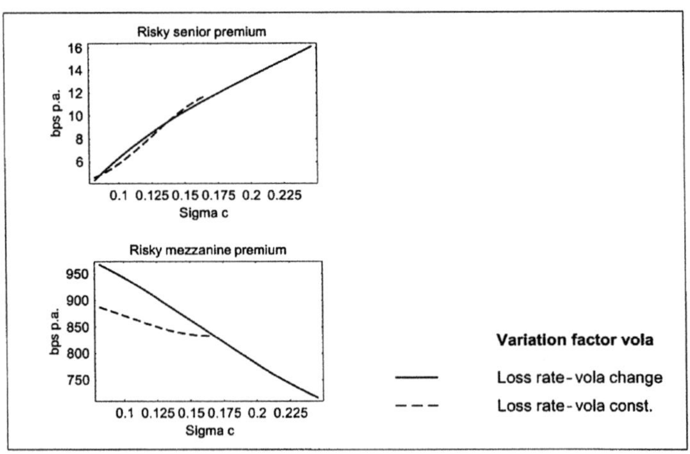

Figure 5.11: **Variation of factor volatilities: premia of *Risky* CDO tranches as functions of the common factor volatility parameter.**

Being exposed only to severe loss risk, senior tranches of both subordination schemes are

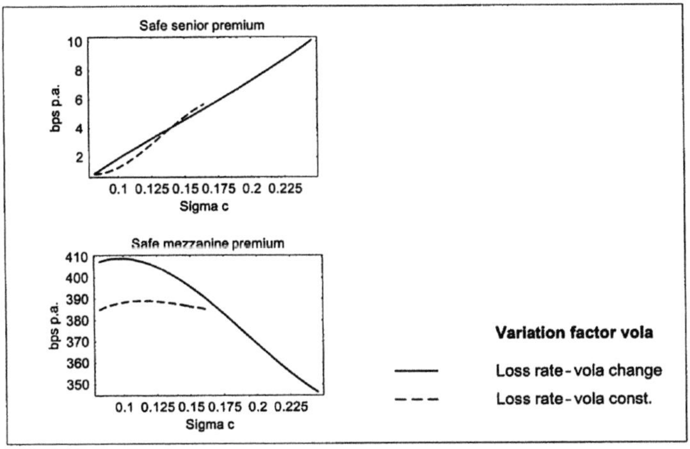

Figure 5.12: **Variation of factor volatilities: premia of *Safe* CDO tranches as functions of the common factor volatility parameter.**

highly sensitive to common factor volatility. The dependence of premia on a change in σ_c turns out to be approximately linear for both subordination schemes, where the *Risky* senior tranche premium exhibits higher sensitivity towards a change in the volatility parameter σ_c than the *Safe* senior premium: An (absolute) increase of the σ_c-parameter value by 0.1 causes the *Risky* senior premium to increase by 9 bps, where the increase of the of the *Safe* senior premium amounts to 6 bps within the examined parameter range.

Considering the second scenario where mean-loss rate volatilities remain at their estimated levels, both senior tranches show no response to the reduction of class-specific factor volatility.

Mezzanine tranches exhibit a fundamentally different dependence on common factor volatility. Consider the *Risky* scheme first: The mezzanine premium is decreasing in common factor volatility, with a change of σ_c by 0.1 causing the mezzanine premium to change by 187 bps throughout the examined range. This finding appears striking when compared to the results on factor space dimensionality obtained in section 5.1.3.2.1 before: By construction, portfolio loss dispersion c.p. diminishes both if the factor space dimensionality is increased and if common factor variation is reduced. Notably, both approaches to a change in loss dispersion produce contrary effects on the mezzanine tranche valuation: Whereas the *Risky* mezzanine tranche experiences a slight premium reduction when the factor space is enlarged, and thus reacts like a senior tranche or standard debt, the *Risky* mezzanine premium actually increases as a consequence of a common factor volatility reduction. This intriguing result – decreasing mezzanine riskiness both in the number of independent factors and in common factor volatility – is explained by the response of different quantiles of the loss distribution to the two scenarios. Whereas a change of factor dimensionality alters mainly the probability mass applying to losses of moderate size, an increase of common factor volatility shifts probability mass towards the tails of the distribution. A common factor variation increase thus reduces the probability mass falling into the range of a mezzanine tranche obtaining little support by the junior loss piece, thus lowering the expected value of loss allocation. Albeit small, the effect is still visible for the *Safe* mezzanine tranche that benefits slightly from a common factor volatility increase.

Furthermore, unlike the senior tranches, the mezzanine tranches examined are sensitive to sector-specific concentration risk. An adjustment of specific factor volatilities such that mean-loss rate volatilities are held constant lowers mezzanine riskiness, thus partly compensating for the effect of a common factor volatility change.

5.2.2 Impact of portfolio quality

The model has been estimated on the basis of investment grade corporate debt and thus applies to CDO transactions securitising the respective risk classes. However, securitisations of below-investment grade bank loans playing a prominent role in Germany and distressed debt transactions are characterised by higher expected values of losses. The factor model allows for a credit quality decline through an increase in factor means.

Moreover, a decrease of factor means is of interest because of the possible illiquidity bias incurred by the use of single-name bond spreads with the inherent tendency to overestimate true default risk compensation, as opposed to CDS premia. An examination of the translation of a possible reduction of factor means constitutes an experiment on how the alternative use of presumably lower CDS premia would have translated to CDO issuance premia.

I thus determine the sensitivity of loss distributions and CDO issuance spreads for the two proposed capital structures *Risky* and *Safe* on a change of the θ_k–parameter of all default risk factors. Note that a variation of mean factor levels necessarily affects process volatilities as a consequence of the CIR model heteroscedasticity. Therefore, a level change of factors that is not fully diversified alters the dependence structure of the portfolio, as indicated by the correlation equation (3.40) and related statistical properties. Note that a change of the mean factor level affects the dispersion of portfolio losses as a consequence of the Poisson default mechanism. An examination of the response of CDO premia to a reference portfolio quality change, modelled as a change in loss expectations, thus inevitably incorporates changes in loss dispersion.

As for the study of factor variation and dependence performed before, a consideration of the *Sectors* portfolio must take specific factor volatility into account.

In order to isolate the effect of a change in the dependence structure, two setups merit closer investigation. Firstly, all default risk-related mean parameters θ_k are varied jointly by an identical multiplier, such that mean-loss rates of all claims experience an increase by the same factor. In the first scenario, changes in factor variation are allowed for, whereas in the second scenario, factor variation is held fixed by an appropriate adjustment of volatility parameters.

For both scenarios, the mean parameters θ_k of all default risk-related factor processes experience a joint variation within 0.5 and 1.5-times their point estimates, marked by a roof below.

In the first scenario, an increase of θ_k only translates to the unconditional factor variance with a multiplier $\frac{\hat{\sigma}_k^2}{2\hat{\kappa}_k}$. In the second scenario, factor heteroscedasticity is controlled for by setting

$$\sigma_k = \sqrt{\frac{\hat{\theta}_k \hat{\sigma}_k^2}{\theta_k}} \tag{5.18}$$

upon a change in θ_k, the roofs again indicating the parameters that are held fixed at the estimated values. Note that initial factor values remain unchanged at the estimated time-series means obtained by Kalman filtering. The *conditional* factor process forecast averages therefore experience a lower increase than applied to the unconditional risk-neutral θ_k-parameters.

The change in single-name loss expectations obviously affects single-name risk premia. The implied five-year single-name par spreads are reported in table 5.5, again for the scenarios entailing minimal and maximal parameter change.

Now consider the portfolio context: Figure 5.13 depicts the standard deviations of the resulting loss distributions for both quality change assumptions. As all credit factor means are altered by a common multiple, the abscissa depicts the value of the multiple as the relative factor level change.

The difference between the graphs measures the amount of loss variation that is induced by the factor volatility change, as opposed to the level-dependent Poisson volatility. As the difference is notable, derivative prices are expected to behave differently in both quality change scenarios. Tranche premia of the two subordination scenarios *Risky* and *Safe* are depicted in figures 5.14 and 5.15.

Premia of all tranches are strongly increasing in factor means θ_k and convex for all tranches considered, the convex relationship being pronounced for senior tranches. With regard to senior tranches, the progressive increase is a consequence of the exposure to extreme losses

	Variation factor mean, vola change		
	Minimum	Estimate	Maximum
risk=1	48.6	78.2	107.8
risk=2	68.8	110.2	151.5
risk=3	80.0	126.7	173.2
$\mathcal{S}_{pool}(0)$	71.3	113.6	155.8

	Variation factor mean, vola const.		
	Minimum	Estimate	Maximum
risk=1	47.2	78.2	108.7
risk=2	67.0	110.2	152.7
risk=3	78.0	126.7	174.6
$\mathcal{S}_{pool}(0)$	69.4	113.6	157.1

Table 5.5: **Reference asset par spread adjustment on mean factor level changes.** The upper table refers to the scenario where only the risk-neutral stationary mean parameters θ_k of credit factor processes are varied by a common multiplier. The lower table refers to the scenario where the unconditional factor process volatilities are held constant by a suitable adjustment of volatility parameters σ_k. The column 'Minimum' refers to the scenario in which risk-neutral process means are reduced by a half, the column 'Maximum' refers to the scenario with a 1.5-fold increase of all credit factor means. The weighted average spread of the base case reference portfolio is reported.

only. Consider the tranches' reactions towards a severe reference asset quality decline, as would be mirrored by a strong factor mean level increase: For instance, expanding the θ_k-parameters around the estimated value, an increase of the risk-neutral factor means by 50% to the values relating to the maximum parameter change causes the *Risky* senior premium to increase by 6.5 bps, amounting to 56% of the *Risky* senior premium obtained at the estimates for the scenario where factor volatilities are held constant. Considering the scenario where a factor mean increase by 50% is accompanied by a corresponding volatility increase, senior sensitivities are higher: the *Risky* senior premium experiences an increase of 9.3 bps or 79% of the value obtained at the estimates. It is interesting to see that both scenarios on the adaption factor volatilities yield pronouncedly different results for the *Safe* senior premium: Rather insensitive with regard to a mean factor increase when process volatilities remain unchanged, an expansion around the estimate of 50% merely yields a *Safe* senior premium increase of 1.3 bps or 23.4%. By contrast, the scenario with increasing process volatilities yields a pronounced premium increase by 4.2 bps or 75.8% of the premium obtained at the estimate. This pronounced difference with regard to the volatility adjustment is a consequence of the *Safe* senior tranche being exposed to extreme losses, captured by systematic factor risk.

It is interesting to note that mezzanine premia of both capital structures exhibit different behaviour towards the process volatility adjustment: Upon a 50% factor mean increase,

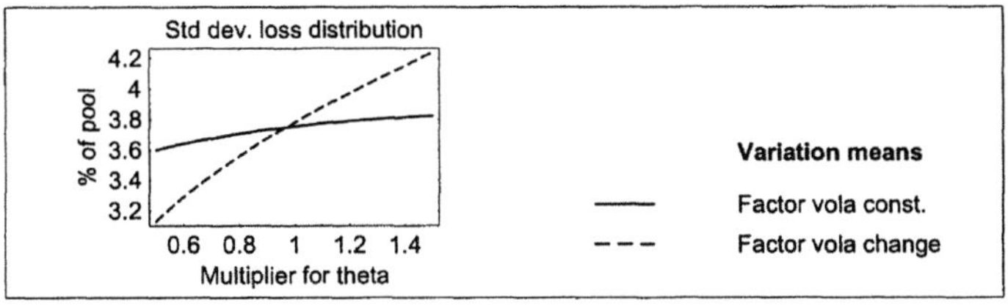

Figure 5.13: **Standard deviation of discounted losses as a function of reference portfolio quality.**

holding factor volatilities constant, the *Risky* mezzanine premium increases by a notable 573.1 bps or 68.8% of the premium obtained for the θ_k-estimates. When factor process volatilities are allowed to increase accordingly, the *Risky* mezzanine premium increase only amounts to 476.4 bps or 57.2%. The *Safe* mezzanine premium exhibits the same pattern: The scenario of holding process volatilities constant yields a premium increase of 333.2 bps or 86.5% of the premium evaluated at the estimated means, whereas a volatility increase yields a lower premium increase of 288.0 bps or 74.8%.

5.2.3 Impact of market price of risk parameters

The market valuation of factor volatility risk as derived from corporate bond spreads affects the loss distribution under the EMM, under which expectations for CDO pricing are formed in several ways.

The CIR model specification, i.e. the factor processes under the physical measure together with the functional form of factor risk premia, causes factor process means θ_k to increase by a factor of $\frac{\kappa_k^*}{\kappa_k}$ as a consequence of the change of measure. The unconditional factor variance, determined by equation (3.41), either applied to empirical or risk-neutral process parameters, is also affected by the change of measure: The change of the reversion speed κ_k, a pure volatility parameter, alters the steady-state factor variances proportionally by a factor of

$$\frac{Var(f_k(t))}{Var^*(f_k(t))} = \frac{\kappa_k^*}{\kappa_k}, \tag{5.19}$$

hence, the variance proportion being a function in λ_k.

Together with the level-dependency of loss dispersion induced by the Poisson mechanism, the market price of risk parameters are expected to have considerable impact, both on location and shape of the loss distribution.

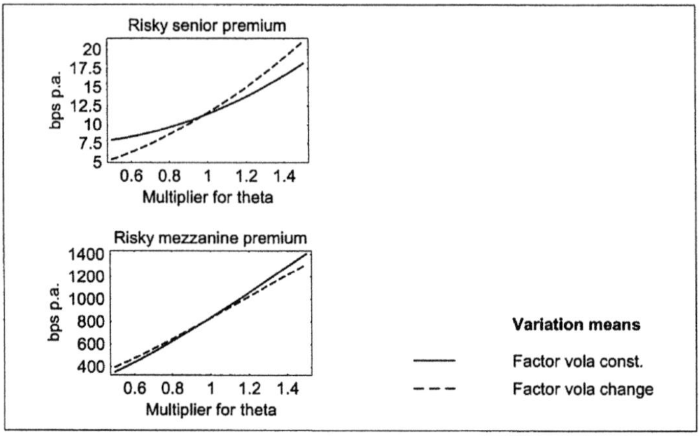

Figure 5.14: **Variation of reference portfolio quality: premia of *Risky* CDO tranches as functions of factor means.**

A comparative-static analysis of the market price of risk parameters quantifies the impact of factor risk valuation on security prices. Note that the comparative-static analysis of the portfolio characteristics performed so far has only been based on risk-neutral parameters. The relevance of factor risk valuation, by contrast, is based on the actual estimates obtained for λ_k and thus permits the decomposition of CDO tranche premia into compensation for actual loss risk and the premium for factor change risk.

The variation of the market price of risk parameters proceeds as follows: Starting by setting all λ_k−parameters equal to zero imposes risk-neutrality of investors with respect to factor change risk. All securities, underlying reference bonds and CDOs, are priced according to their discounted cash-flow expectations under the physical measure. In the limiting case, reference par spreads only compensate for default risk and evaluate to 30.4 bps, 40.9 bps and 61.3 bps for the three respective risk levels, implying a portfolio average $\mathcal{S}_{pool}(0)$ of 48.0 bps.

The impact of increasing risk aversion on tranche premia and loss expectations is assessed by varying all λ_k− parameters jointly between zero and the actual (negative) estimates depicted in table (4.8), holding physical parameters κ_k^*, θ_k^* constant at their point estimates. A further parameter increase beyond the estimated level, however, results in badly-behaved factor processes: The resulting values for κ_k quickly approach zero and become negative. The persistent and then mean-averting factor behaviour causes factor variation to become infinite. Therefore, I restrict the attention to parameters between

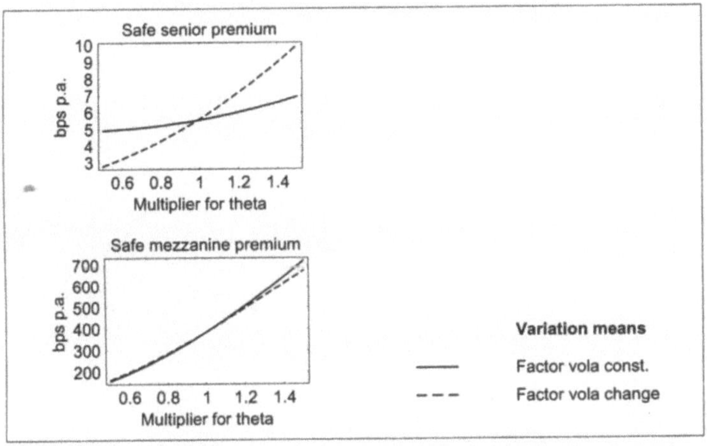

Figure 5.15: **Variation of reference portfolio quality: premia of *Safe* CDO tranches as functions of factor means.**

zero and the estimates.

Figure 5.16 illustrates the change of the loss distributions incurred by factor risk pricing: Starting from default risk expectations that are formed under the physical measure, factor processes are allowed to change by an increasing risk adjustment, again by a multiplier applied to the λ_k−parameters. The solid lines correspond to the limiting cases, i.e. the scenario where factor risk is priced in neither market and to the estimated case.

The relevance of risk aversion for location and dispersion of the distribution formed under the risk-neutral probabilities is striking. Both loss expectation and variance are convex in λ_k, which shows that the increase in the risk-neutral factor reversion speed incurred by an increase in $|\lambda_k|$ is overcompensated by the variance increase incurred by the level-dependent variance of the Poisson-default mechanism. The pronounced impact of risk pricing on the entire shape of the risk-neutral loss distribution suggests that small deviations of the λ_k−parameters from their estimates are expected to have strong impact on CDO valuation.

The dependence of tranche valuation on the multiple applied to λ_k is depicted in figure 5.17, collecting the two subordination schemes considered.

The high sensitivity of the right tail of the loss distribution to deviations of the λ_k from their estimated levels is highly relevant to senior premia: A reduction of all $|\lambda_k|$ by 10% of the estimated values reduces senior premia of both subordination structures by one third. Seen from the zero risk premium scenario, however, the marginal effect of an increase in

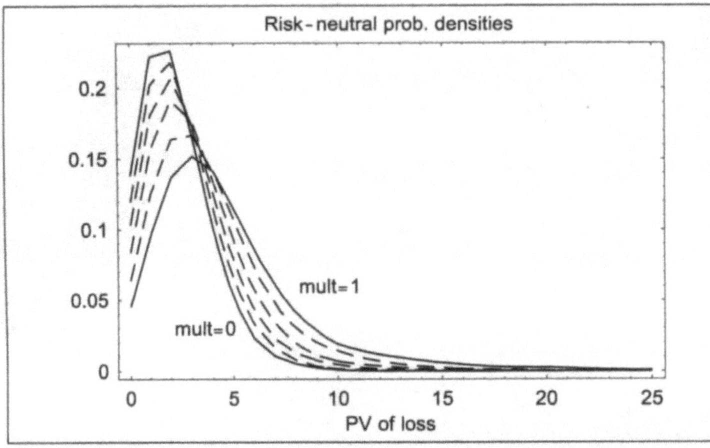

Figure 5.16: **Variation of factor risk valuation: response of loss distribution to a change in market price of factor risk parameters.**
The dashed functions refer to intermediate values of the multiplier applied to the λ_k-parameters, increasing in increments of 0.2.

$|\lambda_k|$ on (risk-neutral) senior loss allocation and resulting premia is small over a wide range of values of λ_k.

The *Risky* mezzanine premium exhibits sensitivity towards an increase in $|\lambda_k|$ already at low levels, whereas the sensitivity of the *Safe* scheme on the market price of risk parameters is less pronounced.

Table 5.6 reveals the impact of factor risk pricing on tranche riskiness: It compares discounted expected tranche loss rates on the basis of the factor evolution under the physical measure, with their counterparts when pricing under the risk-neutral measure at the estimated λ_k parameters. As previously introduced, a tranche loss rate denotes the gross tranche-CDS value normalised by the tranche principal.

Whereas expected loss allocation under the risk-neutral measure directly determines arbitrage-free premia, loss expectations that are formed under the physical measure can be mapped into a tranche agency rating.[16]

[16] See section 4.4.4 for a discussion of the relationship between agency ratings and the real-world loss expectations. A direct comparison between the valuation results, i.e. the premia obtained when setting λ_k to zero and those obtained for the estimators, however, should be interpreted with care. As the reduced-form model requires that claim valuation at default and the default stochastic are defined under the same risk-neutral measure derived from the factor market, the evaluation of the CDO pricing model for λ_k implies that *all* securities, both reference assets and CDOs, are required to be priced at zero risk premia. This is not true for exogenously-given reference claims, as their contractual coupons clearly incorporate market risk valuation.

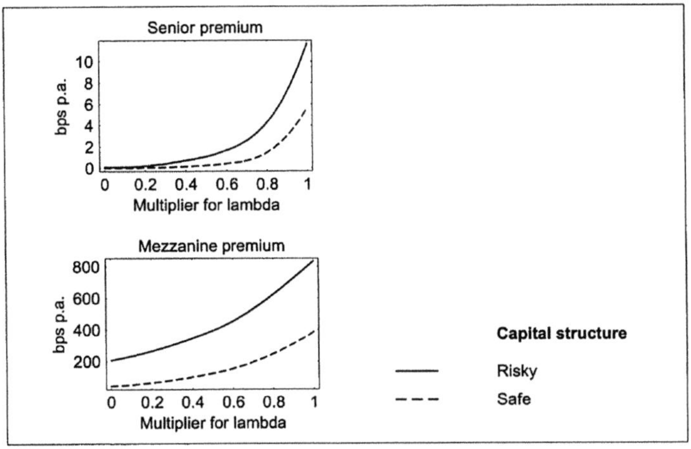

Figure 5.17: **Variation of factor risk valuation: premia of CDO tranches as a function of market price of factor risk parameters.**

The three-tranche capital structures show that factor risk components in CDO issuance premia are increasing in tranche overcollateralisation and size. Whereas *Risky* junior loss expectations are least affected by factor risk pricing, issued tranches carry a factor risk premium that by far exceeds factor risk compensation identified in the single-name bond market (see figure 4.3 for the analogous comparison applied to singe-name expected loss rates). The comparison of mean senior tranche loss allocation to the loss expectation of Aaa/Aa-rated corporate bonds, inferred from figure 4.3 for a five-year maturity horizon, clearly indicates that even the *Risky* senior tranche would obtain an implicit rating above corporate Aaa.

5.3 Summary of results

The pricing model values CDO tranches as senior/subordinated portfolio default swaps, taking the capital structure as expressed by the principal overcollateralisation ratios into account. For the basic senior/subordinated model, premia have been obtained for a variety of capital structures, such that a functional relationship between tranche position, size and the issuance premium has been established by loss simulation and loss allocation to tranche protection sellers.

Valuation results indicate that the underlying loss stochastic puts a heavy probability mass on losses affecting the mezzanine range. This is a direct consequence of five-year

	$P_{tr}(0)$	**Physical**	**EMM**
Risky			
Senior	90	0.004	0.52
Mezzanine	8	8.94	32.54
Junior	2	69.02	86.33
Safe			
Senior	84	0.00	0.25
Mezzanine	10	1.87	16.30
Junior	6	31.86	73.77

Table 5.6: **Expected loss allocation to tranches: effect of factor risk valuation.** Loss expectations taken under the physical measure may be mapped into a tranche's agency rating.

loss expectations formed under the risk-neutral measure: A comparison of the single-name loss expectations (see figure 4.3), translating into the expected value of portfolio losses (see table 5.2), with the mezzanine loss ranges examined shows that tranches are consistently impaired by losses of the expected amount. The exposure of senior tranches only to severe losses is mirrored by the premia consistently falling below 12 bps for the model estimates.

Two identification problems have been addressed and the impact on portfolio losses and CDO tranche pricing has been studied. Firstly, the lack of sector specification within the estimation setup has been studied in the light of CDO pricing. A comparison of two limiting cases of factor space dimensionality derives upper and lower bounds on premia that are in line with the factor model class assignments, restricted so far to risk levels. Five-year premia of senior and mezzanine tranches are fairly robust against the number of independent class-specific factors, and both are decreasing in factor space dimensionality. This robustness supports the restriction of the analysis to a class partition into nine fictive risk/sector-related subportfolios, adhering to the risk-level representation of typical investment grade reference portfolios. Secondly, the impact of uncertain recovery of reference assets on CDO pricing has been studied: As a perfectly diversified risk factor, recovery risk has no impact on granular portfolio risk. A comparative-static exercise on the non-granular investment grade reference portfolio setting shows that the error incurred by the assumption of zero LGD has little impact on resulting tranche premia for the relevant parameter constellations.

Within the senior/subordinate portfolio derivative setup, the impact of the factor realisation at origination and the maturity-dependence of tranche premia have been studied: Due to low reversion rates, especially of the common factor, factor start values have notable impact over the entire horizon of a five-year CDO, such that the current spread environment is highly relevant to issuance conditions. The contractual tenor of a CDO has a clear impact on senior risk exposure. Mezzanine tranches, by contrast, are less vulnerable to the extension of the tenor of the transaction beyond five years, due to early premium accrual in conjunction with low expected exposure at later periods.

A comparative-static simulation study determines sensitivities of tranche premia to factor process parameters, representing the average credit quality (identified by mean factor levels), the dependence structure (determined by volatility parameters) within a reference portfolio, and the sensitivities of tranche premia towards the market prices of credit factor risk. Whereas senior premia feature the expected increase in systematic factor variation, mezzanine premia show a somewhat surprising response to a change in factor variation: Premia of mezzanine tranches receiving little support by the junior piece turn out to be decreasing in factor volatilities, hence the sensitivity against a change in underlying loss dispersion having the opposite sign to the similar case where the factor-space dimensionality is varied. Factor expectations determining portfolio loss expectations have a clear impact on all tranches, whereas the effect of the incurred change in factor volatilities is strongest for highly-overcollateralised senior tranches. The analysis of the relevance of credit factor risk pricing on tranche valuation permits a comparison of the premium paid for actual loss allocation risk with the premium component payable due to the market pricing of factor change risk. As in the bond market, factor risk premia on CDO tranches are substantial: The change of measure causes not only factor and thus loss expectations to increase considerably, but also yields a notable factor and loss variation increase. Both effects work strongest on highly-overcollateralised tranches, such that positive senior premia are almost entirely due to risk pricing. Accordingly, the risk premium component of the mezzanine premium is both increasing in mezzanine position and size.

Overall, the analysis of the basic structure shows that high loss expectations are allocated to the mezzanine range and high factor risk premia are payable to senior tranches. Premium reductions can be achieved by the use of credit enhancements in the structure. Therefore, the effectiveness of credit enhancements that apply to synthetic structures is investigated in the next chapter.

Chapter 6

The Relevance of Credit Enhancements

6.1 Effect on tranche loss allocation

Under the senior/subordinate portfolio derivative assumption, CDOs are immediately affected by portfolio losses, once losses exceed the size of a retained first-loss piece. The riskiness of all or selected tranches can be altered by the inclusion of credit enhancements, whose relevance for tranche risk reduction is to be examined in this chapter.

For the present work, credit enhancements refer to all elements that reduce the risk of at least one tranche when compared to the simple senior/subordinate portfolio derivative transaction, leaving the underlying reference portfolio risk unaffected. Means that alter the reference portfolio risk profile, such as default protection of individual large exposures (either in form of credit insurance or protection through single-name derivatives) are precluded due to lack of generality.

Every credit enhancement reduces the level of riskiness as expressed in expected losses of at least one tranche, and thus the respective tranche spread. The cost of risk reduction may be borne by the originator in form of lower expected revenue from his protected portfolio. Alternatively, credit enhancement of senior tranches can be implemented at the expense of more subordinate tranches.

Credit enhancements can be classified according to their impact on reference portfolio loss ranges transferred to tranches.[1]

Modification of thresholds: improvement of OC-ratios. Loss buffers have the

---

[1] The mere increase of overcollateralisation ratios by subordinate tranches and first-loss retention is not considered as credit enhancement in this contribution.

effect that the aggregate loss amount to occur until a tranche suffers losses may exceed $\underline{K}_{tr}$. Protection is provided through weakly positive-valued cash balances that may take different forms. One analytically interesting variant, the 'spread account', is subject to formal analysis in this chapter. Third-party guarantees towards specified tranches also increase overcollateralisation of the tranches under consideration, but shall not be considered further.

Modification of tranche size: early redemption. Principals $P_{tr}(t)$ of tranches not yet impaired may be dynamically changed contingent on loss occurrence. This is achieved through put rights of the tranche investors in case of unfavourable collateral performance or by automatic redemption rules, such as amortisation triggers. Early amortisation of senior tranches generally aims at maintaining the original degree of overcollateralisation provided by subordinate tranches, rendering the lower threshold of the most senior tranche $\underline{K}_{sen}$ unattainable by portfolio losses.[2]

In synthetic structures, a dynamic modification of tranche thresholds, increasing overcollateralisation, is achieved by the use of so-called spread accounts. Early senior tranche redemption upon unfavourable collateral performance is a typical true-sale feature and shall no be considered further.[3]

Spread accounts, a credit enhancement available to synthetic transactions, collect all or part of the weakly positive excess spread generated over time. Instead of accruing directly to the originator, the account's balance is put at stake to protect some or all tranches against future loss allocation. Expected tranche loss allocation decreases, as the overcollateralisation ratio, as defined in equation 2.1, of a tranche receiving credit enhancement by the account with value $SA(t^{pay})$ increases to

$$OC_{tr}(t^{pay}) = \frac{\sum_{sub=1}^{tr-1} P_{sub}(t^{pay}) + SA(t^{pay})}{P_{pool}(t^{pay}) + SA(t^{pay})}. \tag{6.1}$$

Hence, overcollateralisation ratios improve dynamically with excess spread growth. Spread accounts appear particularly interesting to the originator, as no initial funding is required. The provision of additional funding clearly improves the effectiveness of the account, but is uncommon in synthetic transactions.

The effects of the presence of a spread account on synthetic CDO valuation can again be

---

2 See Schorin and Weinreich (1998) p. 10 for credit enhancement through early redemption.

3 Clearly, the provision of termination of a super-senior CDS would have comparable effect, reducing the senior premium to zero given timely redemption upon the breach of predefined overcollateralisation levels. However, it is unlikely that the risk transfer is recognised by the regulation authorities with regard to capital relief.

appraised by the portfolio default swap interpretation: On the loss leg, spread accounts lower both probability and severity of tranche loss allocation. On the premium leg, it is expected that, in the dynamic context, periodical premium payments are determined on a higher principal exposure basis, as in the senior/subordinated portfolio derivative case examined so far. Therefore, the improvement of OC-ratios through spread accounts is expected to be an effective means for protection cost reduction and is indeed widely used under different forms. These are subject to further investigation.

6.2 Spread accounts: dynamic improvement of overcollateralisation ratios

The relation between premia payable to the tranche investors and the spread income generated by the reference claims entails that through the life of both true-sale and synthetic CDOs, excess cash-flow is generated, such that any structure, true-sale or synthetic, disposes of a cash position with dynamically increasing value. So far, it has been assumed that the generated excess spread accrues to the issuer at the final maturity when consolidating the SPV or through his stake in an on-balance sheet reference portfolio. Alternatively, the entire cash balance or part of it may be used to cover losses in the reference portfolio, respectively, and thus modify the riskiness of all or some tranches of the capital structure.

Whereas in principle, credit enhancement by spread accumulation may also be used in true-sales, all calculations are again performed for the synthetic case, as derivative contracts provide a higher degree of transparency and generality. The possible extension of results to true-sales is indicated when appropriate.

Excess spread available for credit enhancement is naturally identified for synthetic structures using an SPV. Two variants have been introduced in Chapter 2, see figures 2.3 and 2.4 for graphical representation of the contracts in use, the role of the SPV and related cash-flows. The risk transfer from the originator to the SPV requires a premium payable to the SPV, in exchange for credit protection on the transferred loss range. The spread component of the reference claims is therefore separated from the riskless coupon part, determining the cash inflow to the SPV. This separation is either performed under a full-portfolio transfer that is replicated by single-name CDSs (see figure 2.3) or a partial risk transfer (see figure 2.4) to the SPV under a portfolio default swap referring to the specified loss range. For both alternatives, an increasing spread differential requires the issuance of a minimum of two tranches by the SPV.

The loss allocation rule and corresponding cash-flows are straightforwardly determined by the priority order given by the following extension of the basic loss allocation scheme developed in Chapter 2. The general outline accommodates two possibilities: tranches may either be subordinate to the spread account, or they may receive credit enhancement by the account. From a practical perspective, subordination to a spread account may be the case for a retained junior tranche, but also for a sub-mezzanine stake transferred to a counterparty that is not included into the SPV. Protection by the spread account is normally granted to tranches that are issued by the SPV and consequently, more senior tranches.

(i) If applicable, tranches that are subordinate to the SPV-issued tranches bear losses until the threshold of the lowest tranche issued by the SPV is reached, such that loss allocation is described by (2.3). Accordingly, tranches subordinate to the spread account remain unaffected as long as (2.4) holds.

(ii) When the subordinate position principal is reduced to zero, losses in the reference portfolio are covered through payments from the current spread account balance $SA(t^{pay})$. Neither are settlement payments to be made by the tranche investors, nor do principal reductions take place. Assuming that the spread account gains riskless interest, its balance is recursively determined as

$$\begin{aligned} SA(t^{pay}) &= XS_{SPV}(t^{pay}) + \exp\left(\Delta t^{pay} R_r\left(t^{pay} - \Delta t^{pay}, \Delta t^{pay}\right)\right) \\ &\quad \cdot \max\left[\left(SA(t^{pay} - \Delta t^{pay}) - \max\left[\left(loss(t^{pay} - \Delta t^{pay})\right.\right.\right.\right. \\ &\quad \left.\left.\left.\left. - \sum_{sub=1}^{SA-1} P_{sub}(t^{pay} - \Delta t^{pay})\right), 0\right]\right), 0\right]. \end{aligned} \tag{6.2}$$

The spread account's position in the capital structure is indicated by the subordination index, starting at 1 for junior, such that tranches subordinate to the account are denoted as $sub = 1, ..., SA - 1$.

(iii) Period portfolio losses that are not covered by the current spread account balance are then allocated to tranches issued via the SPV and, if applicable, to the directly-written senior default swap tranche

$$\begin{aligned} P_{tr}(t^{pay}) &= \max\left[P_{tr}(t^{pay} - \Delta t^{pay}) - \max\left[\left(loss(t^{pay}) - SA(t^{pay})\right.\right.\right. \\ &\quad \left.\left.\left. - \sum_{sub=SA+1}^{tr-1} P_{sub}(t^{pay} - \Delta t^{pay})\right), 0\right], 0\right]. \end{aligned} \tag{6.3}$$

The presence of a spread account causes the tranche thresholds to be path-dependent. Consequently, the exact identification of portfolio loss ranges with tranche thresholds $\underline{K}_{tr}$ of tranches senior to the spread account no longer applies. Instead, the current tranche principal evaluates to $P_{tr}(0)$ as long as

$$\sum_{s} (loss(s) - SA(s)) < \underline{K}_{tr},\ s = \Delta t^{pay}, ..., t^{pay}. \tag{6.4}$$

As opposed to the basis structure, the originator's residual claim providing compensation for first-loss retention now consists of two positions: Firstly, the originator is entitled to the final value $SA(T)$ of the spread account held by the SPV. Secondly, a residual claim may be generated on the originator's balance sheet, in the case where only part of the reference portfolio risk has been transferred via the SPV: As in the base case, risk premia of reference claims weakly exceed protection costs payable to the SPV under the swap agreement, creating dynamic excess spread income $XS_{orig}(t^{pay})$ immediately accruing to the originator. Regardless of the actual implementation of the structure, the no arbitrage-condition now requires that both positions are valued equivalently to the first-loss position.

The effectiveness of the spread account on tranche risk reduction is determined by the following structural parameters:

Cash outflow. Premium outflows from the SPV to tranche protection sellers are a function of the tranche principals and the endogenously determined premia.

Cash inflow. Contractual inflows to the SPV differ for both cases under consideration: Promised inflows from the originator to the SPV under a full-portfolio transfer are uniquely determined by the reference claims' par spreads and therefore increasing in reference portfolio riskiness. In case of partial risk transfer via the SPV, cash inflow is a function of the transferred loss range and the portfolio default swap premium, which in turn must be sufficient to meet payment obligations towards trancheholders.

Position. The tranche directly superior to the spread account benefits most from additional overcollateralisation. The first-loss position that is often taken by the account is therefore not necessarily optimal when a maximal premium reduction of issued tranches is to be achieved.

Spread differential. Excess spread accumulation gains momentum with a large spread differential among several tranches.

As excess spread accumulation is determined by the credit derivatives effectuating the risk transfer between the originator and the SPV, the institutional implementation becomes a valuation issue. The contract constellations give rise to a large number of contractual variants. Due to the considerable computational burden associated with premia determination, I restrict the attention to some relevant cases: To start with, full-portfolio risk transfer by an SPV shall be examined. This structure permits to quantify the effect of maximal protection on tranche premia that is attainable, whilst assuring cash-flow sufficiency within the protected portfolio. The analysis is then extended to the forms of credit enhancement encountered in the empirical study, performed in Chapter 7, where partial risk transfer is performed under a portfolio default swap.

The large number of parameters to be chosen when structuring a credit enhanced synthetic transaction obstructs the view that spread accumulation is indeed a straightforward approach to the provision of protection: The originator receives the identical degree of protection as in the senior/subordinate portfolio structure. The key difference is that the protection payment is originally made from the collected spread instead of the tranche protection sellers. As the originator achieves the same degree of protection as in the basis structure, the residual claim must be valued identically to the first losses allocated to a retained junior position. However, the entire originator's position becomes increasingly uncertain the more excess spread is put at stake for credit enhancement, such that maximum effectiveness with respect to tranche premium reduction is a contrary goal to maximum risk transfer.

6.3 Full-portfolio risk transfer

6.3.1 Problem

The structural variant yielding maximal protection through the exploitation of a spread differential is characterised through a transfer of the entire portfolio default risk to the SPV, making excess premia based on the entire portfolio nominal available for tranche protection. Consider again figure 2.3: The cash-account (i.e. the hatched area) held by the SPV, serves the purpose of excess spread accumulation. Albeit less common in synthetic structures, it is the natural choice for fully-funded transactions, characterised by a true-sale of the entire portfolio.[4] Both in the traditional, fully-funded, and the less common synthetic full-portfolio transfer case, the SPV obtains all reference assets' spread payments. Given the separability of the reference spreads from the riskless coupon part,

[4] From a practitioner's view, Hatstadt (2001), for instance, uses a full transfer synthetic structure to highlight the effect of protection through excess spread accumulation.

both structures are indeed equivalent, such that the restriction to the analysis to the synthetic case is without loss of generality.

In order to guarantee that the structure is self-financing, i.e. at no point in time, neither the originator, nor the credit-constrained SPV are required to raise additional funds, it is assumed that portfolio default risk is transferred to the SPV under separate single-name CDSs on the reference bonds. In exchange for portfolio loss protection, the quarterly spread income of the portfolio, as defined by the relationship (2.7) is paid to the SPV.

The single-name CDS risk transfer makes the entire amount of excess spread derived from the reference portfolio $XS_{orig}(t^{pay}) = XS_{SPV}(t^{pay})$, defined according to (5.8), available for credit protection.

The effectiveness of the feature is reduced by premium outflows to trancheholders, defined by (2.8). Two limiting cases are studied, varying with respect to the terms of the junior tranche. The premium of a retained or, from an institutional viewpoint, repurchased junior tranche can be set arbitrarily between zero and the maximum that is fully financed by the reference claims' spread income. The excess spread growth rate is decreasing in the junior premium size, such that the credit enhancing effect of the account is reduced by a large junior premium. Thus, it is indeed a contract parameter that can be chosen to modify superior tranche premia. The two limiting cases are studied:

Variant I: Zero junior premium. Maximum credit enhancement is obtained within a scheme mimicking first-loss retention, the contract scheme examined in the base case. Institutionally, retention of the first-loss piece is equivalent to allocation of the junior tranche to the originator, who receives no premium and obtains no settlement payments until $\underline{K}_{mez}$ is reached. The spread account gains value right from the start, as $\mathcal{S}_{pool}(0) > \mathcal{S}_{tr}(0)$.

Variant II: Maximum junior premium. The lower bound on protection, or the upper bound on tranche premia, respectively, that can be achieved within a full-portfolio transfer structure, is characterised by a setting where the entire initial spread proceeds are used to refinance tranche premia, i.e. $\mathcal{S}_{pool}(0) = \mathcal{S}_{tr}(0)$. The junior premium claim is therefore set equal to

$$s_{jun} = \frac{\mathcal{S}_{pool}(0)P_{pool}(0) - s_{sen}P_{sen}(0) - s_{mez}P_{mez}(0)}{P_{jun}(0)}. \tag{6.5}$$

The spread account will gain positive value after the first default event time.

An alternative solution, providing a degree of enhancement falling between the two limiting cases, as for instance has been presented by Hatstadt (2001), can be implemented under a trigger mechanism: Whereas in low-default scenarios, the junior claimant obtains a contractual premium payment, excess accumulation is triggered once a pre-specified overcollateralisation requirement is violated, such that a positive balance is available before superior tranches suffer losses.

A short note on cash-flow sufficiency is in order: The assumption of premium fixing on the basis of tranche principals at the beginning of the coupon period causes a zero SPV balance to become negative upon the first default event. The incurred SPV insolvency is transitory, as excess spread generation starting next period fills the negative balance with certainty. As the impact of the insolvency problem on tranche valuation is negligible, I do not rule it out. In practice, the provision of a small liquidity reserve by the originator would solve the problem.

The valuation of the issued and retained tranches is formally described by the portfolio default swap pricing equations (5.1) for the issued mezzanine and senior tranches and by (5.6) for junior pieces, respectively. As opposed to the base case, however, the path dependency of the tranche threshold has the effect that CDO tranches are not valued mutually independently, neither with regard to expected loss allocation, nor with regard to average premia, as the spread account balance depends on aggregate premium outflows during previous periods. Therefore, senior and mezzanine tranche premia are determined simultaneously. If applicable, the junior premium is determined by rule (6.5) that enters the valuation system equation. Furthermore, the senior premium is not independent of the partition of the subordinated loss range between the mezzanine and junior tranche: Both junior and mezzanine principals determine the absolute premium payments towards the protection sellers and the contractual premium inflows from the originator, hence determining the cash balance of the spread account held by the SPV.

In the synthetic setting studied, the spread account write-down is used to provide loss protection to the originator under the portfolio of single-name CDSs entered with the SPV. This synthetic variant may also be implemented within a true-sale transaction. In case of fully-funded collateral sale to the SPV, the spread account's balance would be assigned to the protected trancheholder, gaining riskless interest until maturity in order to guarantee contractual coupon and redemption payments.

The originator receives no cash-flows from the reference portfolio until maturity, i.e. $XS_{orig}(t^{pay}) = 0$. Instead, the terminal value of the spread account accrues to him as his residual claim with value $RC_{orig}(0)$. For both scenarios, the originator's no arbitrage-condition (5.10) can be expressed by the terminal value of the spread account

$$RC_{orig}(0) := D_r(0,T)\mathbb{E}_0\left[SA(T)\right] = -CDS_{jun}(0) + \mathbb{E}_0\left[PV(savings)\right]. \tag{6.6}$$

Again, the discretisation error due to loss determination in arrears is taken into account. In variant I, the time-zero value of the junior CDS depends only on expected loss allocation, whereas the value of the junior CDS in variant II takes also a positive periodic premium into account.

The standard deviation of the originator's entire position, comprising the cash-flows that occur under the junior CDS and the final value of the spread account, is computed as

$$\begin{aligned} StdDev_{orig}(0) &= StdDev\left[\sum_{t^{pay}} D_r(0,t^{pay})\left[P_{jun}(t^{pay}) - P_{jun}(t^{pay} - \Delta t^{pay})\right]\right. \\ &\quad \left. + D_r(0,T)SA(T)\right] \end{aligned} \tag{6.7}$$

for variant I and as

$$\begin{aligned} StdDev_{orig}(0) &= StdDev\left[\sum_{t^{pay}} D_r(0,t^{pay})\left[(s_{jun}\Delta t^{pay} - 1)\, P_{jun}(t^{pay} - \Delta t^{pay})\right.\right. \\ &\quad \left.\left. + P_{jun}(t^{pay})\right] + D_r(0,T)SA(T)\right] \end{aligned} \tag{6.8}$$

for variant II. Note that for both variants, the value of the spread account $SA(t^{pay})$ has a different growth rate, causing the final value $SA(T)$ to differ for both full-portfolio transfer variants. For the ease of notation, $SA(t^{pay})$ shall refer to any spread account in this chapter, however, its balance evaluates differently for the structural variants examined. Finally, it shall be annotated that the three-months interest rate $R_r\,(t^{pay} - \Delta t^{pay}, \Delta t^{pay})$ earned on the spread account during future periods is modelled as the time-zero forward rate applicable for the period starting at $t^{pay} - \Delta t^{pay}$ with length Δt^{pay}.

6.3.2 Fair premia

Fair premia for the senior and mezzanine tranches are determined for the principal proportions examined in the base case. Figures 6.1 and 6.2 depict the annualised premia for variants I and II where the entire spread income collected from the reference portfolio is made available for credit enhancement.

Comprehensive valuation results for the different positions of the structures are collected in tables C.2 for variant I and C.3 for variant II in Appendix C. For better comparison, the valuation results for the junior CDS position in variant II are split up into discounted

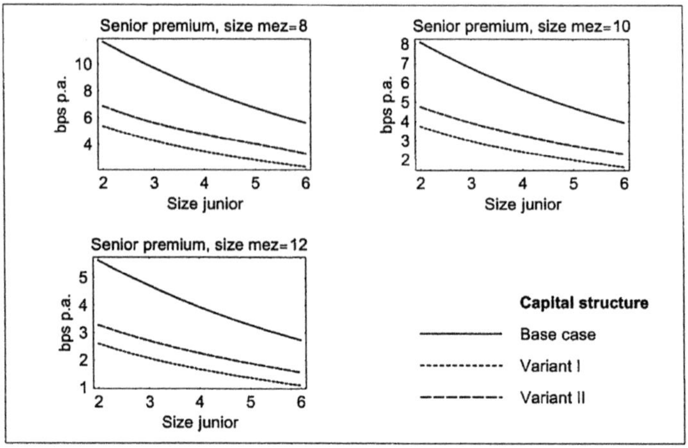

Figure 6.1: **Annualised premium of senior tranche: synthetic SPV spread account collecting the spread income of the entire reference portfolio.**
Variant I provides the maximum degree of protection by minimising premium outflow to liabilities. Variant II provides the minimum degree of protection by setting a premium payable to the junior claimant equal to the maximum that is financed by the reference portfolio.

losses allocated to junior, the loss leg of the swap, as documented for the base case, and the time-zero value of the premium-paying swap. As for the base case, the entire claim of the originator for the respective positions summarises to 0.13, the small discretisation error incurred by late loss determination.

The two assumptions on junior premia characterise the limits of the region of senior and mezzanine premia that are attainable through the choice of the junior premium.

The high premium inflow available for credit enhancement has a considerable effect: Comparison of the loss allocation rates depicted in tables C.2 and C.3 with loss allocation rates for the base case (see table 5.1) shows that protection by spread accumulation reduces expected loss allocation to senior and mezzanine tranches by the order of a half, with the corresponding effect on tranche premia. Premium differences are diminishing in tranche size, as less risky tranches have less need for protection.

The difference between both limiting cases, implying zero and maximal early outflow to the originator, however, depends on the tranche considered. The senior tranche already receives strong protection if the less effective variant II is implemented. When reducing the junior premium to zero in variant I, loss allocation is only slightly reduced, and the premium differences do not exceed two basispoints for the two alternatives I and II. For mezzanine tranches, the availability of additional funds in case of zero early outflow has

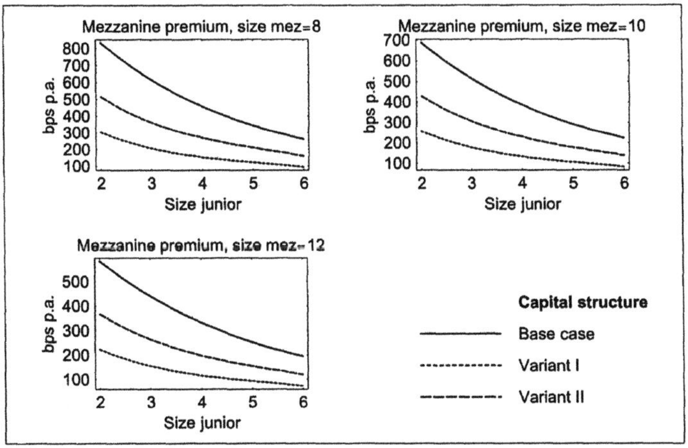

Figure 6.2: **Annualised premium of mezzanine tranche: synthetic SPV spread account collecting the spread income of the entire reference portfolio.**

a notable effect on loss allocation. The difference for the two variants amounts to almost two percentage points for schemes characterised by low overcollateralisation provided by junior. The absolute premium difference diminishes with an increasing threshold $\underline{K}_{mez}$, providing stronger protection by junior.

As secured from primary loss allocation, the junior tranche itself benefits most from additional credit enhancement. As can be seen from a comparison of junior loss allocation shown in tables C.2 and C.3, the expected junior loss rate is highly sensitive to the distinction of the two variants. Albeit irrelevant to the valuation of the originator's claim, which is determined by the aggregated position of the junior CDS cash-flows and the final value of the spread account, the studied credit enhancements are of different desirability under the objective of bank portfolio risk reduction.[5] The volatility of the originator's claim $StdDev_{orig}$ shown in tables C.2 and C.3 as compared with table 5.1 increases heavily upon the introduction of the spread account. The alternatives suggest that residual volatility is clearly decreasing in the contractual size of the junior premium, causing early outflow towards the originator.

[5] A comparison of the structural variants' hedge efficiency is carried out at the end of the chapter.

6.3.3 Funded reserve accounts

The effectiveness of a spread account can still be ameliorated by the provision of initial funding by the originator. Funded accounts are uncommon in synthetic structures, as these are normally easily constructed to meet investor preferences and aim at effective risk transfer rather than liquidity creation. Traditional structures, by contrast, make use of funded reserve accounts to increase the proportion of the structure that attracts cheap funding. The analysis, however, is again facilitated by the CLN-decomposition, such that only the valuation of the tranched CDSs only is required. Thus, albeit performed in the synthetic framework, the analysis applies equally to the true-sale fully-funded case, given that the collateral assets' coupons can be separated into a riskless component and a component for single-name default risk compensation.

Essentially, funding a spread account subordinate to junior extends the first-loss position, thus increasing the overcollateralisation ratios of all tranches. However, the growth rate of the spread account balance is expected to be smaller than in an alternative scenario where the junior tranche is simply enlarged by the spread account initial balance. Excess spread generation is expected to be slower, as the mezzanine and, if applicable, junior tranches, causing high premium outflows are affected later than in the case where the junior tranche is simply extended. The effectiveness of funding for tranche premia reduction therefore merits an investigation.

I determine tranche premia as functions of the initial spread account balance $SA(0)$. With respect to liquidity constraints of an SPV, shortages may occur upon the reduction of the funded reserve account to zero, as the outstanding tranche principals, protected by the reserve account, exceed the current, already reduced reference portfolio nominal. However, as for the unfunded case, excess spread generation fills the negative balance right from the next period, rendering the significance for tranche valuation negligible.

With respect to tranching, I consider only the proportions *Risky* (90/8/2) and *Safe* (86/10/4) that have served as the reference cases for the comparative-static analysis of factor process parameters in section 5.2.

The tranche premium reduction incurred by additional credit enhancement in variants I and II is depicted in figures 6.3 and 6.4 for the *Risky* and *Safe* capital structures, respectively.

Obviously, the extension of the first-loss position is an effective means to reduce tranche premia, notwithstanding the growth rate reduction of excess spread. Further insight is gained from consideration of the positions held by the originator. The valuation of the respective positions is shown in tables 6.1 and 6.2 for the two junior premium variants. The intercepts for both alternatives correspond to the premia obtained for the (90/8/2)

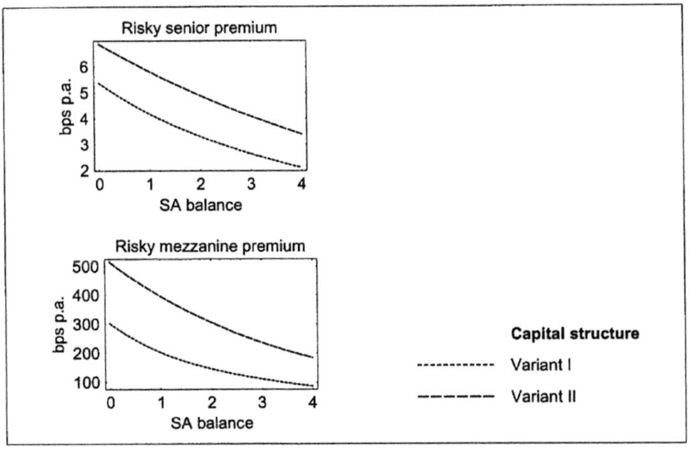

Figure 6.3: **Credit enhancement by a funded reserve account: *Risky* structure.**

and (86/10/4) capital structures examined in the previous section, where the accounts have been initialised at zero balance.

Risky	**Reserve account balance** 0	1	2	3	4
Junior	-1.02	-0.63	-0.40	-0.27	-0.19
Reserve acc.	1.14	1.76	2.53	3.40	4.33
Std dev. orig.	1.56	2.03	2.35	2.59	2.80

Safe	**Reserve account balance** 0	1	2	3	4
Junior	-1.33	-0.86	-0.58	-0.41	-0.31
Reserve acc.	1.44	2.00	2.71	3.54	4.44
Std dev. orig.	2.25	2.55	2.76	2.93	3.09

Table 6.1: **Credit enhancement by a funded reserve account: positions held by the originator, variant I.**

As for the unfunded spread account case, absence of arbitrage requires identity (6.6) to hold, where the initial funding provided by the originator is taken into account

$$RC_{orig}(0) := D_r(0,T)\mathbb{E}_0\left[SA(T)\right] = -CDS_{jun}(0) + SA(0) + \mathbb{E}_0\left[PV(savings)\right]. \quad (6.9)$$

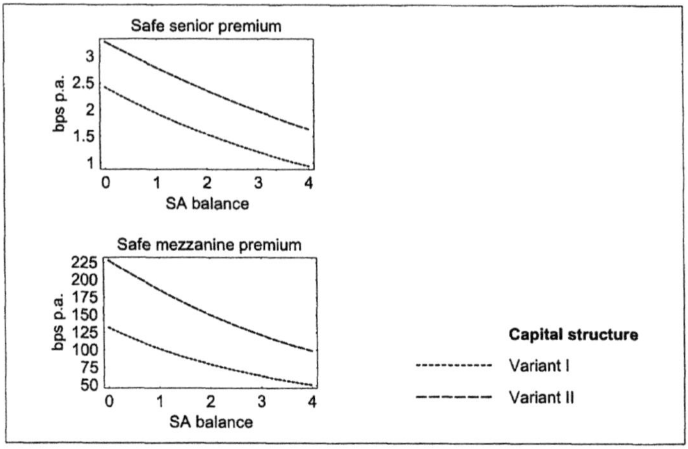

Figure 6.4: **Credit enhancement by a funded reserve account: *Safe* structure.**

It remains to be noted that the provision of funding is indeed costless to the originator, which is easily verified by the computation of the above equation for the obtained values collected in tables 6.1 and 6.2. The reduction of premium outflows to superior tranche protection sellers and the strong protection of the junior claim by the reserve account, on expectation, compensate exactly for the provision of funding. Clearly, the entire position becomes more volatile when the account's initial balance is raised, which makes the structure less desirable from a supervisory perspective.[6]

In case of variant II, an interesting result concerning the marketability of the junior tranche is obtained. As table 6.2 shows, the value of the junior swap is always positive if the reserve account is equipped with a time-zero balance of $SA(0) \geq 1$ and increases in $SA(0)$. As the first-loss position is borne by the reserve account, the junior claim becomes marketable as a standard tranche CDS, issued at par at a contractual premium that is fully financed by portfolio spread income. As opposed to the maximally-set junior premium, the spread generation mechanism will be more effective due to lower early outflows, still lowering issued tranche premia.

6 BCBS (2003) no. 504 requires that a reserve account dedicated to credit enhancement but recorded as an asset by the originator is to be treated as a securitisation exposure, hence attracting regulatory capital to the same extent as a retained CDO tranche at the respective position.

	Reserve account balance				
Risky	0	1	2	3	4
Junior CDS	-0.37	0.68	1.66	2.48	3.14
Loss jun.	-1.63	-1.41	-1.14	-0.88	-0.65
Reserve acc.	0.49	0.45	0.48	0.65	1.00
Std dev. orig.	1.06	1.37	1.65	1.92	2.17

	Reserve account balance				
Safe	0	1	2	3	4
Junior CDS	-0.31	0.77	1.74	2.55	3.18
Loss jun.	-2.61	-2.23	-1.77	-1.35	-1.00
Reserve acc.	0.43	0.36	0.40	0.59	0.96
Std dev. orig.	1.75	2.00	2.22	2.42	2.61

Table 6.2: **Credit enhancement by a funded reserve account: positions held by the originator, variant II.**

6.4 Synthetic partial portfolio risk transfer

6.4.1 Problem

Whereas the full-portfolio risk transfer case corresponds closely to what is observed for true-sales, most synthetic structures accomplish partial risk transfer via an SPV only, usually comprising the loss range whose risk is securitised by CLN-issuance, as depicted in figure 2.4. The senior loss piece is transferred directly under a super-senior swap. Senior tranche premia are therefore directly payable by the originator, which, on one hand, reduces the cash outflow from the SPV. On the other hand, maintaining the premise that protection costs shall be entirely financed through spread proceeds from the reference portfolio, partial risk transfer cannot be financed by the full-portfolio risk premia. Instead, partial risk transfer from the originator to the SPV is performed under a portfolio default swap for the respective loss range.

Unlike as for the full transfer case, the portfolio default swap premium payable in exchange for partial risk transfer is not identified from single-name market spreads. Instead, a constant premium rate s_{SPV} is named in the contractual documentation, applicable only to the currently outstanding principal exposure of the loss range transferred by the SPV. As before, principals are subject to reduction in the case of loss allocation.

Considering cash inflows and outflows of the SPV, weakly positive excess spread is again generated over the tenor of the transaction. The net period excess spread, to be collected on the riskless cash-account included into figure 2.4, is determined as

$$XS_{SPV}(t^{pay}) = (s_{SPV} - S_{tr\,by\,SPV}(t^{pay})) \cdot \sum_{tr\,by\,SPV} P_{tr}(t^{pay}). \tag{6.10}$$

Note that the equivalence of loss determination rules, applying to the originator/SPV portfolio default swap and the CDO tranches, yields identity of principal exposures on both sides of the SPV. The premium payable by the originator to the SPV is normally defined as the initial average premium of tranches issued by the SPV (2.11), such that the net income of the SPV prior to default amounts to zero. Excess spread accumulation stops when the principals of all tranches issued by the SPV are reduced to zero.

As opposed to the full-portfolio risk transfer, excess spread is not only generated within the SPV, but also by the protected portfolio held by the originator: It can be seen from the positions included in figure 2.4, that not only the relationship between the SPV and the note investors represents a loss cascade, but also the relationship between the originator and the SPV. Hence, as long as the reduction of the premium amount $s_{SPV} \sum_{tr\,by\,SPV} P_{tr}(t^{pay})$ payable to the SPV in exchange for credit portfolio protection exceeds the defaulted reference asset spread payment, weakly positive spread is also created, examples to be introduced below. Generally speaking, $XS_{orig}(t^{pay})$ is a function of the spread differential between the portfolio spread income as well as of the premia payable to directly issued, generally super-senior, tranches and the premia payable to the SPV under the portfolio default swap:

$$\begin{aligned} XS_{orig}(t^{pay}) &= S_{pool}(t^{pay}) \\ &\quad \cdot [\#(t^{pay}, risk = 1) + \#(t^{pay}, risk = 2) + \#(t^{pay}, risk = 3)] \\ &\quad - \sum_{tr\,direct} s_{tr} P_{tr}(t^{pay}) - s_{SPV} \sum_{tr\,by\,SPV} P_{tr}(t^{pay}). \end{aligned} \tag{6.11}$$

As the final value of the spread account accrues to the originator, both claims add up to the residual claim, evaluated at the origination date to

$$RC_{orig}(0) := \mathbb{E}_0 \left[\sum_{t^{pay}} D_r(0, t^{pay}) XS_{orig}(t^{pay})) \right] + \mathbb{E}_0 \left[D_r(0, T) SA(T) \right], \tag{6.12}$$

where $XS_{orig}(t^{pay})$ accrues directly to the originator. This component of reference portfolio spread is therefore not available to the spread account providing additional overcollateralisation.

In order to assess the effectiveness of partially-financed spread accounts, I consecutively alter the contract parameters as follows:[7]

Variant I: SPV for junior and mezzanine transfer. To start with, the loss range transferred via the SPV is set to its maximum excluding the directly-written super-senior CDS by including both the junior tranche and a single mezzanine tranche into the SPV.

As for the full-portfolio transfer case, the junior premium is a free parameter, which can be set arbitrarily to alter the effectiveness of protection. I set the junior premium to its maximum, such that solvency of the SPV is guaranteed when the premium payable to the SPV is set equal to the weighted average at origination $s_{SPV} = \mathcal{S}_{tr\,by\,SPV}(0)$.[8] As for the full-portfolio transfer analogue, the SPV experiences maximal early outflow, such that excess spread generation starts upon the first default event. The spread account takes the first-loss position.

The standard deviation of the originator's entire position, made up by the premium-bearing junior CDS, the final value of the spread account and the residual on-balance sheet spread claim is determined as

$$\begin{aligned} StdDev_{orig}(0) &= StdDev\Bigg[\sum_{t^{pay}} D_r(0,t^{pay})\left[\left(s_{jun}\Delta t^{pay}-1\right)P_{jun}(t^{pay}-\Delta t^{pay})\right. \\ &\quad \left. + P_{jun}(t^{pay}) + XS_{orig}(t^{pay})\right] + D_r(0,T)SA(T)\Bigg]. \end{aligned} \tag{6.13}$$

Variant II: splitting the mezzanine tranche. Variant II explores the effect of the creation of an additional spread differential, leaving other elements unaltered. This is achieved by splitting the mezzanine loss range into two tranches, $mez2$ being subordinated to $mez1$. Three tranches are issued by the SPV, of which the junior is assigned to the originator. The rule for junior and portfolio default swap premium determination is unaltered. The exploitation of a larger spread differential is expected to reduce tranche riskiness further. With respect to the volatility of the originator's stake in the structure, (6.13) applies.

Variant III: SPV for mezzanine only. Finally, the loss range transferred by the SPV is reduced to mezzanine only, which in turn issues two tranches, as in variant II. The portfolio premium payable for the entire mezzanine transfer is determined as the

7 The structural variants to be examined are defined in anticipation of the empirical comparison with observed spreads of synthetic structures.

8 Clearly, the junior premium in connection with the portfolio default swap premium payable to the SPV is again a degree of freedom to the capital structure.

weighted average premium at issuance, whilst the specification of a junior premium is irrelevant to the valuation problem. Institutionally, the originator simply leaves the first-loss piece unprotected. The reduction of the loss range transferred by the SPV reduces cash-inflows from the structure. As excess spread accumulation starts once the junior principal is written-down to zero, the spread account only provides protection to the issued mezzanine and senior tranches and therefore takes a second-loss position. The volatility of the originator's position is described by

$$
\begin{aligned}
StdDev_{orig}(0) &= StdDev\Bigg[\sum_{t^{pay}} D_r(0,t^{pay})\left[P_{jun}(t^{pay}) - P_{jun}(t^{pay} - \Delta t^{pay})\right.\\
&\quad \left. + XS_{orig}(t^{pay})\right] + D_r(0,T)SA(T)\Bigg]. \qquad (6.14)
\end{aligned}
$$

The valuation problems are again solved by the simultaneous determination of two or three tranche issuance premia, taking the modified loss allocation scheme into account. Furthermore, the rules determining the respective portfolio default swap and junior premia as functions of the issued tranche premia must be integrated.

6.4.2 Fair premia

Figures 6.5 and 6.6 compare the resulting senior and mezzanine premia of the three variants using the SPV for partial risk transfer with the base case without credit enhancement.

Comprehensive valuation results are documented in tables C.4, C.5, and C.6 for the three variants under consideration.

Senior tranche premia depicted in figure 6.5 solve the swap pricing equation (5.1). The risk reducing-effect of the spread account collecting the premium inflows from partial risk transfer is clearly smaller when compared to the structures where the full-portfolio spread income is made available for tranche enhancement, see figures 6.1 and 6.2 for comparison of fair issuance premia.

The senior premium reduction is small for all variants: The most effective variant II, combining a large principal basis with a high spread differential, yields a premium reduction of less than two basispoints compared with the base case for all capital structures examined. The effect of splitting the mezzanine tranche can be assessed by comparing the base case with variant III (issuing two mezzanine tranches via the SPV) and by comparing variant I and variant II (both issuing junior and mezzanine via the SPV, where variant II splits the mezzanine range). It is seen that mezzanine splitting yields only a very small

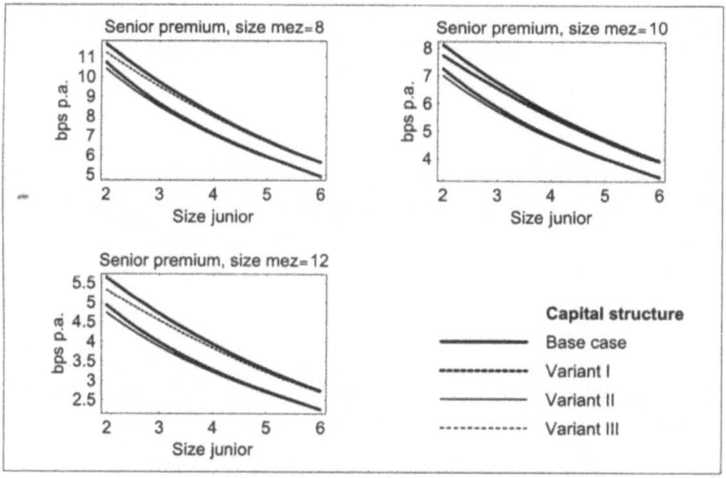

Figure 6.5: **Senior premium: partial risk transfer via SPV.**
Variant I transfers both junior and mezzanine via the SPV, variant II splits the mezzanine range in two tranches, hence accelerating excess spread growth, and variant III transfers a two-tranche mezzanine range only via the SPV, thus reducing the principal basis for spread accumulation.

reduction of fair senior premia.

Mezzanine tranches, by contrast, do indeed receive significant support from the spread account when compared to the base case: For better comparison of the one-mezzanine variants (base case and variant I) with the two mezzanine variants (II and III), figure 6.6 depicts the weighted average of both mezzanine premia $\mathcal{S}_{pool}(0)$ as defined in the basic valuation setup (see equation (5.2)). For variant III, the weighted average premium corresponds to the portfolio default swap premium that applies to the entire mezzanine range payable by the originator to the SPV. The average mezzanine premium thus quantifies nominal protection costs at origination. A puzzling observation is made when average mezzanine premia of the base case and variant III are compared, and the same holds true if variant I and II are compared: The credit enhancing excess spread accumulation mechanism of variant II and III, including two mezzanine tranches, is supposed to be more efficient with regard to tranche risk reduction, as has been confirmed for senior tranches above. However, the figure shows that average mezzanine premia indeed experience an increase when a second mezzanine tranche is introduced. The puzzle is solved by reconsidering the asymmetric principal reduction rule in the event of default occurrence, which has been discussed for the basic valuation model in Chapter 5. The nominal premium increase required by the more subordinate $mez2-$investors, applicable to a fast decreasing principal basis exceeds the decrease in the more senior nominal $mez1-$premium, appli-

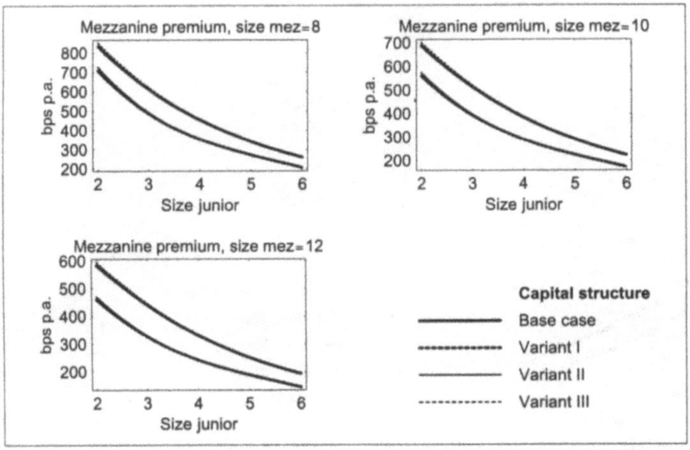

Figure 6.6: **Mezzanine premium: partial risk transfer via SPV.**
In case of issuance of two mezzanine tranches, the weighted average premium at origination is given.

cable to a more stable principal basis than in the one-mezzanine capital structures. The actual effectiveness of the spread account collecting the spread differential of two mezzanine tranches is therefore better assessed by a comparison of total loss allocation, which must equal total premium outflows to mezzanine tranche investors. Mean loss rates of the entire mezzanine loss piece are depicted in figure 6.7.

The increase of the spread differential obtained by mezzanine splitting does indeed improve the efficiency of the spread account. However, the differences to the otherwise equivalent one-mezzanine structures is small, as has already been stated for senior tranches.

6.5 Summary and evaluation of the hedging quality of spread accounts

To summarise, the effectiveness of excess spread accounts, making the excess income generated within an SPV transferring all or part of credit portfolio risk to market participants, is judged as follows: In principle, a spread account can be implemented as a powerful feature to reduce both senior and mezzanine tranche riskiness, leaving the value of the originator's stake unaltered, even when no additional funding is provided. The comparison not only between the full-portfolio risk transfer variants and the partial-portfolio risk transfer alternatives, but also among the partial risk transfer variants including different

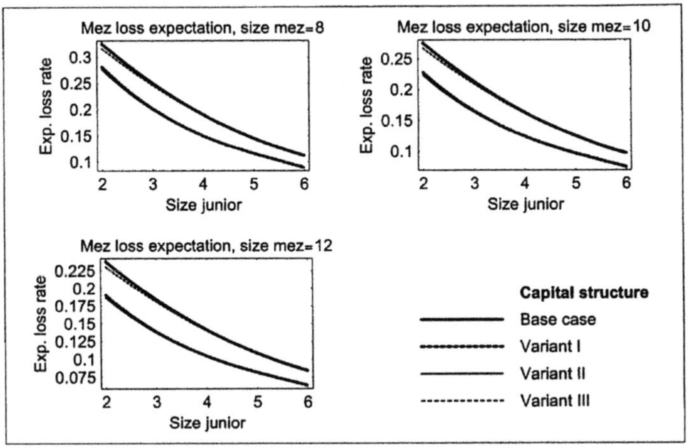

Figure 6.7: **Expected mezzanine loss rate: partial risk transfer via SPV.**

tranches in the SPV for the purpose of spread accumulation, shows that the principal range included into the SPV turns out to be the most relevant contract parameter for the credit-enhancing effect: The effect on expected loss allocation is increasing in the absolute principal exposure that is transferred by the SPV.

Full-portfolio transfer to the SPV, implemented through single-name CDSs for the analysis at hand, but capturing the risk profile of a well-designed true-sale, does indeed open the way to effective credit enhancement by excess spread accumulation. I find that combined with additional funding of the account, marketability of the junior piece under form of CDS or sinking-fund debt can be even achieved.

Synthetic structures using partial risk transfer by the SPV, by contrast, exhibit little scope for effective cash accumulation. The aim of maximising the principal of the directly-written senior swap tranche opposes the implementation of an effective credit enhancement, as the loss range in which excess spread is being generated is small. The inclusion of the junior tranche in the SPV is the only means to yield a significant premium reduction. Note that if the junior premium is reduced, potentially to zero, while maintaining the entire portfolio default swap premium at the exactly refinanced level, further mezzanine- and senior premium reductions would be achieved. Additional subdivision of the mezzanine range yields almost no improvement in overcollateralisation by the account.

The spread differential between several tranches on the liability side, determining the outflow reduction upon loss occurrence, appears to be largely realised by the basic three-tranche capital structure. As mezzanine tranche principals, to which further tranching

			SPV: full		SPV: partial		
Originator	**Unprotected**	**Base case**	**I**	**II**	**I**	**II**	**III**
Risky							
Std dev. orig.	3.96	0.44	1.60	1.07	0.60	0.59	0.64
95%-Quantile	-7.53	-0.30	-1.84	-1.36	-0.62	-0.62	-0.55
Safe							
Std dev. orig.	3.96	1.05	2.31	1.78	1.43	1.42	1.12
95%-Quantile	-7.53	-0.77	-3.53	-2.51	-1.63	-1.62	-0.97

Table 6.3: **Effectiveness of risk transfer under the examined capital structures.** Standard deviations and quantiles refer to risk-neutral distributions of the discounted sum of period cash-flows accruing to the originator.

applies, are small when compared to the full transaction nominal, the effect of mezzanine spread differential is almost negligible. Protection costs incurred by the originator at origination even experience an increase, as the reduction of total loss allocation takes effect over time.

The installation of an effective tranche enhancement, however, comes at the cost of an increase in uncertainty about the aggregate payoff to the originator, and thus lowers the degree of credit risk transfer achieved by the structure. The amount of risk actually transferred by a given structure is revealed by the dispersion of cash-flows allocated to the originator. However, only the loss stochastic defined under the risk-neutral measure may be considered within the approach taken. Table 6.3 compares the hedging quality of all capital structures under consideration from the originator's viewpoint for the tranche dimensions *Risky* and *Safe*.

The standard deviation of the discounted sum of period cash-flows accruing to the originator is reported, together with the 5%-quantiles of the same variable, characterising the undesirable outcomes. Even the most effective full-portfolio spread mechanisms have a considerable effect on obligor exposure reduction, when compared to the dispersion measures of discounted cash-flows from the unprotected portfolio.

It is evident that the originator retains a higher residual exposure when entering a full transfer structure than when entering a partial transfer structure or the base case. The originator's residual exposure in the partial transfer structures, however, is not monotonic in the impact of credit enhancement on tranche premium reduction. This is a consequence of the number of mezzanine tranches issued, altering nominal premia and the loss allocation sequence.

A concluding remark on the role of SPVs in synthetic structures is in order: Whereas SPVs currently appear to be primarily used in order to guarantee bankruptcy-remoteness of deposited cash collateral, their role may straightforwardly be altered towards the collection of excess spread in order to provide cost-efficient credit enhancement, given that the loss range transferred by the intermediary provides enough potential for cash accumulation.

Chapter 7

Empirical Pricing Comparison: the Case for Synthetic CBOs

7.1 Market environment and sample selection

In this final chapter, an empirical pricing comparison for a specific class of CDOs, namely synthetic CBOs, is carried out.

The introductory outline given in Chapter 2 distinguishes CBOs and CLOs, that may both be implemented as true-sale and as synthetic transactions. Within this context, the selection of sample transactions has been made on the basis of the following considerations. In addition, the possibility of active collateral trading, distinguishing market-value CDOs from cash-flow CDOs, has been addressed.

Consider CLOs, the transaction type dominating the German market: As a consequence of banking confidentiality, both traditional and synthetic bank balance sheet CLOs only communicate collateral composition on an aggregate basis. Furthermore, the empirical approach pursued so far relies on the availability of market spreads. Obligor default risk pricing on the basis of market-traded assets is normally not available when considering loan portfolios, as these often consist of a large number of small corporate debtors having little access to market-based refinancing. Hence, CLOs appear to some extent unsuitable for a precise pricing comparison.

A slightly different picture results from the consideration of CBOs: On one hand, the lack of market risk pricing also applies to true-sale CBOs. As has been argued in section 2.2.1, the need for bond securitisation arises from restricted trading in sub-investment grade collateral, which indicates a lack of credit risk pricing. Synthetic bond securitisation, on the other hand, relies on the availability of market-priced reference claims. The disclosure of the identity of the reference assets underlying the single-name or portfolio default swaps involved in the transactions is not affected by legal confidentiality constraints. The manageable number of reference names, mostly linked to market-traded bonds with a certain degree of liquidity, and the pure transfer of default loss risk facilitate the analysis of this product class considerably. The incentives created by the regulatory recognition of risk transfer and lower protection costs, as compared to an on-balance sheet hedge by single-name CDSs achieved by first-loss retention, indicate the significance of this type.

Relevance of market risk to the structure poses minor problems to a valuation model. However, a dynamic change of the reference portfolio composition requires an a priori characterisation of trading behaviour according to transaction-specific contractual trading restrictions, such that the obtained results would be of little generality. Therefore, the restriction of the analysis to static cash-flow deals is maintained.

The identification of deals to be considered as synthetic CBOs is hampered by the fact that CDOs are bespoke securities, usually considered as buy-and-hold investments. The availability of CDO issuance information is clearly affected by confidentiality concerns towards counterparties. Deal-specific publicly available information is therefore rather limited and must be complemented by contractual documentation on the implementation of risk transfer. A publicly available source of information is the web-based magazine Structured Finance International.[1] The magazine publishes quarterly data on the origination of transactions securitising non-US assets, partly including tranche dimensioning and issuance spreads together with an indication of the collateral type. Additional offering information has been provided by banks involved in the transactions, either as structuring parties or acting on behalf of customers. For the transactions considered, the description of reference claims has been disclosed to investors on a single-obligor basis. In order to respect confidentiality concerns regarding the lending relationships among the originating bank and the creditors whose risk has been securitised, a breakdown to the single-issuer level shall not be reported. The bond sample selection for model estimation has been made on the basis of the issuers indicated in the offering information.

In addition to these practical considerations, it is desirable that the transactions considered have been issued in the same market environment. The time of the sample selection decision, the end of the year 2001, is related to the fact that synthetic CBOs firstly emerged in 2001 – the period with the most pronounced sudden spread widening ever observed. Reconsidering the selection of bond data used for spread estimation, discussed in detail in section 4.2, corporate bond issuance activity has been considerable in the years following the EMU currency accord. It has been argued that the data requirements for the factor model estimation could be fulfilled. Since mid-2000, spread availability based on recently-issued, comparatively liquid corporate bonds has been satisfactory.

---

1 See http://www.ew.sfi.com.

The synthetic transactions finally selected originate from between April and December 2001. On one hand, the spread widening appears undesirable with respect to transaction comparison. On the other hand, the factor model parameter estimates have turned out to be rather robust against the extreme event.[2] With regard to the timing structure, it should be noted that the pricing analysis is performed within sample: The sample period for factor model estimation starts in July 2000 and ends in December 2001, exploiting the spread series depicted in figure 4.1 for factor model estimation. All CDO origination dates therefore fall into the period used for underlying factor estimation. This has the desirable implication that for every transaction, estimates for the factor realisations at origination are available: These have been obtained from the update step of the Kalman filter recursion, such that portfolio loss forecasts for all four transactions can be made taking into account the appropriate initial values of factors. With regard to model-based loss forecasting, I maintain the assumption made so far that initial values of credit factors are determined only by the risk levels. As has been stated in section 5.1.2.4, all factors evolve independently over time, maintaining the orthogonal structure when conditioning on the initial values.

The timeline of the origination dates of synthetic CBOs selected for empirical study, together with the estimated factor series, is depicted in figure 7.1. Three of the four transaction analyses rely on information that has been publicly available. One transaction is a private placement, of which contractual information is considered as confidential. It is thus encoded as 'Private'.

The lower graph includes five-year par spreads of the three risk levels, as determined by the affine factor model. These are obtained by model evaluation at the factor realisations observed on the date depicted on the abscissa. Par spreads firstly give a picture of the current market pricing of credit at the origination dates of the transactions. With regard to CDO pricing, they determine the spread income that is obtained from the reference asset portfolio, hence, the variable $\mathcal{S}_{pool}(t^{pay})$.

The factor series is rather unstable, albeit well in line with observed volatile spread time-series behaviour, see again figure 4.1. CDO issuance has taken place at points in time with different factor estimates. The issuance timeline is related to estimated factor paths and the current credit market environment as follows. The first transaction, Repon 15, is characterised by spread factor realisations moderately exceeding the time-series averages used for loss forecasting so far. $f_c(t)$ exhibits a peak, such that default risk pricing is considered to be high at origination of Repon 15. Scala 3, by contrast, benefits from overall low factor estimates, especially for the common $f_c(t)$. Anticipating model-based loss forecasting, one expects that mutual dependence of loss events is built up over time

---

2 See tables 4.8 and C.1.

Repon 15	Life[years]					5
	Nominal mio. EUR					3000
	Aaa/Aa : A : Baa[%]					10.00 : 53.33 : 36.67
	#reference assets					120
	Risk transfer					Direct swap/CLN
	Spread account					None
	Origination date					11/04/01
	Single-name valuation					
	Model spreads Aaa/Aa : A : Baa[bps]					88.5 : 117.2 : 138.4
	$S_{pool}(0)[bps]$					122.1
	Capital structure		**Spread $s_{tr}[bps]$**		**Exp. loss rate[%]**	
	$P_{tr}(0)[\%]$	**Rating**	**Market**	**Model**	**Valuation**	**Rating**
Senior	92.0	CDS	-	20.7	0.9	0.0
Mezzanine	3.4	AAA	38	703.8	28.6	2.8
	0.8	AAA	75	1338.0	48.7	11.4
	1.0	BBB+	220	1836.4	48.4	21.7
	0.7	BBB-	375	2558.2	72.4	37.6
Junior	2.1	Retained	-	-	87.8	73.2

Table 7.1: **Term sheet Repon 15.**

Model valuation results are included. Expected tranche loss allocation is normalised by the initial tranche principal and has been computed under the risk-neutral measure as the normalised gross value of a tranche swap. Expected tranche loss rates computed under the empirical measure may provide the basis of a tranche rating assignment.

by the mean-reversion effect. Repon 16 has been issued in the most difficult market environment observed: The high $f_c(t)$ estimate causes overall default risk and reference spreads to be high after issuance. Origination conditions for Private are still adversely affected by the spread increase in 2001.

7.2 Sample transactions

Sample term sheets collecting the relevant facts on the four structures to be studied are given in tables 7.1 to 7.4, together with valuation results and tranche loss expectations to be discussed later in the next section.

All structures are similar with respect to underlying credit quality. Exposure is only to investment grade corporate credit, with an overall emphasis on European names. Indeed, the issuance information reveals that the European reference names included largely intersect. With respect to regional diversification, Repon 15 and 16 both exhibit considerable exposure to US names, whereas Private exclusively and Scala 3 to a large extent securitise European credit risk. All transactions are widely diversified among industries.

Scala 3	Life[years]					5
	Nominal mio. EUR					805
	Aaa/Aa : A : Baa[%]					11.25 : 55.00 : 33.75
	#reference assets					80
	Risk transfer					SPV mezzanine
	Spread account					Partial, variant III
	Origination date					27/06/01
	Single-name valuation					
	Model spreads Aaa/Aa : A : Baa[bps]					66.4 : 96.3 : 108.8
	$\mathcal{S}_{pool}(0)[bps]$					97.2
	Capital structure		**Spread $s_{tr}[bps]$**		**Exp. loss rate[%]**	
	$P_{tr}(0)[\%]$	Rating	Market	Model	Valuation	Rating
Senior	92.30	CDS	-	12.1	0.3	0.0
Mezzanine	3.38	A1	120	545.0	15.0	1.3
	0.62	A3	180	973.2	30.7	5.9
	1.30	Baa3	330	1528.6	45.1	14.1
Junior	2.40	Retained	-	-	75.0	50.6

Table 7.2: **Term sheet Scala 3.**

Model valuation results are included. Expected tranche loss allocation is normalised by the initial tranche principal and has been computed under the risk-neutral measure as the normalised gross value of a tranche swap. Expected tranche loss rates computed under the empirical measure may provide the basis of a tranche rating assignment.

With respect to the adaption of the model such that the reference portfolio characteristics are captured, I take the actual risk-level assignment as conveyed by the letter rating at origination as a classification device. I adhere to the subdivision into nine fictive sector-related subportfolios, exhibiting identical spread and risk evolution.

The reference claims' contract specifications have not been fully disclosed in the sales information available. However, the results are expected to be fairly robust towards payment dates, as payments among counterparties depend only upon the reference claims' specification in the case of default. Pre-default coupon bond prices are rather insensitive towards coupon period and maturity, such that the cash-flow timing assumptions made so far are maintained.[3] Reference claims are again assumed to trade at par on issuance, by setting coupons equal to the par coupons implied by the factor model. Par spreads as the single-issuer default risk premia payable in arrears are given in the tables. These are obtained as the model spreads at origination and can be read from the lower graph of figure 7.1. In addition, the average portfolio spread $\mathcal{S}_{pool}(0)$, weighted according to the breakdown of reference assets among rating classes is reported.

3 The minor relevance of maturity is a consequence of the assumption of interest rate and credit risk independence.

Repon 16	Life[years]					5
	Nominal mio. EUR					3000
	Aaa/Aa : A : Baa[%]					14.18 : 48.51 : 37.31
	#reference assets					134
	Risk transfer					Direct swap/CLN
	Spread account					None
	Origination date					26/09/01
	Single-name valuation					
	Model spreads Aaa/Aa : A : Baa[bps]					84.8 : 154.2 : 123.2
	$S_{pool}(0)[bps]$					132.8
	Capital structure		**Spread** $s_{tr}[bps]$		**Exp. loss rate[%]**	
	$P_{tr}(0)[\%]$	**Rating**	**Market**	**Model**	**Valuation**	**Rating**
Senior	94.44	CDS	-	49.0	2.2	0.1
Mezzanine	1.51	CDS	-	1598.5	55.3	10.1
	0.67	AA	80	2272.4	68.5	21.8
	0.30	A	150	2544.4	72.4	28.2
	0.56	private	230	3217.6	79.9	39.2
	0.60	CDS	-	3975.1	84.8	53.3
	0.25	CDS	-	4603.1	87.8	65.0
Junior	1.66	Retained	-	-	94.6	85.5

Table 7.3: **Term sheet Repon 16.**

Model valuation results are included. Expected tranche loss allocation is normalised by the initial tranche principal and has been computed under the risk-neutral measure as the normalised gross value of a tranche swap. Expected tranche loss rates computed under the empirical measure may provide the basis of a tranche rating assignment.

Private	Life[years]					5.5
	Nominal mio. EUR					910
	Aaa/Aa : A : Baa[%]					10.00 : 50.00 : 40.00
	#reference assets					100
	Risk transfer					SPV jun & mez
	Spread account					Partial, variant II
	Origination date					19/12/01
	Single-name valuation					
	Model spreads Aaa/Aa : A : Baa[bps]					97.1: 144.7 : 143.6
	$S_{pool}(0)[bps]$					139.5
	Capital structure		**Spread $s_{tr}[bps]$**		**Exp. loss rate[%]**	
	$P_{tr}(0)[\%]$	**Rating**	**Market**	**Model**	**Valuation**	**Rating**
Senior	90.44	CDS	-	21.6	1.1	0.0
Mezzanine	2.53	Aa1	90	495.2	22.4	1.0
	3.74	A3	190	1202.1	47.0	9.3
Junior	3.30	Repurch.	1243	1243.0	84.5	59.6

Table 7.4: **Term sheet Private.**

Model valuation results are included. Expected tranche loss allocation is normalised by the initial tranche principal and has been computed under the risk-neutral measure as the normalised gross value of a tranche swap. Expected tranche loss rates computed under the empirical measure may provide the basis of a tranche rating assignment. The interest-bearing junior tranche is repurchased by the originator.

Granularity is comparably high for all reference portfolios considered: Portfolios are of comparable size and neither portfolio exhibits concentrations in single positions.

With respect to the subordination schemes, the transactions differ in tranche dimensioning, institutional implementation, and the provision of credit enhancement. Whereas the transactions considered are comparable with respect to the senior tranche, directly issued as a super-senior CDS comprising between 90.44% and notable 94.44% of the reference portfolio nominal, mezzanine dimensions are quite diverse. The number of mezzanine tranches ranges from two to six, whereas information on premia is only publicly available for tranches issued as CLNs. This is due to the fact that CLN-tranches receive an agency rating, such that the agencies' risk assessments may provide information on which tranches may be offered. Monitoring and rating updates through the life of a structure provide a basis for secondary trade. Rating assessments for CDSs, however, are uncommon, as these do not provide investment opportunities. As for the super-senior CDS, a highly-rated financial institution is an appropriate counterparty, ensuring that capital relief is granted. Overcollateralisation provided by a retained or repurchased junior tranche, however, is small for all transactions, measured by the alternative capital structures examined in detail in Chapters 5 and 6.

The institutional implementation of risk transfer is related to the exploitation of excess spread providing credit enhancement by increasing OC ratios of issued tranches. The contract details included in the term sheet tables 7.1 to 7.4 convey the mode of risk transfer and the variant of excess spread mechanism that actually apply to the transactions: The Repon-transactions are directly issued by the originator or use single-tranche SPVs whose only purpose is to hold CLN cash collateral and to pass-through payments between originator and protection seller. Thus, excess spread is not available for tranche protection, such that the Repon 15 and 16 transactions correspond precisely to the basic senior/subordinate portfolio derivative structure examined in detail in Chapter 5. Scala 3 and Private, by contrast, use SPVs for multi-tranche issuance, such that excess spread is exploited for credit enhancement. Full-portfolio transfer, associated with maximum excess spread efficiency, is not observed in the synthetic CBO transactions considered. Instead, the partial portfolio risk transfer concepts examined in section 6.4 are applied: Private uses the partial risk transfer variant II, combining junior inclusion with further mezzanine tranching, which has shown to be rather efficient for credit enhancement. The free contract parameter, the junior premium s_{jun}, determining early outflows from the account towards the originator, is reported to amount to 12.43%. Scala 3 makes use of excess spread generated within an SPV transferring only three mezzanine tranches (partial portfolio risk transfer, variant III), which has been judged as rather inefficient with regard to tranche premium reduction. For both structures, Scala and Private, risk transfer between the originator and SPV is established under portfolio default swaps, whose premium is set equal to the weighted average of SPV-issued tranche spreads at origination. For model application, this contract parameter is obtained by evaluating 5.2 as a function of premia of those tranches issued by the SPV.

7.3 Rating assessments and tranche valuation

7.3.1 Variables of interest

Evaluation of the factor model for the four sample transactions takes all contract parameters described above into account: Slight deviations in reference asset quality, as conveyed by the agency ratings, are accounted for. I respect the slight maturity extension of Private (see table 7.4). Tranche dimensions are chosen in accordance to the issuance information available. In addition, spread-based credit enhancements are integrated, precisely as was explored in the general sections before.

Valuation results are reported in the lower parts of the transaction tables: I include fair tranche issuance premia, reported in the column 'Spread'. In addition, loss expectations are included. Those are again normalised by the tranches' principal values. As indicated in the tables, loss expectations are obtained in two distinct ways. The loss measure applying to the valuation context is subsumed under the column 'Valuation': Expected tranche loss rates normalise the gross value of the tranche swap legs by the tranche principal. In addition, an approximate measure for real-world loss forecasts can, at the very least, be obtained. In principle, factors that determine loss rates under the empirical measure are obtained by assuming zero factor risk pricing. Hence, I extend the analysis performed for zero market pricing of factor risk (see section 5.2.3) to the four sample transactions: The column 'Rating' depicts the loss rate expectations taken under the physical measure, determined by evaluating all expectations for zero market price of risk parameters. Effectively, the relative tranche loss rates, as depicted in table 5.6 within the comparative-static model analysis, are computed for all tranches of the four sample transactions.

The rating-relevant tranche loss rates can be mapped into letter ratings using the agency classifications: For not only CDOs, but also for single-name defaultable zero-bonds, an indication of expected values taken under the physical measure is obtained by evaluating the bond pricing relationships for zero market-price of risk parameters. For graphical representation, reconsider figure 4.3, depicting the term structures of expected losses of one unit of zero-bond principal as a function of the time horizon. The expected values of losses of bond rating classes provide an approximate measure of an according rating assignment of CDO tranches, presumed that rating is indeed performed on the basis of an expected value of losses, expressed in absolute terms.

The valuation results and evidence of a tranche rating assignment, corresponding to CDO tranche model loss expectation taken under the real-world measure, are summarised in the following sections.

7.3.2 Timeline of CDO issuance

Consider the timeline of the CDO issuance sample in conjunction with the estimated factor series and single-name spreads depicted in figure 7.1: Both in the valuation context and with regard to model-based tranche rating, the differences between transactions are pronounced. The origination timeline, as depicted in figure 7.1 together with estimated factor paths, is important for transaction model valuation, as the initial state vector is highly persistent due to low risk-neutral mean reversion rates (reconsider table 4.8 on reversion rates and half-lives).

A glance at the tranches' agency ratings and reported real-world issuance spreads reveals that the spread widening in autumn 2001, observed in the bond market as depicted in figure 7.1, has not translated to the CDO market at the same scale. This is seen by the following comparison of mezzanine tranches receiving an AA/Aa-rating.[4]

Repon 15 and Repon 16 are closely comparable: Both transactions are directly issued by the originator without performing credit enhancement. However, the first transaction has been issued in a stable environment and the second has been issued during the high-spread period. Despite the differences in the tranching scheme, a common aspect is that both transactions exhibit a mezzanine tranche rated AA. In both transactions, the tranche under consideration relates to the loss ranges $\underline{K}_{AA}(R15) = 3.80$, $P_{AA}(R15) = 0.80$ and $\underline{K}_{AA}(R16) = 3.37$, $P_{AA}(R16) = 0.67$. Both tranches have been issued at comparable spreads of $s_{AA}(R15) = 75$ bps and $s_{AA}(R16) = 80$ bps. The slightly better pool quality as expressed by reference obligor ratings of the Repon 16 transaction appears the only factor to account for a meager 5 bps spread increase, given the difficult credit market environment.

Observed rating assignments and reported issuance spreads of the Scala 3 transaction issued in the low-spread environment are in line neither with the fair valuation according to the origination timeline nor with factor estimates: Even for the superior mezzanine tranche, comprising a considerably less risky range of $\underline{K}_{A1}(Scala) = 4.32$, $P_{A1}(Scala) = 3.38$, only a A1-rating is being granted, the tranche therefore issued at $s_{A1}(Scala) = 120$ bps. The slightly worse reference pool quality as compared to Repon 15 again appears unlikely to account for the considerably higher reported issuance spread, given the stable credit market environment.

When relating CDO origination timing to the estimated factor series, Private stands out from the remaining transactions: The rating and reported issuance valuation of Private corresponds to some extent to the spread evolution. Issued at the end of the sample period, a comparatively large overcollateralisation ratio together with the spread account on mezzanine and junior, is being required such that the tranche defined by $\underline{K}_{Aa1}(Private) = 7.04$, $P_{Aa1}(Private) = 2.53$ receives an Aa1-rating.[5] The issuance spread $s_{Aa1} = 90$ bps is comparable to the AA-tranches of the Repon transactions.

Altogether, I conclude that observed CDO issuance terms are detached from the single-name credit market environment.

---

4 It is beyond the scope of the present work to discuss the differences in the CDO rating approaches determining the Moody's and Standard and Poor's CDO tranche letter ratings, all the more so, as the precise numerical assumptions entering rating approaches are undisclosed. I only use letter ratings for identification of the tranches under consideration, the tranche riskiness is identified by position $\underline{K}_{tr}$ and size $P_{tr}(0)$ as before.

5 It should be reconsidered that the form of the spread account included into the transaction has been shown to be comparatively efficient: Both junior and mezzanine tranches are included, hence, the comparatively large principal basis allows for effective excess spread accumulation.

7.3.3 Comparison of tranche valuation

Observed issuance spreads and rating assignments shall be compared to the fair model premia and to the tranche loss expectations taken under the physical measure. Consider senior tranches first, consistently issued as unfunded swaps: A precise pricing comparison is hampered by the lack of senior swap premium indication. However, the perceived absence of loss risk suggests that senior swaps should trade at virtually zero premium. However, some evidence on non-zero premia is obtained the requirement imposed by the current regulatory environment: As senior risk transfer is required in order to obtain regulatory capital relief, one expects that senior protection is sought after by originators. Hence, positive premia must prevail to incite possible counterparties to enter a contract.

Consider the model results of the four transactions: A substantially positive senior swap premium of 49 bps is obtained for Repon 16. This is a straightforward consequence of both the low overcollateralisation level of the transaction and the high factor realisations at origination. For the remaining transactions, senior swap premia amount to between 12 and 21 bps, depending on overcollateralisation and factor realisations. The slight maturity extension of Private has no visible impact on tranche pricing. A rough appraisal on an implied rating of senior swaps may be obtained by a comparison of senior losses with discounted loss rates that are obtained under the physical measure in the single-name bond market: Reconsideration of the term structures of loss expectations, depicted in figure 4.3 on the left-hand side, together with the analogue, subsumed under the column 'Rating' in the sample sheets, tables 7.1 to 7.4 indicates that pure default risk of super-senior tranches justifies a rating exceeding corporate Aaa/Aa. Except for Repon 16, nonzero senior premia are largely due to the market pricing of factor risk, rather than pure default loss risk.

A comparison of transactions illustrates how multi-mezzanine tranching extends to a wide variety of claims differing in loss expectations and thus requiring pronouncedly different premium rates. All results that have been obtained for mezzanine tranches indicate an enormous discrepancy in risk perception of CDO market participants and model forecasts: Consistently, mezzanine premia indicate that market participants value loss allocation to the mezzanine range considerably lower than agents forming expectations under the factor model. It is interesting to inquire if this result is primarily driven by factor risk pricing, which has been the case for senior tranches. Alternatively, the pure default risk contribution can be quantified, again along the lines of the market price of risk analysis. Hence, default loss expectations taken under the real-world measure as depicted in the column 'Rating' in tables 7.1 to 7.4 convey a market-based view on the information underlying rating assignments.

Examine expected tranche loss rates defined under the risk-neutral measure for valuation purposes with their counterparts defined under the physical measure for rating purposes: Notable differences reveal that tranche loss expectations are subject to a notable increase upon the change of measure. Nevertheless, high model premia are not entirely a consequence of the high pricing of factor risk. Tranche loss expectations taken under the physical measure tend to be higher than would be consistent with investment grade rating assignments. For discussion, consider highly-overcollateralised superior mezzanine tranches first, where some noteworthy exceptions can be identified: The most superior mezzanine tranches of Scala 3 and Private receive an A1-rating for Scala 3 and a Aa1-rating for Private. For both tranches, discounted losses expressed as a proportion of principal amount to 1.3 and 1.0% of the tranche nominal. Comparison with the single-name loss expectations, illustrated in figure 4.3 on the left-hand side, confirms that the risk level of those superior mezzanine tranches is well in line with corporate investment grade risk of a five-year time horizon, amounting to loss expectations, amounting to 1.5% for low-risk Aaa/Aa corporates. Valuation implications, however, again mirror the results obtained within the comparative-static analysis of the market prices of factor risk performed in section 5.2.3: As illustrated for the fictive transactions subject to comparative-static analysis, the response of the expected value of loss allocation to non-zero market pricing of factor risk is stronger the more overcollateralisation by subordinate tranches is provided. This finding becomes even more salient when multi-mezzanine capital structures are considered. Valuation results show that highly-overcollateralised mezzanine tranches exhibit fair model premia exceeding those applicable to single-name debt of comparable quality, as conveyed by rating and real-word loss expectations given in the tables.

For subordinate mezzanine tranches, all transactions provide similar results: All mezzanine tranches in the four transactions for which pricing information is available, are rated investment grade rating by the agencies. However, model results obtained for zero factor risk pricing reveal that expected values of losses allocated to subordinate mezzanine investors by far exceed those corresponding to the investment grade rating benchmark. According to this, fair premia are high. As opposed to superior mezzanine tranches, however, it may be stated that a comparison of loss allocation rates obtained under both measures, i.e. the columns 'Rating' and 'Valuation', consistently conform to highly-speculative grade debt characteristics.

The comparison of model spreads with observed issuance premia of synthetic CBOs in 2001 appears somewhat puzzling. Especially mezzanine CDO issuance premia appear to be de-linked from the corporate debt market, whose risk is being repackaged under the examined securitisation programmes.

A final discussion addresses the following questions: A first argument investigates specification issues, taking into account the impact of parameter variations and possible estimation biases. A second argument relates the mispricing phenomenon to the institutional environment, especially to the counterparties' motivations to engage in securitisations.

7.4 Discussion

7.4.1 Model specification error

Severe mispricings of mezzanine CDO tranches provide an clear indication of disparate portfolio default risk perceptions prevailing in the securitisation market when mezzanine CDO tranches are compared to the market-data based model benchmark. This section seizes some of implications derived from the model specification analysis performed in the comparative-static framework in Chapter 5, chiefly those obtained within the parameter analysis in section 5.2. These shall be related to estimation issues, especially to a possible bias incurred by the use of bond data for spread estimation.

Reconsider the exposure of mezzanine tranches to the entire portfolio loss distribution: Referring to losses of moderate size, mezzanine tranches have shown a high responsiveness towards a change in expected values of loses, as identified by the single-name credit riskiness and the according single-name market spreads. At least within the model class examined, I find that the pricing of mezzanine tranches is only influenced by overall loss dispersion to a small extent.[6]

Therefore, a short review of those parameters affecting expected values of losses, as conveyed by the single-name default risk premia, is in order. Reconsider the latent factor framework, where spreads are explained by two factors adding up to the mean-loss rate of the defaultable asset. The level of the random mean-loss rate is primarily determined by the current factor realisations $f_c(0), f_{class}(0)$, the risk-neutral unconditional means of the factor processes θ_k and the market pricing of factor risk.

Consider the effect of a notable reduction in these three parameters on mezzanine CDO pricing: Referring to the comparative-static analysis performed in Chapter 5, a model transaction with tranche principal dimensions very similar to the four synthetic CBO sample transactions has been studied in great detail. The fictive transaction *Risky*, a direct issuance senior/subordinate portfolio derivative transaction with a capital structure of (90/8/2) tranche principals has been defined in order to study a hypothetical synthetic

6 Note that the choice of a modelling approach that allows for higher dependencies, such as a heavy-tailed copula model or the common-jump model suggested by Duffie and Gârleanu (2001) would not solve the problem: Effectively, a mean-preserving spread on the loss distribution is performed, still accommodating single-name risk premia. This may indeed yield a mezzanine riskiness reduction. However, the senior premium would inevitably experience an increase, as more probability mass applies to severe loss scenarios.

CBO transaction comparable to the four sample transactions. For this *Risky* structure, referring to a portfolio with sector-related concentration groups, a premium of 832.8 bps has been obtained, compensating for mezzanine losses occurring during a five-year time horizon.[7] Five-year reference bond par spreads yield a weighted reference portfolio average $\mathcal{S}_{pool}(0)$ of 113.6 bps for the estimated model applied to a portfolio with a breakdown among Aaa/Aa, A, and Baa assets of (10:50:40). Departing from this case, a decrease in expected values of portfolio losses, as obtained by variations of the parameters mentioned above, affects mezzanine tranches in the following manner:

First, reduce the initial factor values to zero: The portfolio mean risk pricing benchmark $\mathcal{S}_{pool}(0)$ decreases to 84.7 bps, the *Risky* mezzanine premium drops to 550.9 bps.[8] Second, consider a reduction of risk-neutral factor means to one half of the estimated value: In this case, the average par spread $\mathcal{S}_{pool}(0)$ drops to 71.3 bps or 69.4 bps (the discrepancy depending on a possible volatility adjustment according to equation (5.18)). Mezzanine spreads diminish to 397.3 bps or 353.8 bps, respectively.[9] Finally, consider the market price of factor risk parameters: The model analysis for zero factor risk pricing yields an average pool spread of 48.0 bps and a fair *Risky* mezzanine premium of 207.4 bps.[10]

The sensitivities of the *Risky* mezzanine tranche against notable changes in parameters indicate that a 'correct model' explaining observed mezzanine spreads would require pronouncedly lower mean-loss rates than those obtained from bond market spreads: Not even a reduction of factor values or the market price of risk parameters to zero reduce mezzanine premia to the observed market levels. A reduction of risk-neutral factor averages by more than half of the estimated process averages would be required to explain mezzanine spreads.

The findings shall be related to the sources of possible uncertainties about the estimate of mean default risk. Recall the discussion of the choice of a reference market for model estimation, put down at the outset of the estimation chapter in section 4.1: It has been argued that despite the presumed presence of illiquidity components in bond market spreads, causing bond spreads to be upward-biased estimates for appropriate default risk compensation, bond data may be preferable to single-name CDS quotes. In fact, the originator generates spread income from an on-balance sheet bond or even illiquid

---

7 See table 5.1.

8 See table 5.3 for par spreads and figure 5.9 on resulting issuance premia. The mezzanine premium at zero factor start value corresponds to the intercept of the solid line in the lower graph.

9 See table 5.5 for par spreads and figure 5.14 for resulting issuance premia. The mezzanine premia of both scenarios correspond to the intercepts in the lower graph.

10 $\mathcal{S}_{pool}(0)$ have not been reported in previous analysis, see figure 5.17 for resulting issuance premia. The mezzanine premium for $\lambda = 0$ corresponds to the intercept in the lower graph.

loan portfolio, that he attempts to protect by synthetic securitisation. Seen from the origination side, illiquid defaultable claims either require a higher par coupon at closing time or can be purchased at a discount. Therefore, funds for redistribution among tranche investors are clearly available. Seen from the side of a CDO investor, it can clearly be stated that CDO tranches are bespoke securities. Hence, CDO tranches should exhibit even lower secondary marketability than investment grade corporate bonds, the estimation benchmark. As a result, notable illiquidity premia should be offered to induce investors to enter buy-and-hold positions in CDO tranches. Compensation for restricted secondary trading of CDO investments must be payable from portfolio spread income, which is fulfilled by income generated on illiquid bonds.

However, it is interesting to inquire to what extent a possible bias incurred by the choice of the reference market for estimation translates into mezzanine CDO pricing. Implicitly, I examine the conjecture whether market participants refer CDO risk to the credit derivatives market, instead of the corporate bond market to which the originator is exposed. A good explanation of mezzanine premia, by a model taking into account typical characteristics of single-name CDS premia, would support this casual suggestion.

Consider a link between corporate bond and single-name CDS pricing: Five-year par spreads have been consistently reported throughout the study for reference collateral of transactions. These give a picture of the current bond market condition, reconsider the timeline of the empirical valuation exercise depicted in figure 7.1, lower graph. These compare closely to market premia of single-name CDSs.

A rough appraisal of a reasonable CDS premium level can be drawn from the empirical pricing literature: For instance, Blanco, Brennan, and March (2003) report five-year bond yield spreads against government debt to exceed maturity-equivalent single-name CDS premia by an average of 23.3 bps over their sample period. The difference between maturity-equivalent bond spreads and CDS premia is referred to as the 'credit basis' in the literature.[11]

The effect on mezzanine premia that would be incurred by the use of on average lower CDS data for estimation is roughly quantified by a parametric comparison. Recall the comparative-static results re-established earlier in this section, relating single-name par spreads and the mezzanine premium of the *Risky* capital structure to variations in factor mean parameters: Severe reductions of those model parameters affecting factor means have a strong impact on the average five-year portfolio par spread $S_{pool}(0)$, being reduced from (estimated) 113.6 bps to values between 48.0 bps and 84.7 bps. The scenarios conform roughly speaking to recalibrating the model to a market exhibiting a 'credit

---

[11] See Blanco, Brennan, and March (2003), table B, breakdown for Europe. Their estimation period runs from January 2001 to July 2002.

basis' of 65.0 bps or 28.9 bps when compared to the bond market estimates. As even those scenarios do not produce the desired effect on fair *Risky* mezzanine spreads, model estimation using CDS premia implying a mean credit basis of 23.3 bps would only alleviate mispricing.

To summarise, the specification analysis shows that the presumed illiquidity-induced bias prevailing in bond market spreads accounts only to some extent for mezzanine mispricing. This finding holds all the more, as the alternative single-name CDS market neither provides perfectly unbiased estimates for accurate default risk compensation.

7.4.2 Relation to the institutional environment: 'arbitrage' CDOs?

It is interesting to assess the relevance of the mispricing relationship in absolute terms: Mezzanine tranches are of small principal nominal, hence it is conceivable that the value of expected cash-inflow incurred by mezzanine premium inflows exceeding mezzanine loss legs may be negligible when expressed as a fraction of total transaction nominals.

The value additivity framework provides a benchmark for the quantification of a possible 'arbitrage' gain, exploiting the notion of the arbitrage as discussed in the introductory chapter, section 2.2.2. The valuation results clearly indicate that discounted expected mezzanine premia do not compensate for discounted expected losses. Straightforwardly, this may be expressed as overpriced CLN issuance. Disregarding the provision of funding, the pricing error of every tranche may be quantified as the time-zero value of the portfolio swap, which has positive value for the originator in case of overpriced CLN issuance. Quantification of the pricing error is therefore performed by evaluation of the basic swap pricing equation (5.1), for those premia s_{tr} that have been actually reported for the four transactions. The difference between the value of the premium leg and the value of the loss leg (CDS_{tr} according to the notation in (5.1)), both relying on the estimated portfolio model default stochastic, quantifies the time-zero model gain incurred by the originator when issuing an overpriced tranche. The total gain incurred by issuing the entire capital structure is obtained as $\sum_{tr=1}^{\#tr} CDS_{tr}(0)$, where tranches that are issued at their fair model spreads simply evaluate to zero.

Presuming that in the transaction sample, all tranches on which no premium information is provided, are priced according to the model, this quantity is computed for the Repon 15, Repon 16, Scala 3, and Private transactions: Cumulated mispriced mezzanine tranches of the four respective transactions turn out to have a time-zero value of 2.25%, 0.85%, 0.98%, and 1.77% of the portfolio nominal. Given the large portfolio volumes reported in the transaction tables, the model gains incurred by mezzanine mispricing are indeed substantial.

This result leads to the conclusion that CDO issuance may be judged as highly desirable from the originator's viewpoint, even if substantial transaction costs are faced at CDO origination. However, the question addressing the disclosure of an 'arbitrage' opportunity incurred by the violation of the value additivity conditions should be negated: The exploitation of the arbitrage opportunity in order to realise a riskless time-zero gain requires either shorting of tranches, or trading of the junior piece at the model values. Neither of these conditions may be expected to be fulfilled in highly-sophisticated markets: Secondary trading of CDO tranches is severely restricted. Low marketability of equity pieces prevents sure gains from being realised either, a result well-founded by the sensitivity of the junior piece to asymmetric information, discussed in the introductory chapter, section 2.1.2.

The final result for the 'arbitrage' notion is therefore relaxed to the statement that investment grade corporate portfolio protection is obtained in the market at very favourable conditions.

Valuation results, however, provide evidence on the translation of preferences of market participants into prices. Some incentives of counterparties to enter CDO transactions have been identified in the introductory chapter, section 2.2.2: Among other things, the 'arbitrage' motive together with the purpose regulatory capital relief from the originator's viewpoint, and the tailor-made exposure to diversified credit portfolio risk as seen from the perspective of a note investor suggest that securitisation is beneficial for both counterparties. All results support the 'arbitrage' motive, holding with the limitation established above. Investors, by contrast, pay dear for the structuring effort, receiving too little compensation for the provision of protection against leveraged portfolio risk.

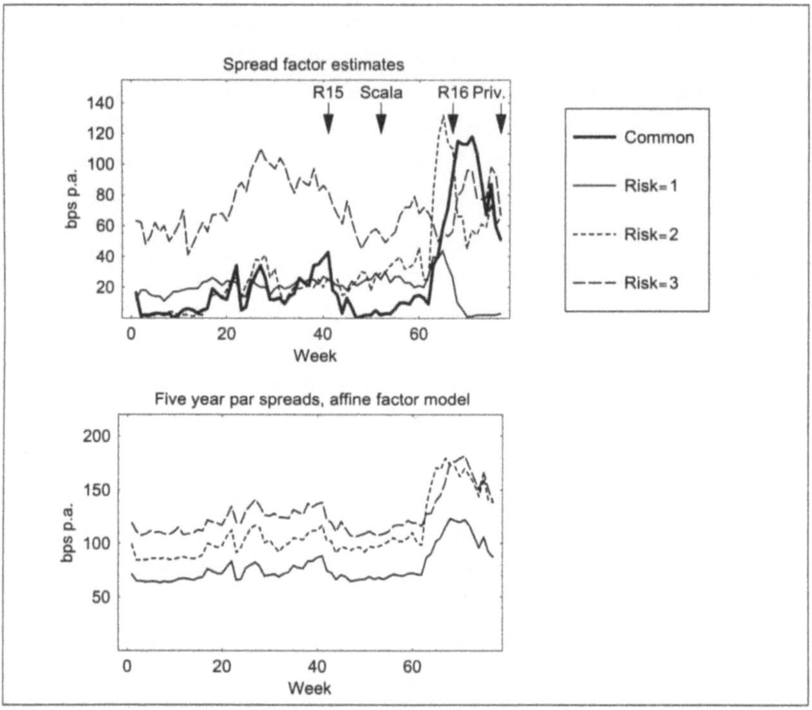

Figure 7.1: **Timeline of synthetic CBO issuance activity, estimated factor paths, and five year model par spreads.**

Factor series have been obtained by the update step of the Kalman filter recursion conditional on the parameter estimates. Five-year par spreads are computed according to the affine solution of the factor model. The sample period (weeks 1-77) starts on 5 July 2000 and ends on 19 December 2001.

Chapter 8

Conclusion

My contribution started from the notion that CDOs, especially the synthetic variants dominating the European market, represent suitable guinea pigs for analysing the pricing of credit portfolio risk in a market environment: Whereas the quantification of single-name default risk, amounting to a measurement of the determinants of the losses from default over a given time horizon, may be considered as comparatively well-understood, the quantification of the systematic aspects of credit portfolio risk provides significant challenges. My contribution addresses the portfolio default risk pricing issue from a strongly empirical perspective, setting the research agenda for the questions that are dealt with.

Both qualitative and quantitative results obtained during the course of the study consistently suggest that CDOs are a novel investment highly sought-after by market participants: The discussion of structural variants and risk factors of various forms of credit risk securitisation performed in Chapter 2 has shown that credit risk securitisation is attractive for both sides of a transaction, especially if it is cost-efficiently implemented synthetically by the use of credit derivative agreements. Comparatively narrow European bond markets provide limited opportunities for non-banks to hold reasonably diversified corporate debt portfolios. As a consequence, securitisation may be judged as a valuable contribution to financial market completeness.

CDO valuation relies on careful modelling of underlying portfolio losses, constituting the first empirical issue on the research agenda: For this purpose, Chapter 3 develops a model of the reduced-form type that is tractable enough to be readily estimated from corporate market spreads, albeit integrating risk components that are common to all or a subset of the reference assets.

Model estimation, performed in Chapter 4, does not just provide the information required for the implementation of the CDO pricing model. The insight that is gained both on corporate spread explanation and on latent-factor model estimation may clearly be considered as more than a by-result: In a first estimation step, it is shown that term structures of default risk premia of European corporate issuers are highly interlinked, providing strong evidence on the presence of a common factor. A second estimation step is of interest not just because of the evidence provided on stochastic latent factor behaviour. Estimation methodology itself provides insight on simultaneous factor estimation using multi-term structure spread data, in the present case restricted to term structures of three rating classes. Kalman filter-based QML estimation exploits the full panel data structure of the information set, in the present case comprising the term structures of credit spreads of several rating classes. As a result, a stochastic characterisation of factors is obtained. I find that the contribution of the systematic effects to overall spread variation turns out to be substantial. Furthermore, parameter estimates imply high factor risk premia prevailing in the bond market. Both estimation results are of central relevance for portfolio credit derivatives pricing, examined in the remainder of the work for for the case of CDOs.

The pricing of CDOs using the portfolio loss model is studied in great detail in Chapter 5, followed by an extension of the basic modelling framework to more involved payout schemes in Chapter 6.

All model specification issues derived in Chapter 5 are dealt with assuming the simplest portfolio derivative structure observed in the market for synthetic CDOs, senior/subordinate portfolio derivatives, often issued as credit-linked notes. As they are immediately affected by reference portfolio losses exceeding a normally retained junior piece, I find that mezzanine tranches exhibit expected values of loss allocation that clearly conform to highly speculative debt. With respect to senior tranches, I find that albeit virtually riskless when portfolio loss forecasts are obtained under the real-world measure, strong factor risk pricing causes senior tranches to trade at nonzero issuance spreads. Besides deriving the basic results on CDO pricing, a comprehensive comparative-static analysis has been carried out for the senior/subordinate portfolio derivative capital structure. A palpable result of the specification analysis states that the restriction of the estimation procedure to rating classes imposes almost no uncertainty on CDO pricing: Estimation could clearly be improved by classifying bonds used for estimation and the reference assets both by the agency rating and the industry affiliation of the issuer. However, the weak response of fair CDO issuance spreads to an expansion of the factor space, mimicking the risk/sector-subportfolio formation, shows that the simplification made for feasibility is innocuous for CDO valuation. Origination timing and the tenor of the transaction, by contrast, turn out to be crucial contract parameters for fair CDO valuation.

The direct exposure of issued tranches to portfolio losses exceeding the first-loss piece may be mitigated by the provision of credit enhancement. Synthetic transactions that effectuate risk transfer by arranging some or all derivative contracts via an SPV often make use of so-called spread accounts. Building on the excess spread generation mechanism, detected and quantified in Chapters 2 and 5, Chapter 6 evaluates the relationship between the contract parameters determining excess spread accumulation and its importance with regard to the reduction of fair tranche issuance premia. The formal study shows that among the structural parameters considered, the principal proportion of total portfolio nominal actually transferred via the SPV is the key determinant for effective credit enhancement, causing absolute cash-inflows to the SPV to exceed absolute outflows towards the CDO counterparties by a large amount. Hence, structures that collect excess spread that is created by a transaction transferring the full portfolio exposure via the SPV, which in turn, issues the full capital structure, trade at considerably lower tranche issuance spreads than structures using only an SPV for partial portfolio risk transfer.

The valuation results obtained in Chapters 5 and 6 are related to the market benchmark in Chapter 7: The comparison of model implications with observed CDO issuance conditions, the second empirical issue on the agenda, keeps the promise made at the outset of the study: I compare the pricing of different stakes in credit portfolio risk that is appropriate within a market spread-based model with the risk and valuation information available for synthetic CBOs conforming to my modelling methodology.

Results obtained for all sample transactions consistently reveal that the exposure of mezzanine tranches to portfolio losses is notably understated by market participants, notwithstanding remaining modelling uncertainty. Although the pricing discrepancies cannot actually be exploited in highly-sophisticated securitisation markets, the conjecture that the unique risk profile provided by CDOs is highly demanded by investors is strongly supported by my contribution.

Appendix A

Annotations to the CIR Model

Closed-form solution for defaultable zero bond prices

The coefficients $a_k(\tau, \phi_k)$ and $b_k(\tau, \phi_k)$ of the pricing relationship

$$P_{class}(t, \tau) = \exp\left(\sum_{k=r,c,class} (a_k(\tau, \phi_k) - b_k(\tau, \phi_k) f_k(t))\right)$$

of a defaultable zero bond whose price is determined by the three relevant term structures of the CIR model are given by Cox, Ingersoll, and Ross (1985) as

$$\begin{aligned}
a_k(\tau, \phi_k) &= \ln\left(\frac{2\gamma_1(\phi_k)\exp\left(\frac{1}{2}\gamma_2(\phi_k)\tau\right)}{\gamma_4(\tau, \phi_k)}\right)^{\gamma_3(\phi_k)} \\
b_k(\tau, \phi_k) &= \frac{2\left(\exp\left(\gamma_1(\phi_k)\tau\right) - 1\right)}{\gamma_4(\tau, \phi_k)} \\
\gamma_1(\phi_k) &= \sqrt{\kappa_k^2 + 2\sigma_k^2} \\
\gamma_2(\phi_k) &= \kappa_k + \gamma_1(\phi_k) \\
\gamma_3(\phi_k) &= \frac{2\kappa_k\theta_k}{\sigma_k^2} \\
\gamma_4(\tau, \phi_k) &= \gamma_2(\phi_k)\left(\exp\left(\gamma_1(\phi_k)\tau\right) - 1\right) + 2\gamma_1(\phi_k),
\end{aligned}$$

where process parameters have been substituted by their risk-neutral counterparts identifiable from the term structures. The yield for an infinite maturity horizon of a risk class is determined as

$$R_{class}(\infty) = \sum_{k=r,c,class} \frac{2\kappa_k\theta_k}{\gamma_1(\phi_k) + \kappa_k}.$$

Conditional factor probability distributions

As given by Cox, Ingersoll, and Ross (1985), a linear transformation of the realisation of factor $f_k(t+\Delta t)$ conditional on its previous value $f_k(t)$ is distributed as

$$\begin{aligned}
2c_k f_k(t+\Delta t) &\sim \chi^2\left[2q_k+2, 2u_k\right], \\
c_k &= \frac{2\kappa_k}{\sigma_k^2\left(1-\exp(-\kappa_k \Delta t)\right)} \\
u_k &= c_k f_k(t)\exp(-\kappa_k \Delta t) \\
q_k &= \frac{2\kappa_k\theta_k}{\sigma_k^2} - 1,
\end{aligned}$$

with $df = 2q_k + 2$ and the level-dependent noncentrality parameter $2u_k$.

Random number generation

In order to obtain random variates from the respective noncentral χ^2-distributions, I adapt the algorithm suggested by Duan and Simonato (1995). The algorithm makes use of the rule stated by Johnson and Kotz (1970) that the noncentral χ^2-distribution can be represented as the mixture $\chi^2\left[2q_k+2+Poi(h^{Poi}(f_k(t)))\right]$, i.e. a central χ^2–distribution, whose degrees of freedom are determined by an affine transformation of a Poisson-distributed random variate.[1] Factor realisations are simulated for weekly time intervals $\Delta t = 1/52$. For each time step with a given previous factor realisation $f_k(t)$ I generate

(i) the degrees of freedom as $df = 2q_k + 2 + Poi(h^{Poi}(f_k(t)))$:

The Poisson-distributed variable with mean (intensity parameter) $h^{Poi}(f_k(t)) = c_k f_k(t)\exp(-\kappa_k\Delta t)$ is straightforwardly obtained as the number of events that occur at exponentially-distributed event times during the unit interval. Exponentially-distributed variates are obtained by the transformation of $U[0,1]$-distributed random variates by the inverse exponential CDF.

(ii) the χ^2-distributed current realisation of $2c_k f_k(t+\Delta t)$ with the simulated df :

This is straightforwardly obtained by the transformation of $U[0,1]$-distributed random variates by the inverse central χ^2 CDF, which is provided by the software package.

[1] See Johnson and Kotz (1970), p. 132.

Appendix B

Outline of the Kalman Filter Recursion

Estimation is performed separately for the riskless rate model and for the corporate spread model. The prediction and the update step are thus given separately for both sets of observables and state variables. For ease of notation, the time interval is normalised to $\Delta t = 1$ and the dependencies on the relevant parameter sets are suppressed

$$\begin{aligned}
\mathbf{T} &:= \mathbf{T}(\phi^{*}) \\
\boldsymbol{\Sigma} &:= \boldsymbol{\Sigma}(\phi^{*}) \\
\mathbf{R}_{r}(t) &:= \mathbf{R}_{r}(t, \phi_{r}) \\
\mathbf{S}(t) &:= \mathbf{S}(t, \phi_{s}) \\
\mathbf{A}_{r} &:= \mathbf{A}_{r}(\phi_{r}) \\
\mathbf{A}_{s} &:= \mathbf{A}_{s}(\phi_{s}) \\
\mathbf{B}_{r} &:= \mathbf{B}_{r}(\phi_{r}) \\
\mathbf{B}_{s} &:= \mathbf{B}_{s}(\phi_{s}).
\end{aligned}$$

Prediction step

Conditional on the estimate of the factor realisations in the previous period $f_r^{update}(t-1)$ and $\mathbf{f}_s^{update}(t-1)$, respectively, the first two moments of the current realisations of the state variables are predicted according to the transition equation (4.8), taking no information arriving in t into account:

Riskless rate model

$$\begin{aligned} f_r^{pred}(t) &= \mathbb{E}\left[f_r(t)\left|f_r^{update}(t-1)\right.\right] = \mathbf{T}_r f_r^{update}(t-1) \\ p_r^{pred}(t) &= Var\left[f_r(t)\left|f_r^{update}(t-1)\right.\right] = \mathbf{T}_r^2 p_r^{update}(t-1) + \mathbf{\Sigma}_r \end{aligned}$$

Corporate spread model

$$\begin{aligned} \mathbf{f}_s^{pred}(t) &= \mathbb{E}\left[\mathbf{f}_s(t)\left|\mathbf{f}_s^{update}(t-1)\right.\right] = \mathbf{T}_s \mathbf{f}_s^{update}(t-1). \\ \mathbf{p}_s^{pred}(t) &= Var\left[\mathbf{f}_s(t)\left|\mathbf{f}_s^{update}(t-1)\right.\right] = \mathbf{T}_s \mathbf{p}_s^{update}(t-1)\mathbf{T}_s' + \mathbf{\Sigma}_s. \end{aligned}$$

$\mathbf{T}_r$ and $\mathbf{T}_s$ represent the relevant partitions of the transition matrix of the full system $\mathbf{T}$, where $\mathbf{T}_s$ is a diagonal $(4x4)$-matrix and $\mathbf{T}_r$ is a scalar. $\mathbf{\Sigma}_r$ and $\mathbf{\Sigma}_s$ analogously denote the relevant $(4x4)$ and $(1x1)$ partitions of the transition variance $\mathbf{\Sigma}$.

The functional dependence of the term structures of rates and spreads on the state variables permits a translation of factor predictions into the cross section of observables:

$$\begin{aligned} \mathbf{R}_r^{pred}(t) &= \mathbf{A}_r + \mathbf{B}_r f_r^{pred}(t) \\ \mathbf{S}^{pred}(t) &= \mathbf{A}_s + \mathbf{B}_s \mathbf{f}_s^{pred}(t). \end{aligned}$$

Update step

Firstly, information arrival, i.e. the observations of term structures of spot rates and spreads in period t as represented by the five maturity classes, permits inference on an error structure. The residual distribution provides the basis for estimation.

The observation errors (with zero expectation) are computed given the model prediction, whilst their respective variances are determined by the affine measurement equation variances (4.11):

Riskless rate model

$$\begin{aligned} \mathbf{v}_r(t) &= \mathbf{R}_r(t) - \mathbf{R}_r^{pred}(t) \\ \mathbf{V}_r(t) &= \mathbf{B}_r p_r^{pred}(t)\mathbf{B}_r' + \mathbf{M}_r \end{aligned}$$

Corporate spread model

$$\begin{aligned}\mathbf{v}_s(t) &= \mathbf{S}(t) - \mathbf{S}^{pred}(t)\\ \mathbf{V}_s(t) &= \mathbf{B}_s\mathbf{p}_s^{pred}(t)\mathbf{B}_s' + \mathbf{M}_s.\end{aligned}$$

The distributional properties of prediction errors are exploited for likelihood construction assuming normality, as outlined in the text.

Secondly, the Kalman filter allows for inference on the actual factor realisation in t, i.e. the derivation of factor estimates taking the full information available in period t into account.

The factor updates are obtained by a correction of the factor predictions, the correction being proportional to the observation errors occurred. The slope coefficients are referred to as the 'Kalman gain', the entire update of the factor prediction effectively amounts to a variance proportion: The magnitude of the corrections is increasing in the informative factor prediction variances and decreasing in the variances of uninformative measurement noise.

The update variances are reduced upon information arrival.

Riskless rate model

$$\begin{aligned}KGain_r(t) &= p_r^{pred}(t)\mathbf{B}_r'\mathbf{V}_r(t)^{-1}\\ f_r^{update}(t) &= f_r^{pred}(t) + KGain_r(t)\mathbf{v}_r(t)\\ p_r^{update}(t) &= p_r^{pred}(t) - KGain_r(t)\mathbf{B}_r p_r^{pred}(t)\end{aligned}$$

Corporate spread model

$$\begin{aligned}KGain_s(t) &= \mathbf{p}_s^{pred}(t)\mathbf{B}_s'\mathbf{V}_s(t)^{-1}\\ \mathbf{f}_s^{update}(t) &= \mathbf{f}_s^{pred}(t) + KGain_s(t)\mathbf{v}_s(t)\\ \mathbf{p}_s^{update}(t) &= \mathbf{p}_s^{pred}(t) - KGain_s(t)\mathbf{B}_s\mathbf{p}_s^{pred}(t).\end{aligned}$$

By incrementing t by one, the subsequent recursion step is performed, setting the initial information equal to the factor updates.

Appendix C

Complementary Tables

	Factors			
Processes	$f_c(t)$	$f_1(t)$	$f_2(t)$	$f_3(t)$
κ_k^*	1.3771	2.042	1.5806	2.0888
	(0.086)	(0.260)	(0.718)	(0.380)
θ_k^*	0.0014	0.0013	0.0023	0.0037
	(0.00009)	(0.00023)	(0.00105)	(0.00070)
σ_k	0.1801	0.1733	0.1366	0.1164
	(0.004)	(0.008)	(0.004)	(0.005)
λ_k	-1.1948	-1.1734	-1.1290	-1.0790
	(0.085)	(0.272)	(0.719)	(0.385)
κ_k	0.1824	0.8690	0.4516	1.0077
θ_k	0.0109	0.0031	0.0081	0.0077
Std dev.				
phys.	0.0041	0.0031	0.0037	0.0035
EMM	0.0311	0.0073	0.0129	0.0072
Half life				
phys.	0.5033	0.3394	0.4385	0.3318
EMM	3.8001	0.7976	1.5349	0.6879

	Std dev. of noise for maturity $\tau[bps]$				
TS	**2**	**4**	**6**	**8**	**10**
$S_1(t,\tau)$	14.3	5.8	2.7	0.6	2.9
$S_2(t,\tau)$	23.2	7.7	3.9	4.7	9.7
$S_3(t,\tau)$	17.0	6.6	1.8	6.7	11.8

Table C.1: **Parameter estimates for the factor model and estimated standard deviations of measurement noise, short period.**

Heteroscedasticity-consistent White-estimators of the asymptotic standard errors of estimates are given in parentheses. The upper table comprises process properties (unconditional standard variation and half life) obtained both under the physical and the risk-neutral measure. Sample period ends on 5/9/2001.

	$P_{jun}(0) = 2$				$P_{jun}(0) = 3$				$P_{jun}(0) = 4$				$P_{jun}(0) = 6$			
			$E[PV(loss_{tr})]$				$E[PV(loss_{tr})]$				$E[PV(loss_{tr})]$				$E[PV(loss_{tr})]$	
Tranches	$P_{tr}(0)$	$s[bps]$	Abs.	Rate[%]	$P_{tr}(0)$	$s[bps]$	Abs.	Rate[%]	$P_{tr}(0)$	$s[bps]$	Abs.	Rate[%]	$P_{tr}(0)$	$s[bps]$	Abs.	Rate[%]
Senior	90	5.3	-0.22	0.24	89	4.2	-0.17	0.19	88	3.4	-0.14	0.15	86	2.3	-0.09	0.10
Mezzanine	8	299.7	-1.02	12.77	8	205.1	-0.71	8.91	8	151.6	-0.53	6.66	8	93.6	-0.33	4.16
Junior	2	0	-1.02	52.01	3	0	-1.21	41.06	4	0	-1.33	33.82	6	0	-1.47	24.98
Spread acc.			1.14				1.32				1.44				1.58	
Std dev. orig			1.56				1.95				2.25				2.66	
Senior	88	3.7	-0.15	0.17	87	2.9	-0.12	0.13	86	2.4	-0.09	0.11	84	1.6	-0.06	0.07
Mezzanine	10	254.4	-1.09	10.94	10	175.9	-0.77	7.69	10	130.8	-0.58	5.77	10	81.4	-0.36	3.62
Junior	2	0	-1.02	51.97	3	0	-1.21	41.05	4	0	-1.33	33.82	6	0	-1.50	24.98
Spread acc.			1.14				1.32				1.44				1.58	
Std dev. orig			1.56				1.95				2.25				2.66	
Senior	86	2.6	-0.10	0.12	85	2.0	-0.08	0.09	84	1.7	-0.06	0.07	82	1.1	-0.04	0.05
Mezzanine	12	220.1	-1.14	9.52	12	153.3	-0.81	6.72	12	114.5	-0.61	5.06	12	71.7	-0.38	3.19
Junior	2	0	-1.02	51.95	3	0	-1.21	41.04	4	0	-1.33	33.81	6	0	-1.47	24.98
Spread acc.			1.14				1.32				1.44				1.58	
Std dev. orig			1.57				1.96				2.25				2.66	

Table C.2: **Tranche valuation: full risk transfer via SPV, variant I.**

In addition to the positions reported in table 5.1, the time-zero value of the spread account is included.

Tranches	$P_{jun}(0) = 2$				$P_{jun}(0) = 3$				$P_{jun}(0) = 4$				$P_{jun}(0) = 6$			
			$E[PV(loss_{tr})]$				$E[PV(loss_{tr})]$				$E[PV(loss_{tr})]$				$E[PV(loss_{tr})]$	
	$P_{tr}(0)$	$s[bps]$	Abs.	Rate[%]	$P_{tr}(0)$	$s[bps]$	Abs.	Rate[%]	$P_{tr}(0)$	$s[bps]$	Abs.	Rate[%]	$P_{tr}(0)$	$s[bps]$	Abs.	Rate[%]
Senior	90	6.8	-0.24	0.27	89	5.6	-0.18	0.21	88	4.7	-0.15	0.16	86	3.3	-0.09	0.11
Mezzanine	8	510.2	-1.23	15.43	8	360.5	-0.82	10.22	8	266.1	-0.59	7.33	8	159.0	-0.35	4.38
Junior CDS	2	3334.8	-0.37		3	2659.2	-0.34		4	2205.0	-0.31		6	1634.2	-0.21	
Loss jun.			-1.63	81.55			-2.19	72.92			-2.61	65.32			-3.19	53.24
Spread acc.			0.49				0.47				0.43				0.34	
Std dev. orig			1.06				1.43				1.74				2.25	
Senior	88	4.7	-0.16	0.18	87	3.9	-0.13	0.14	86	3.2	-0.10	0.11	84	2.3	-0.06	0.08
Mezzanine	10	425.4	-1.32	13.16	10	303.9	-0.88	8.79	10	226.1	-0.63	6.34	10	136.5	-0.38	3.81
Junior CDS	2	3347.9	-0.37		3	2662.3	-0.35		4	2205.9	-0.31		6	1634.4	-0.22	
Loss jun.			-1.63	81.53			-2.19	72.91			-2.61	65.32			-3.19	53.24
Spread acc.			0.49				0.47				0.43				0.34	
Std dev. orig			1.06				1.43				1.75				2.25	
Senior	86	3.2	-0.11	0.13	85	2.7	-0.09	0.10	84	2.2	-0.07	0.08	82	1.5	-0.04	0.05
Mezzanine	12	364.0	-1.37	11.44	12	261.7	-0.92	7.68	12	195.7	-0.67	5.56	12	119.1	-0.40	3.36
Junior CDS	2	3358.0	-0.36		3	2664.8	-0.35		4	2206.7	-0.30		6	1634.5	-0.22	
Loss jun.			-1.63	81.51			-2.19	72.91			-2.61	65.32			-3.19	53.24
Spread acc.			0.48				0.46				0.43				0.34	
Std dev. orig			1.07				1.43				1.75				2.25	

Table C.3: **Tranche valuation: full risk transfer via SPV, variant II.**

In addition to the positions reported in table 5.1, the time-zero value of the spread account is included. The junior position is both disclosed as the time-zero value of the premium-paying swap ('Junior CDS') and as the gross value loss allocation leg ('Loss jun.').

	$P_{jun}(0)=2$				$P_{jun}(0)=3$				$P_{jun}(0)=4$				$P_{jun}(0)=6$			
			$E[PV(loss_{tr})]$				$E[PV(loss_{tr})]$				$E[PV(loss_{tr})]$				$E[PV(loss_{tr})]$	
Tranches	$P_{tr}(0)$	$s_{tr}[bps]$	Abs.	Rate[%]	$P_{tr}(0)$	$s_{tr}[bps]$	Abs.	Rate[%]	$P_{tr}(0)$	$s_{tr}[bps]$	Abs.	Rate[%]	$P_{tr}(0)$	$s_{tr}[bps]$	Abs.	Rate[%]
Senior	90	10.7	-0.43	0.48	89	8.6	-0.34	0.38	88	7.1	-0.28	0.32	86	4.9	-0.19	0.22
Mezzanine	8	708.3	-2.25	28.15	8	487.8	-1.62	20.21	8	354.4	-1.20	15.03	8	205.8	-0.72	8.94
Junior CDS	2	2365.7	-0.81		3	2230.9	-0.79		4	1975.7	-0.74		6	1549.0	-0.63	
Loss jun.			-1.70	85.16			-2.32	77.50			-2.81	70.18			-3.47	57.78
Exc. Spread			0.80				0.73				0.68				0.60	
Spread acc.			0.14				0.19				0.20				0.17	
Std dev. orig			0.60				0.99				1.37				1.98	
Senior	88	7.2	-0.28	0.32	87	5.9	-0.23	0.26	86	4.8	-0.18	0.21	84	3.3	-0.12	0.15
Mezzanine	10	560.0	-2.28	22.79	10	392.7	-1.65	16.51	10	289.2	-1.24	12.39	10	171.3	-0.75	7.48
Junior CDS	2	2562.8	-0.73		3	2308.9	-0.71		4	2014.1	-0.67		6	1561.7	-0.57	
Loss jun.			-1.70	84.81			-2.31	76.99			-2.79	69.63			-3.44	57.29
Exc. Spread			0.67				0.62				0.58				0.51	
Spread acc.			0.19				0.23				0.23				0.19	
Std dev. orig			0.66				1.06				1.43				2.03	
Senior	86	4.9	-0.19	0.22	85	4.0	-0.15	0.18	84	3.3	-0.12	0.15	82	2.3	-0.08	0.10
Mezzanine	12	459.9	-2.28	19.03	12	326.6	-1.66	13.87	12	242.6	-1.26	10.46	12	145.5	-0.76	6.37
Junior CDS	2	2710.3	-0.66		3	2368.7	-0.65		4	2044.2	-0.62		6	1572.0	-0.52	
Loss jun.			-1.69	84.52			-2.30	76.59			-2.77	69.19			-3.41	56.90
Exc. Spread			0.57				0.52				0.49				0.44	
Spread acc.			0.23				0.26				0.26				0.21	
Std dev. orig			0.72				1.12				1.48				2.06	

Table C.4: **Tranche valuation: partial risk transfer via SPV, variant I.**

In addition to the positions reported in table 5.1, the time-zero value of the spread account is included. The junior position is both disclosed as the time-zero value of the premium-paying swap ('Junior CDS') and as the gross value loss allocation leg ('Loss jun.'). The value of the claim on excess spread created on the originator's balance sheet is included.

	$P_{jun}(0) = 2$				$P_{jun}(0) = 3$				$P_{jun}(0) = 4$				$P_{jun}(0) = 6$			
			$E[PV(loss_{tr})]$				$E[PV(loss_{tr})]$				$E[PV(loss_{tr})]$				$E[PV(loss_{tr})]$	
Tranches	$P_{tr}(0)$	$s[bps]$	Abs.	Rate[%]	$P_{tr}(0)$	$s[bps]$	Abs.	Rate[%]	$P_{tr}(0)$	$s[bps]$	Abs.	Rate[%]	$P_{tr}(0)$	$s[bps]$	Abs.	Rate[%]
Senior	90	10.4	-0.42	0.46	89	8.5	-0.34	0.38	88	7.0	-0.28	0.31	86	4.9	-0.19	0.22
Mezzanine 1	4	303.1	-0.52	12.99	4	224.2	-0.39	9.72	4	176.5	-0.31	7.70	4	118.3	-0.21	5.21
Mezzanine 2	4	1151.1	-1.69	42.28	4	764.6	-1.21	30.27	4	537.7	-0.89	22.17	4	294.5	-0.51	12.63
Total mezzanine		727.1	-2.21	27.64		494.4	-1.60	19.99		357.1	-1.19	14.94		206.4	-0.71	8.92
Junior	2	3376.4	-0.84		3	1570.0	-0.80		4	868.8	-0.75		6	345.3	-0.63	
Loss jun.			-1.70	85.23			-2.33	77.53			-2.81	70.19			-3.47	57.78
Exc. Spread			0.80				0.73				0.68				0.60	
Spread acc.			0.17				0.20				0.20				0.17	
Std dev. orig			0.74				1.24				1.68				2.35	
Senior	88	7.0	-0.27	0.31	87	5.7	-0.22	0.25	86	4.7	-0.18	0.21	84	3.3	-0.12	0.15
Mezzanine 1	5	201.3	-0.44	8.75	5	157.0	-0.34	6.87	5	127.2	-0.28	5.59	5	86.7	-0.19	3.83
Mezzanine 2	5	945.8	-1.80	35.97	5	638.4	-1.29	25.77	5	455.3	-0.95	19.00	5	256.8	-0.55	11.07
Total mezzanine		573.5	-2.24	22.36		397.7	-1.63	16.32		291.3	-1.23	12.30		171.8	-0.75	7.45
Junior	2	3175.2	-0.75		3	1491.5	-0.72		4	830.2	-0.68		6	332.6	-0.57	
Loss jun.			-1.70	84.88			-2.31	77.02			-2.79	69.64			-3.44	57.30
Exc. Spread			0.67				0.62				0.58				0.51	
Spread acc.			0.22				0.24				0.23				0.19	
Std dev. orig			0.80				1.28				1.70				2.35	
Senior	86	4.7	-0.18	0.21	85	3.9	-0.15	0.17	84	3.2	-0.12	0.14	82	2.2	-0.08	0.10
Mezzanine 1	6	142.9	-0.38	6.27	6	114.5	-0.30	5.04	6	93.7	-0.25	4.14	6	64.2	-0.17	2.85
Mezzanine 2	6	796.9	-1.86	31.07	6	546.1	-1.34	22.37	6	394.6	-1.00	16.62	6	227.5	-0.59	9.85
Total mezzanine		469.9	-2.24	18.67		330.3	-1.64	13.71		244.2	-1.25	10.38		145.9	-0.76	6.35
Junior	2	3022.8	-0.68		3	1430.9	-0.66		4	800.1	-0.62		6	322.3	-0.52	
Loss jun.			-1.69	84.58			-2.30	76.62			-2.77	69.20			-3.41	56.90
Exc. Spread			0.56				0.52				0.49				0.44	
Spread acc.			0.25				0.27				0.26				0.21	
Std dev. orig			0.84				1.31				1.72				2.35	

Table C.5: **Tranche valuation: partial risk transfer via SPV, variant II.**

In addition to the positions reported in table 5.1, the time-zero value of the spread account is included. The junior position is both disclosed as the time-zero value of the premium-paying swap ('Junior CDS') and as the gross value loss allocation leg ('Loss jun.'). The value of the claim on excess spread created on the originator's balance sheet is included. For the two mezzanine tranches, 'Total mezzanine' reports the weighted average mezzanine premium and the value of loss allocation to the entire mezzanine range.

	$P_{jun}(0) = 2$				$P_{jun}(0) = 3$				$P_{jun}(0) = 4$				$P_{jun}(0) = 6$			
			$E[PV(loss_{tr})]$				$E[PV(loss_{tr})]$				$E[PV(loss_{tr})]$				$E[PV(loss_{tr})]$	
Tranches	$P_{tr}(0)$	$s_{tr}[bps]$	Abs.	Rate[%]	$P_{tr}(0)$	$s_{tr}[bps]$	Abs.	Rate[%]	$P_{tr}(0)$	$s_{tr}[bps]$	Abs.	Rate[%]	$P_{tr}(0)$	$s_{tr}[bps]$	Abs.	Rate[%]
Senior	90	11.2	-0.45	0.50	89	9.5	-0.38	0.42	88	8.0	-0.31	0.36	86	5.6	-0.21	0.25
Mezzanine 1	4	353.8	-0.60	15.08	4	275.4	-0.47	11.87	4	216.5	-0.38	9.41	4	141.7	-0.25	6.22
Mezzanine 2	4	1346.2	-1.93	48.13	4	970.7	-1.50	37.43	4	703.1	-1.14	28.44	4	380.5	-0.65	16.17
Total mezzanine		850.0	-2.53	31.60		623.0	-1.97	24.65		459.8	-1.51	18.92		261.1	-0.90	11.20
Junior	2	0.0	-1.73	86.33	3		-2.41	80.21	4	0.0	-2.95	73.77	6	0.0	-3.68	61.36
Exc. spread			1.82			0.0	2.52				3.08				3.81	
Spread acc.			0.04				0.02				0.01				0.00	
Std dev. orig			0.59				0.73				1.00				1.60	
Senior	88	7.7	-0.30	0.34	87	6.5	-0.25	0.29	86	5.5	-0.21	0.25	84	3.9	-0.15	0.17
Mezzanine 1	5	240.0	-0.52	10.39	5	193.4	-0.42	8.43	5	157.3	-0.34	6.89	5	106.9	-0.24	4.71
Mezzanine 2	5	1163.9	-2.15	42.96	5	848.6	-1.67	33.37	5	619.2	-1.27	25.35	5	340.7	-0.73	14.56
Total mezzanine		701.9	-2.67	26.68		521.0	-2.09	20.90		388.2	-1.61	16.12		223.8	-0.96	9.64
Junior	2	0.0	-1.73	86.33	3	0.0	-2.41	80.21	4	0.0	-2.95	73.77	6	0.0	-3.68	61.36
Exc. spread			1.81				2.52				3.07				3.81	
Spread acc.			0.05				0.02				0.01				0.00	
Std dev. orig			0.56				0.72				1.00				1.60	
Senior	86	5.3	-0.20	0.24	85	4.5	-0.17	0.20	84	3.8	-0.14	0.17	82	2.7	-0.10	0.12
Mezzanine 1	6	171.1	-0.45	7.48	6	141.6	-0.37	6.21	6	117.5	-0.31	5.17	6	80.8	-0.21	3.58
Mezzanine 2	6	1020.3	-2.32	38.59	6	750.1	-1.80	29.95	6	551.6	-1.37	22.81	6	308.8	-0.80	13.25
Total mezzanine		595.7	-2.76	23.04		445.8	-2.17	18.08		334.5	-1.68	13.99		194.8	-1.01	8.41
Junior	2	0.0	-1.73	86.33	3	0.0	-2.41	80.21	4	0.0	-2.95	73.77	6	0.0	-3.68	61.36
Exc. spread			1.81				2.52				3.07				3.81	
Spread acc.			0.05				0.02				0.01				0.00	
Std dev. orig			0.53				0.71				1.00				1.60	

Table C.6: **Tranche valuation: partial risk transfer via SPV, variant III.**

In addition to the positions reported in table 5.1, the time-zero value of the spread account is included. The value of the claim on excess spread created on the originator's balance sheet is included. For the two mezzanine tranches, 'Total mezzanine' reports the weighted average mezzanine premium and the value of loss allocation to the entire mezzanine range.

Bibliography

Anderson, R. W. and S. Sundaresan (1996). Design and valuation of debt contracts. *The Review of Financial Studies 9*, 37–68.

BaFin (1997). Bundesanstalt für Finanzdienstleistungsaufsicht (formerly Bundesaufsichtsamt für das Kreditwesen): Veräußerung von Kundenforderungen im Rahmen von Asset-Backed Securities-Transaktionen durch deutsche Kreditinstitute (Rundschreiben 4/97).

BaFin (1999). Bundesanstalt für Finanzdienstleistungsaufsicht (formerly Bundesaufsichtsamt für das Kreditwesen): Behandlung von Kreditderivaten im Grundsatz I gemäß §§ 10, 10a KWG und im Rahmen der Großkredit- und Millionenkreditvorschriften (Rundschreiben 10/99).

Bakalar, N., M. Herrmann, J. F. Tierney, and D. Folkerts-Landau (2000). The arbitrage CDO market. Deutsche Bank, Global Markets Research.

BCBS (1999). Basel Committee on Banking Supervision: A new capital adequacy framework, consultative paper. Bank for International Settlements.

BCBS (2001a). Basel Committee on Banking Supervision: Asset securitisation, consultative document. Bank for International Settlements.

BCBS (2001b). Basel Committee on Banking Supervision: Working paper on the treatment of asset securitisation. Bank for International Settlements.

BCBS (2003). Basel Committee on Banking Supervision: The new Basel capital accord - 3rd consultative document. Bank for International Settlements.

Bielecki, T. R. and M. Rutkowski (2002). *Credit Risk: Modeling, Valuation and Hedging.* Berlin: Springer.

Black, F. and J. C. Cox (1976). Valuing corporate securities: Some effects of bond indenture provisions. *The Journal of Finance 31*, 351–367.

Blanco, R., S. Brennan, and I. W. March (2003). An empirical analysis of the dynamic relationship between investment grade bonds and credit default swaps. Working paper no. 211. Bank of England.

Böhringer, M., U. Lotz, C. Solbach, and J. Wentzler (2001). Conventional versus synthetic securitisation - trends in the German ABS market. Deloitte & Touche Germany.

Boscher, H. and I. Ward (2002). Long or short in CDOs. *Risk 15*(6), 125–129.

Campbell, J. Y., A. W. Lo, and A. C. MacKinlay (1997). *The Econometrics of Financial Markets*. Princeton: Princeton University Press.

Chan, K. C., A. G. Karolyi, F. A. Longstaff, and A. B. Saunders (1992). An empirical comparison of alternative models of the short-term interest rate. *The Journal of Finance 47*, 1209–1227.

Chapman, D. A., J. B. Long, and N. D. Pearson (1999). Using proxies for the short rate: When are three months like an instant? *The Review of Financial Studies 12*, 763–806.

Childs, P. D., S. H. Ott, and T. J. Riddiough (1996). The pricing of multiclass commercial mortgage-backed securities. *Journal of Financial and Quantitative Analysis 31*, 581–603.

Cox, J. C., J. E. Ingersoll, and S. A. Ross (1985). A theory of the term structure of interest rates. *Econometrica 53*, 385–407.

Crédit Suisse First Boston (1997). CreditRisk+.

de Jong, F. (2000). Time series and cross-section information in affine term-structure models. *Journal of Business and Economic Statistics 18*, 300–314.

Deutsche Bundesbank (2001). Grundsatz 1 über die Eigenmittel der Institute.

Driessen, J. (2002). Is default event risk priced in corporate bonds? Working paper. University of Amsterdam.

Duan, J.-C. and J.-G. Simonato (1995). Estimating and testing exponential-affine term structure models by Kalman filter. Working paper. CIRANO, Série Scientifique 95s-44.

Duffee, G. R. (1998). The relation between treasury yields and corporate bond yield spreads. *The Journal of Finance 53*, 2225–2241.

Duffee, G. R. (1999). Estimating the price of default risk. *The Review of Financial Studies 12*, 197–226.

Duffie, D. (1999). Credit swap valuation. *Financial Analysts' Journal 55*(1), 73–87.

Duffie, D. and N. Gârleanu (2001). Risk and valuation of collateralized debt obligations. *Financial Analysts' Journal 57*(1), 41–59.

Duffie, D. and R. Kan (1996). A yield factor model of interest rates. *Mathematical Finance 6*, 379–406.

Duffie, D. and K. Singleton (1997). An econometric model of the term structure of interest-rate swap yields. *The Journal of Finance 52*, 1287–1321.

Duffie, D. and K. Singleton (1999a). Modeling term structures of defaultable bonds. *The Review of Financial Studies 12*, 687–720.

Duffie, D. and K. Singleton (1999b). Simulating correlated defaults. Working paper. University of Stanford.

Düllmann, K. and H. Scheule (2003). Determinants of the asset correlations of German corporations and implications for regulatory capital. Working paper.

Düllmann, K., M. Uhrig-Homburg, and M. Windfuhr (2000). Risk structure of interest rates: An empirical analysis for deutschemark-denominated bonds. *European Financial Management 6*, 367–388.

Düllmann, K. and M. Windfuhr (1999). Credit spreads between German and Italian sovereign bonds - do affine models work? Working paper. University of Mannheim.

Eom, Y. H., J. Helwege, and J.-Z. Huang (2003). Structural models of corporate bond pricing: An empirical analysis. Forthcoming in *The Review of Financial Studies.*

Fabozzi, F. J. (2000). *Bond Markets, Analysis and Strategies* (4th ed.). New Jersey: Prentice Hall.

Frey, R. and A. McNeil (2001). Modelling dependent defaults. Working paper. ETH Zürich.

FTSE (2002). FTSE Global Classification System.

Fuller, W. A. (1976). *Introduction to Statistical Time Series.* New York: Wiley.

Geyer, A., S. Kossmeier, and S. Pichler (2003). Measuring systematic risk in EMU government yield spreads. Working paper. Vienna University of Technology.

Gordy, M. B. (2000). A comparative anatomy of credit risk models. *Journal of Banking and Finance 24*, 119–149.

Gorton, G. B. and G. G. Pennacchi (1995). Banks and loan sales: Marketing nonmarketable assets. *Journal of Monetary Economics 35*, 389–411.

Gupton, G. M., C. C. Finger, and M. Bhatia (1997). CreditMetrics - Technical Document. JP Morgan, Risk Management Research.

Hamilton, D. (2002). Default and recovery rates of European corporate bond issuers, 1985-2001. Moody's Investor Service, Global Credit Research, July 2002.

Harvey, A. C. (1989). *Forecasting, Structural Time Series Models and the Kalman Filter.* Cambridge UK: Cambridge University Press.

Hatstadt, P. (2001). Collateralised synthetic obligations: A new asset class. *Risk: Credit Risk Special Report 14*, 2–5. September.

Henke, S., H.-P. Burghof, and B. Rudolph (1998). Credit securitisation and credit derivatives: Financial instruments and the credit risk management of middle market commercial loan portfolios. Working paper. Center for Financial Studies, Frankfurt.

Herrmann, M. and J. F. Tierney (1999). The market for CLOs in Germany. Deutsche Bank, Global Markets Research.

Humphries, N. (2002). Reinventing the market. *Credit Risk Special Report*, 10–11. October.

Hüttemann, P. (2000). Financial Engineering mit Kreditderivaten. In H.-P. Burghof, S. Henke, B. Rudolph, D. Sommer, and P. Schönbucher (Eds.), *Kreditderivate: Handbuch für die Bank- und Anlagepraxis*, pp. 309–324. Stuttgart: Schäffer-Poeschel.

International Swaps and Derivatives Association (2003). 2003 ISDA Credit Derivatives Definitions.

Jamshidian, F. (1996). Bond, futures and option evaluation in the quadratic interest rate model. *Applied Mathematical Finance 3*, 93–115.

Jarrow, R. A., D. Lando, and F. Yu (2003). Default risk and diversification: Theory and empirical implications. Working paper.

Jarrow, R. A. and S. M. Turnbull (1995). Pricing derivatives on financial securities subject to default risk. *The Journal of Finance 50*, 53–85.

Jobst, A. A. (2002a). Collateralised loan obligations (CLOs) - a primer. Working paper. Center for Financial Studies, Frankfurt.

Jobst, A. A. (2002b). The pricing puzzle: The default term structure of collateralised loan obligations. Working paper. Center for Financial Studies, Frankfurt.

Johnson, N. L. and S. Kotz (1970). *Distributions in Statistics: Continuous Univariate Distributions, Vol. II.* Houghton Mifflin Company, Boston.

KfWG (2003). Gesetz über die Kreditanstalt für Wiederaufbau.

Krämer-Eis, H., C. Schneider, and C. Tiskens (2001). Die Verbriefung von Mittelstandskrediten durch die KfW. Kreditanstalt für Wiederaufbau.

Kreditanstalt für Wiederaufbau (2003). Banks launch 'True Sale Initiative' for Germany. Press release, 23/4/2003.

KWG (1998). Gesetz über das Kreditwesen.

Lando, D. (1998). On Cox processes and credit risky securities. *Review of Derivatives Research 2*, 99–120.

Lehman Brothers (2003). *The Lehman Brothers Guide to Exotic Credit Derivatives.* Risk Waters Group.

Leland, H. E. (1994). Corporate debt value, bonds covenants, and optimal capital structure. *The Journal of Finance 49*, 1213–1252.

Li, D. X. (1999). On default correlation: A copula function approach. Working paper. RiskMetrics Group.

Liu, J., F. A. Longstaff, and R. E. Mandell (2000). The market price of credit risk: An empirical analysis of interest swap spreads. Working paper.

Longstaff, F. A. and E. Schwartz (1995). A simple approach to valuing risky fixed and floating rate debt. *The Journal of Finance 50*, 789–819.

Merton, R. C. (1974). On the pricing of corporate debt: The risk structure of interest rates. *Journal of Finance 29*, 449–470.

Mortgage Bank Act (2002). Assoc. of German Mortgage Banks.

Nelson, C. R. and A. F. Siegel (1987). Parsimonious modeling of yield curves. *Journal of Business 60*, 473–489.

Pearson, N. D. and T.-S. Sun (1994). Exploiting the conditional density in estimating the term structure: An application to the Cox, Ingersoll, and Ross model. *Journal of Finance 49*, 1279–1304.

Pennachi, G. G. (1991). Identifying the dynamics of real interest rates and inflation: Evidence using survey data. *The Review of Financial Studies 4*, 53–86.

Pykhtin, M. and A. Dev (2003). Coarse-grained CDOs. *Risk 16*(1), 113–116.

Rajendra, G. (2004). European securitisation. Deutsche Bank, Global Markets Research, January.

Repullo, R. and J. Suarez (2003). Loan pricing under Basel capital requirements. Working paper. CEMFI and CEPR.

Riddiough, T. J. (1997). Optimal design and governance of asset-backed securities. *Journal of Financial Intermediation 6*, 121–152.

Sarig, O. and A. Warga (1989). Bond price data and bond market liquidity. *Journal of Financial and Quantitative Analysis 24*, 367–378.

Schmidt, W. and I. Ward (2002). Pricing default baskets. *Risk 15*(1), 111–114.

Schönbucher, P. J. (2000). Factor models for portfolio credit risk. Bonn Econ Dissussion Papers, no. 16.

Schorin, C. and S. Weinreich (1998). Collateralized debt obligation handbook. Morgan Stanley Dean Witter, Fixed Income Research.

Standard & Poor's (1999). Global CBO/CLO criteria.

Standard & Poor's (2003). Criteria for rating synthetic CDO transactions.

Sullivan, K. H., B. M. Collins, and D. A. Smilow (1987). Mortgage pass-through securities. In F. J. Fabozzi and I. M. Pollack (Eds.), *The Handbook of Fixed Income Securities*, pp. 382–403. Homewood, Illinois: Dow Jones-Irwin.

Tavakoli, J. M. (2001). *Credit Derivatives and Synthetic Structures.* New York: John Wiley and Sons.

The Bond Market Association (2003). ESF securitisation: Data report. Data reports dating from 2001 to 2003.

Vasicek, O. (1977). An equilibrium characterization of the term structure of interest rates. *The Journal of Financial Economics 5*, 177–188.

Watzinger, H. (2000). Einsatz von Kreditderivaten zum Zwecke der Eigenmitteloptimierung. In H.-P. Burghof, S. Henke, B. Rudolph, D. Sommer, and P. Schönbucher (Eds.), *Kreditderivate: Handbuch für die Bank- und Anlagepraxis*, pp. 291–308. Stuttgart: Schäffer-Poeschel.

Wei, D. G. and D. Guo (1997). Pricing risky debt: An empirical comparison of the Longstaff and Schwartz and Merton models. *Journal of Fixed Income*, 8–28. September.

White, H. (1980). A heteroskedasticity-consistent covariance matrix estimator and a direct test for heteroskedasticity. *Econometrica 48*, 817–838.

Yoshizawa, Y. (2003). Moody's approach to rating synthetic CDOs. Moody's Investor Service, Global Credit Research, July 2003.

MIX
Papier aus verantwortungsvollen Quellen
Paper from responsible sources
FSC® C105338

If you have any concerns about our products,
you can contact us on
ProductSafety@springernature.com

In case Publisher is established outside the EU,
the EU authorized representative is:
Springer Nature Customer Service Center GmbH
Europaplatz 3, 69115 Heidelberg, Germany

Printed by Libri Plureos GmbH
in Hamburg, Germany